a milit

a militant muse
Harri Webb

Selected Literary Journalism 1948–80
Compiled and Edited by Meic Stephens

seren

seren is the book imprint of
Poetry Wales Press Ltd
Wyndham Street, Bridgend, CF31 1EF, Wales

Text and Introduction © Meic Stephens, 1998

ISBN 1-85411-212-0

A Cataloguing in Publication record for this title
is available from the British Library

*The publisher works with the financial support of the
Arts Council of Wales*

Cover photograph by Richard Watkins

Printed in Plantin by Creative Print and Design Wales, Ebbw Vale

Contents

Introduction

Although Harri Webb was best-known as a poet, he was also a prolific writer of prose. Besides the 350 poems which were included in his *Collected Poems* (1995), he wrote extensively on literary and political subjects for more than three decades. These writings amount to about half-a-million words and there are, in addition, the voluminous diaries in which, over many years and during a busy life, he managed to write something almost every day. Harri was a compulsive writer from his schooldays in Swansea, during his time at Oxford and war-service in the Navy, and into the 1960s when he first came to prominence as a poet. Indeed, it seems that few of his rich experiences meant much to him until they had been written down.

Harri made hardly any distinction in his verse and prose between the literary and the political, the two were so closely linked in his mind. He was a writer whose engagement in left-wing politics, whether as a member of the Labour Party, the Welsh Republican Movement or Plaid Cymru, was an integral part of his outlook, and without an understanding of it his writing loses much of its immediacy and lasting appeal; perhaps in this he was influenced by those French and Spanish writers, especially Góngora (1561-1627), whose work he had read at Oxford. Nevertheless, for the purposes of the present book a line has had to be drawn, however tentatively, and some invidious choices made. Here will be found a selection of Harri Webb's prose that touches upon literary and broadly cultural matters, rather than his more specifically political writing, some of which has been published in the volume *No Half-Way House* (1997). A bibliography of his literary journalism not selected for re-publication here will be found at the rear of the book in hand.

The miscellany of reviews, articles, essays, memoirs and letters assembled here have been taken mainly from the periodicals for which Harri wrote regularly between 1948 and 1980. They begin with a letter to Keidrych Rhys, the editor of the magazine *Wales*, which marked Harri's début on the literary scene and the beginning of his association with a journalist and impresario of Welsh writing in English whose combative personality and iconoclastic views chimed with his own. This letter led to a friendship between the two and, in 1949, to Keidrych's employing Harri, albeit briefly, in the fabulously cluttered office of the Druid Press in Lammas Street, Carmarthen. In it he flies a kite for a National Theatre of Wales: like Keidrych, who was in many ways his mentor, Harri was always ready to take up and promote new ideas, however impractical or unpopular they might appear at the time.

7

This panache of Harri's is also to be seen in his contributions to *The Welsh Republican*, a newspaper to which he began contributing in 1950 and of which he was editor from 1953 to 1957. Many of the articles and editorials he wrote for that paper, often pseudonymously, will be found in *No Half-Way House*. Those of a more literary nature are represented here by a spoof verse interlude satirising certain Welsh politicians, a mordant attack on David Williams, the doyen historian of his day, and a percipient article about the caricature of Wales as projected by radio and television. Harri's impatience with the Welsh Establishment, both literary and political, which was to be a hallmark of so much of his later writing, is also to be seen in his review of Gwyn Williams's early translations of Welsh poetry, in which the egregious Sir Ben Bowen Thomas comes under his lash.

By 1960, after the demise of the Welsh Republican Movement and his disillusionment with the Labour Party, Harri had rejoined Plaid Cymru and, from 1962 to 1964, was to edit the party's newspaper, *Welsh Nation*, from Garth Newydd in Merthyr Tydfil. Although its main function was as an organ of propaganda, the paper under Harri's editorship gave a good deal of space to current literary affairs, especially to coverage of new books by Welsh writers. Four examples are reprinted here, including an appreciation of Augustus John as painter and Welsh patriot and a trenchant reply to an article about Wales which Goronwy Rees had published in *Encounter*. The former Principal of the University College of Wales, Aberystwyth, was among a *galère* of eminent Welshmen (James Griffiths, the first Secretary of State for Wales, was another) for whom Harri felt the keenest antipathy, never missing an opportunity of expressing it. From this period, too, dates the article 'At the Ford of Irfon', a remarkable manifestation of Harri's preoccupation with the figure of Llywelyn ap Gruffudd, the last Prince of independent Wales, from whose death in 1282 he was able to draw conclusions that seemed to him, and to other dissident Nationalists of the New Nation group, to have relevance for the Wales of the 1960s. A more eirenic statement of Harri's Nationalism, which was not always at one with the party line, is to be found in his monograph on 'Hen Wlad Fy Nhadau', the national anthem, which was first published by the Triskel Press in 1964.

For a year or so in the mid-1960s, and intermittently thereafter, Harri was an occasional contributor to the *Western Mail*, writing articles on the contemporary literary scene and on aspects of Welsh history to which he found himself attracted. The newspaper's enlightened policy of commissioning articles from poets and critics allowed him more scope for exercising his wit and displaying his erudition than ever before. He wrote about Owain Glyndŵr, whose defiant example he came to prefer to Llywelyn's, about the London Welsh (whom he consistently deplored), and about David Lloyd George, whom he regarded as the most odious London Welshman of them all. If there is in some of these pieces an animosity bordering on the scurrilous, a portentousness that seems now to be apocalyptic, it may explain part of the appeal of Harri's writing among younger readers who, in the 1960s, were in the vanguard of a rapidly changing Wales. The hyperbole and verbal inventiveness which he habitually employed were essential features of his inimitable style.

Among other subjects on which Harri wrote at this time were urban myths, relations between Wales and Ireland, and the poetry of the Scots. In his review of Maurice Lindsay's anthology, *Modern Scottish Poetry* (1966), we have the first clarification of what Hugh MacDiarmid, the great Scottish poet (both Communist and Nationalist), had come to mean to him. Harri had discovered the work of MacDiarmid, particularly his autobiography *Lucky Poet* (1943), while on shore-leave in Scotland in 1945 and had quickly assimilated his Republicanism and anti-English attitudes. He was to revere the Scottish writer for the rest of his life, seeing in his writing and politics a possible model for his own. When in 1974 he and I spent an afternoon in MacDiarmid's company at Lampeter and Ystrad Fflur, where we visited the memorial to Dafydd ap Gwilym, Harri was to describe it in his diary as 'one of the most wonderful days of my life'.

Another key moment in Harri's development as a writer was the Poetry Conference held in Cardiff in September 1965 as part of the Commonwealth Conference. This circus was inflicted on Wales by the metropolis without any reference to the local situation and few Welsh writers attended it. Harri was appalled by what he saw and heard on this dismal occasion and it only served to confirm his view of what the role of the Welsh writer in English ought to be. In the pages of the *Western Mail*, and subsequently in *Poetry Wales*, he took his stand against the vacuous 'universalism' that had been so stridently preached at the Conference and began to define for himself a function for the Welsh writer that was based on community and social responsibility.

From 1965, when I launched *Poetry Wales*, to 1975, when my successor Sam Adams relinquished the editorship, Harri contributed not only his best poems to the magazine but also many reviews and several substantial articles in which his views continued to be expressed with typical piquancy. A dozen pieces have been chosen to represent his contribution during these ten years, his most productive decade. They include warm appreciations of the work of Caradoc

Evans, A.G. Prys-Jones, Alun Lewis, Euros Bowen, R.S. Thomas and the English poet John Heath-Stubbs. Among other significant pieces from this time are two about the history of Welsh literature which reflect Harri's increasingly profound knowledge of writing in his second language, and a spirited letter to Sam Adams about why the writers of Wales should not seek or need the approval of English critics. This, Harri's most 'literary' phase (although he would not have recognized it as such), came to an end when the editorship of *Poetry Wales*, in whose creation he had played an avuncular part, passed into the hands of those whom he considered to be English academics with no real sympathy for Wales and its literary traditions.

Harri's allegiance now shifted to another magazine, namely *Planet*, founded by Ned Thomas in 1970, on whose editorial board, together with John Tripp, he was to serve for a while. The first of his contributions reprinted here is a reprise, under the guise of a book-review, of his *ad homine* attack on Goronwy Rees, still for Harri the very epitome of the rootless and treasonable Welsh intellectual. Here too is 'Webb's Progress', an account of the writer's childhood in Swansea and his family's background in Gower. This piece, written with a delicately clear-eyed view of his early years and the influences upon him, was to be followed by another autobiographical essay, equally informative and reflective without any of the self-absorption that is so often the weakness of the genre, which first appeared (without a title) in *Artists in Wales 3* (1977); it is reproduced here as if it were the latter part of the earlier essay. Both are important for the light they shed on Harri's life and writing.

Finally, there are the writings of Harri's last phase. Much of his effort between 1976 and 1980 went into writing the monthly 'Preview' column for the Wales edition of *Radio Times*. While this commission paid well, Harri found it something of a chore and did not put his heart into the work, with the result that nothing from the column is reprinted here. He was still having a few articles and reviews accepted by the *Western Mail* and several short talks were broadcast by BBC Wales. But he was now coming to the end of his prodigious life as a writer: his output was shortly to be affected by ill-health and a general loss of vitality. The first heavy blow fell on 1 March 1979 when, in a referendum, a clear majority of the Welsh electorate voted against the modest degree of administrative auton-omy which was on offer from a Labour Government in the form of an elected Assembly. The result was a bitter disappointment to Harri, who for thirty years had been an active worker for the cause of self-government, and as his diaries show, this was a dark hour for him: he raged against what he saw as the spinelessness of his people and their political leaders, especially the Labour Party in Wales which had failed to implement its own policy. He soon rallied, however, regaining the better part of his political faith and his resolute belief that Wales would one day win the independence that had always been his goal. But he now decided that he would write no more journalism. He finished a few scripts for BBC Wales and HTV and worked on his last poems, which were to appear as *Poems and Points* in 1983, but there were no more prose-writings to compare with his earlier work. Two years later, he confirmed in an interview with Mario Basini in the *Western Mail* that he had given up writing in English – 'a dying language' — which meant, in effect, that he had given up writing altogether. Shortly afterwards he suffered his first stroke. Although he was to live for another ten years, his health continued to deteriorate and he became virtually housebound. His last years were sad and lonely: he saw few of his old friends and showed little interest in current literary or political affairs, not even in his own work and reputation. He died in his sleep early on the morning of 31 December 1994.

The selection of Harri Webb's prose-writings reprinted here will be of interest both for themselves and for their relationship to his poems, although it will not be possible to make an overall assessment of his oeuvre without taking into account his political journalism, and perhaps the more relevant passages from his diaries. The reader who wishes to come to a balanced judgement of Harri's work will have to bear in mind that, in his case, 'English standards do not apply', and that it cannot be considered according to the tenets of that 'ghastly good taste' which, in his view, has vitiated so much of Welsh writing in English. It should be remembered, too, that if what he wrote was sometimes closer to doggerel than to poetry, or to polemic than to literary criticism, at least it was in a deliberate response by a fully equipped writer who, putting aside purely aesthetic considerations, chose to write in this way. 'Poetry that makes nothing happen,' he wrote, alluding to Auden's elegy for W.B. Yeats, 'is a luxury we just cannot afford.' No politician, at least not in the usual sense, he therefore used the best means at his disposal in an attempt not to describe his country but to change it. Few of our writers have attempted as much. It is a measure of Harri's success that his writing allows us to think that, without it, the Wales of the last forty years would have been a different, and duller, place. For that small mercy we have cause to be grateful to him.

Meic Stephens,
Whitchurch, Cardiff
May 1998

11

beirdd byd barnant ŵr o galon

A Theatre for Wales

209 City Road,
Cardiff

Dear Mr Rhys,

I notice in your latest issue that one of your correspondents has again referred to the subject of a Theatre for Wales, which I believe was discussed at some length in one of your previous numbers. This time it is put forward as part of a proposal to make the English 'Wales-conscious'. I think the significance and importance of a possible Welsh theatre far transcends this admirable aim, and are indeed, at the moment, of unique value. *A Welsh theatre is necessary to reveal us to ourselves.* It must surely strike everyone as a paradox that a nation so devoted to the spoken word should have produced no dramatic literature worth speaking of, neither in Welsh nor English. A comparison in this respect with Ireland must make us blush. From Goldsmith to O'Casey the best English plays have been written by Irishmen, and this, we are assured, is due to their national cultivation of the art of talking. On this basis, what magnificent if profoundly different contribution remains for the Welsh gift of impassioned speech to make to the literature of our neighbours!

More important for Wales herself: national identity and consciousness reside in the language. As nowhere else I can think of, the language is the nation. That is what we mean when we sing 'O bydded i'r hen *iaith* barhau' ['Oh, long may the old *language* endure']. We, perhaps alone in northern Europe today, are conscious of the unbroken traditions of civilization residing in the very forms of the commonest words of Welsh. It is the sort of sentiment adumbrated by David Jones in *In Parenthesis*, by Saunders Lewis in *Buchedd Garmon*, something unique. For the last three hundred years this heritage has been in the hands of what Arthur Machen called 'the queer half-puritan, half-pagan Calvinism' of our typical religious institutions. The swell of the *hwyl* retains who knows what echoes – overtones of the Roman Mass, the chants to which the megaliths were raised. But fewer people listen to it now. The theatre must step in to supplement and extend the work of the traditional means by which the language is transmitted. It is the only possible agency that can do so. And it is one of the things we can do to save our country, if we put our minds to it, perhaps at the moment one of the few really useful, valuable things we can do at all. It must surely be a matter of amazement that we have never achieved anything like the Abbey Theatre.

For a theatre there are only two real necessities: people and money. The instruments – the stage, the technicians, the actors etc – can by these two powerful voices be conjured from nowhere. So many people, from sheer predilection, want to act, or at least to be associated with a theatre. They are the easiest element to assemble; and money is not all that hard to come by. This may seem a rashly optimistic statement, but I can tell you of a very small-scale business that modestly advertised for £500 capital and received over twenty replies – £10,000 at least, obviously lying idle, waiting to be used. A theatre is, admittedly, not the usual type of business proposition, but even for the hard-headed business man it has a certain appeal. 'There's no business like show-business!', and anyone connected with the amateur stage will testify to the wide and keen public even for the 'average amateur show'. One small place puts on a festival twice a year and makes them pay, packing the local hall for all performances. The stage is ridiculously inadequate and the facilities primitive, the situation is remote, and most noteworthy of all, the actual resident population of the immediate vicinity would not fill the hall on even one night. What obvious thirst for dramatic entertainment in that public, what sublime audacity in the promoters, what a paying proposition for the backers! I think sufficient inducement exists for the investing of relatively substantial sums of capital, if the matter were properly handled. I believe it was Rhys Davies who pointed out that a hard-headed business approach is necessary in this respect. That should not be difficult to achieve. The Welsh are notoriously adept at having their cake and eating it, at being idealistic and at the same time making a good thing out of it.

It is not too much to envisage a theatre with a permanent home in one of the larger towns and at the same time a travelling company to serve halls and institutes throughout the land, whose visit would be an event; an organization capable of putting before the public original work in both languages, that will hold the mirror up to our national life and heritage, of finding live audiences for translations of foreign masterpieces into Welsh, and so bringing home to the Welsh people the potentialities of their own language; which will gather together the best of the scattered talent so often running to seed in half-trained amateurism; an organization above all home-grown and standing on its own feet with real Welsh independence, initiated by official (necessarily alien) subsidy, stopping up yet another trickle of migration, adding a much needed ingredient to our national self-respect. Why, for instance, should the Mid-Rhondda Unity Group be doing *Juno and the Paycock*? Why should the Arts Council, with whatever good intentions, have the field to itself with its subsidised company peddling Priestley in those quaint places whose names they probably can't pronounce? The situation as it stands is a national disgrace.

And the remedy is so eminently practicable, so sweetly possible. The poets and playwrights are the only really imponderable elements. That is why I address myself to you, sir, who have in large measure had to create your own public, and should be able to appreciate the difficulties as well as the potentialities of the idea as a whole. This letter is too long, too discursive and ill-planned for you to publish, but I would be very pleased to hear from you personally, if you do not consider this too presumptuous a request. If you have the time to do so, if you consider the idea has any possibilities at all, please make your remarks as devastating and as obstructionist as possible, because implementing any such scheme would have such great difficulties that the most violent criticism would in the long run be most helpful.

Yours faithfully,
Harry Webb

Wales (vol.VII, no. 29, May 1948)

The Babes in Milk Wood

With acknowledgments to Emrys ap Iwan, Dylan Thomas, Twm o'r Nant and the Parliament for Wales Campaign, we present an INTERLUDE

Characters
JOHN BULLY: a bankrupt Bandit
DAI AND BLOD: two young people whose inheritance he has stolen
SMOG PHILLIPS AND CLIFF SMOTHERO: his hired assassins
THE DEMON JIM: a bad influence
THE FAIRY MEGAN: a good effort
STEPHEN AND GORONWY: and their merry men – King Arthur's Champions.
Y DDRAIG GOCH

SCENE 1. *Outside the back door – or Traitor's Gate – of Mouldering Mansions, London WC Tel. U.S. 49*
Enter John Bully.

15

J.B.   I am John Bully, a bandit bold,
        My motto: 'What I have I hold.'
        I've robbed and looted all my days
        But now I have to mend my ways.
        My victims all hit back at me,
        They have no sense of decency!
        But though my sun is almost set
        The wealth of Wales shall keep me yet.
        Tis Dai's and Blod's, of course, by rights
        My heart bleeds for the little mites –
        I help myself to all they've got
        And they don't seem to care a jot.
        Milk Wood is mine and mine Sheep Hill,
        Coal Valley shall my coffers fill,
        Fish Haven too shall keep me fed –
        While Wales is mine, soft is my bed.

The Demon Jim materialises on the left. During the course of the action he moves gradually to the Right.

D.J.   But Dai and Blod are getting sharper;
        When they are wise you'll have to scarper.
J.B.   For them I do not give two hoots,
        At my command they'll lick my boots:
        Their forebears thrashed me hard and oft,
        Today the Welsh are just plain soft.
D.J.   Well if there's trouble, call on me,
        I'm yours for the usual fee.
J.B.   Pal, if there's dirty work to do
        I know I can rely on you.
        Blind them with sob-stuff, jerk the ready tear
        Use all your arts of smarm and smear
        And Wales will be John Bully's ever.
D.J.   I'm only a simple chap, not clever ...
J.B.   Come off it, keep that stuff for Wales,
        Down there they'll lap it up in pails.
        But look, here comes my trusty staff –
        They'll see Britannia rules the Taff.

Enter the hired assassins, Smog Phillips and Cliff Smothero. Their shambling gait and skulking stance betray their antipathy to the light of day.

Smog   Wot is it, guv? We've 'eard as 'ow

	Some bleeders want to start a row.
Smoth.	Yus, Dai and Blod are playin' 'ell
	We'll settle 'em, and settle 'em well.
J.B.	Their innocent sheep do not disturb,
	Just use a certain poisonous HERB,
	Their simple wits to paralyze
	And all will share a large cash prize.
Smog	For them wot wants to make a packet
	There's nuffink like John Bully's racket.

They all troop out, trying hard to remember the words of the 'Red Flag'. Curtain.

SCENE 2. *The depths of the wood. Dai and Blod are wandering around in circles.*

Dai	Well here we are and here we stay,
	It seems to me we've lost the way,
	We're ditched and diddled – what a game!
Blod	You've only got yourself to blame
	For listening to bad advice.
Dai	They said they'd take us somewhere nice.

Enter the Fairy Megan

F.M.	Courage, my friends, do not despair.
	I'll lead you into the fresh air.
Blod	Oh, who's the nice kind lady, Dai?
F.M.	The bounteous Fairy Megan, I,
	And I will help you all I can.
Dai (aside)	We heard the same from your old man.
F.M.	Fair will your fortune be indeed
	If you will follow where I lead.

She waves her wand and a beautiful vision arises – WALES FREE.

Blod	There's lovely – that's just what we want.

Enter the Demon Jim. The vision vanishes.

D.J.	You'd like to have it but you can't!
	John Bully's claims are paramount
	And British interests only count.

	You wicked Fairy Megan – fly.
F.M.	Oh no, for soon, help may be NYE.
	Hark, I hear voices in the wood,
	I only hope it's someone good.
D.J.	Pah, who will heed your piffling plea?
	Be wise, be sane, be ruled by me.

He distributes copies of an improving tract called 'From the White House to the White House' or 'How an Ammanford Anarchist saw the Light'.

Dai	I think I've read all this before,
	Oh Jim, you're getting quite a bore.

Enter Stephen, Goronwy and their merry men, clad in shining armour.

S.O.	For Wales, for honour, Dai and Blod
	And all whom Bully rides roughshod
	We strive to help, we strive to free.
D.J.	Have you no sense of decency?
S.O.	Avaunt, misleading spirit, shame!
	Do not disgrace our country's name.
D.J.	No name have I that's worth the loss,
	No country either. Bully's boss!
S.O.	But Dai and Blod we will redeem
	From your Imperialistic scheme.
D.J.	Presumptuous rebel, not so fast,
	John Bully's reign is here to last
	I care not for your puny band,
	See what a horde I have at hand.

The woods part. A huge concourse of cosmopolitan degenerates, armed to the teeth and led by Smog and Smothero, hems in the champions.

D.J.	You would not brave a force so large.
S.O.	That's just what you think. Champions, charge!

A confused mêlée follows.

Dai	I fear that things aren't going well
	But I remember an old spell
	I had forgotten till today –
	Y DDRAIG GOCH is not dead they say
	But only sleeping in the wood.

D.J.	Poor Dai, that plan is not much good,
	Myself I killed that useless beast,
	She was not modern in the least.
	Of course I used a humane killer.
Dai	This battle looks like being a thriller,
	Our champions few are hardly pressed.
Smog	Yield and declare that Bully's best.
Dai	First I must take a sword in hand,
	First strike a blow and make a stand.
	Then, only then, will she arise
	In answer to her children's cries.

Dai takes up his sword and wades into the fray.

	See, I unsheath a tireless blade –
	DDRAIG GOCH, come to your country's aid!
Smog	Cor 'ark at 'im, them beasts is dead.
Smoth.	Wot nonsense fills your pretty 'ead.

Enter Y DDRAIG GOCH

Smog	Cor, strike me pink!
Smoth.	You don't exist!
D.J.	Tis time I vanished in the mist!

Y DDRAIG GOCH breathes fire. The Demon Jim vanishes in a murky yellow fog. Smog and Smothero are reduced to ashes. The cosmopolitan rabble flees, squealing.

Y DDRAIG	I am the symbol of our land.
	My scales are bright, my claws are sharp.
	Whoever takes the sword in hand
	Or strikes a warsong on the harp
	Shall ride in triumph on my wings
	And put an end to evil things.
	But those who hold in fearful awe
	John Bully and his hirelings cheap
	For them I will not stir a claw
	For as you sow, thus shall you reap.
	Y DDRAIG GOCH only comes to aid
	Those who are bold and unafraid.
	Possess the land your fathers kept
	By all the arts of peace and war.

For far too long your valour slept
But now the shameful trance is o'er
And courage shall earn its full increase –
Freedom, Prosperity and Peace.

The Welsh Republican (February-March 1955)

Poetry for Radio

An appreciation of 'The Nightfishing', read by W.S. Graham on the BBC Third Programme on Sunday, 6 November 1955.

The problem of communication is at the heart of much modern thought in philosophy as well as in poetry, and a poet reading his own work on the radio is attempting to breach many barriers at once. Here is voice only. The medium offers no distraction from the essential word. It is said that a play does not exist until it is acted, and a play of Eliot's, for instance, which may tantalise on the printed page, becomes lucid and explicit on performance.

Poetry is the first voice of the nations. The lays of Homer were sung before the tedious developments of phonetic script were ready to record them, and the health of poetry is the spoken word – the word of myth, as Graham would say. The growth of literacy has debilitated poetry, overloading its thought content and diluting its impact, until we reach the fine flower of decadence in the typographical fireworks of Mallarmé and Cummings, and Eliot's *vincures de verre*; Auden and Empson are remote and ineffectual dons.

It is the significance and glory of Dylan Thomas that he bust this racket up with his uninhibited booming and baying, as a note of music shatters fine glass. The critic who once remarked to me that Graham was just another leak from Dylan's petrol-tank may have been wide of the mark, but both poets have this much in common – their verse springs from oral tradition and is written for declamation, speaking to blood and sinew and bone as well as to the spongy convolutions of the brain. Graham less so than Dylan, obviously, for Dylan grew up in a community in which eloquence is always on tap, where the last witch-doctors of the western world weave their spells from the pitch-pine pulpits, where tipsy tradesmen declaim satire and love over their thin beer, and versifying schoolmasters are honoured amidst ovations worthy of the rugby-arena, with solid silver crowns of regrettable design.

The background noises in Graham are less overwhelming. The Scoto-Irish balladry of the Clyde coast sings through his writing, clear but subdued. In *The Nightfishing*, his most ambitious work to date, the imagery of work (rather self-consciously proletarian in his earlier poems), the clear melody of Lowland song, and the poet's inner quest, are synthesised into a rare perfection of mood. It takes a very good poet indeed to do justice to such an obviously 'poetical' experience as sailing over a calm night sea, one which haunted Yeats until he wrote it out in 'The Shadowy Waters'. It is the measure of Graham's ability that he maintains unity of mood and variety of resource through the several hundred lines of this chapter of liquefied autobiography.

It has been objected that the treatment is unduly solipsistic, that Graham never once refers to his shipmates and might be the only man on board. But it seems to me that this is the objection of a literary critic who has never leaned over the taffrail watching the wake streaming astern into the darkness, nor stood above the bow-wave gently parted by the ship making steady way through calm water, for these are the most solitary and withdrawn experiences in the world. Indeed, at the lowest level of experience, the recording of external environment, the poem is a striking achievement. To take one triumph among many,

> The last net's gone and we make fast
> And cut the motor ...

Let anyone try to write as factual a line in as melodious a cadence, to appreciate what rare achievements this poet is capable of. Over the facts, so lucidly recorded, play the poet's inner shadows, the various phases of the self, the shifting problems of communication: 'The sea as metaphor of – the sea.'

Graham reading the works of Graham did not challenge the supreme gift of radio to our age, Dylan reading the works of Dylan. His rendering seemed not to do justice to the swell of his lines, though he warmed up about half-way through. He appeared too deliberate and precise, reining in the pleasant singing voice that delights his friends, producing an effect of detachment that was not really appropriate to such a personal poem. But this was, after all, just one performance. We have been told that there has been a previous, better one, and we may hope for more.

> It is now as always this difficult air

21

We look towards each other through. And is there
Some singing look or word or gesture of grace
Or naked wide regard from the encountered face,
Goes ever true through the difficult air?

Promenade (no. 72, November 1955)

Rebecca and her Daughters

David Williams, *The Rebecca Riots.*

'The Rebecca Riots', said Frankland Lewis, one of the actors in the drama, 'are a creditable portion of Welsh History.' At their height, they tied up 1,800 troops, a regiment of cavalry and a demi-brigade of guns, and the advice of the Duke of Wellington himself had to be sought for their discomfiture. They righted wrongs, private and public, forced wholesale reform of the abuses that inspired them, threw up champions and bequeathed a legend that has lasted, and was invoked as recently as the 'Battle of Rhandirmwyn'.

But to their chronicler, Professor David Williams, they were 'outrages', perpetrated by 'tarnished heroes' infected with 'mass hysteria' and 'midsummer madness' in a 'rebellion *pour rire*'. If this is really the case, it is difficult to see why the learned professor has written a book of nearly 400 pages on the subject!

Here, nevertheless, is the first book about Rebecca, and it must be seriously considered. The title must first give us pause. 'Riots' has a derogatory shade of meaning, and its application to Rebecca, as to the Chartist Revolt of 1839, is a misuse of language. Both these great events were Risings of deep significance, not mere brawls. What reception would greet the Irish historian who treated the events of 1798, which were neither so widespread nor so prolonged, as mere 'Riots'.

The first chapters of the book, however, are excellent, giving a detailed picture of the apostate aristocracy and the mean, chiselling middle-class in all their corruption and inefficiency. On the 'gwerin', Professor Williams is not so good. He paints their weaknesses and poor circumstances but gives no indication of the resources of communal and national spirit which were to defy an empire, both in the military and cultural fields right through the century. This lack of understanding is best typified in a passing reference to the Drovers

22

(who do not really come into the story at all) 'whose brutal and evil-smelling occupation has been much romanticised by recent writers'. The economic and cultural importance of the Drovers is completely nullified by their smell. Culture, obviously, is something that goes on in semi-detached villas (H and C, and all mod cons) in Aberystwyth. We might expect the distinguished English scholar who has been described as 'a Rowse on the Rocks of Literature' to pour scorn on a society 'given up to bastardy and balladry' but we look for something better from our Welsh historians in this day and age.

The chapters dealing with the Rising, when we reach it on page 185, fail to do it justice. While admitting the military efficiency of Rebecca, he makes no attempt at a military appraisal of her tactics and strategy. This is admittedly a difficult job, but it leaves us with an incomplete, pointless and indeed, rather dull picture. To have made Rebecca dull and pointless is quite an achievement; if that was Professor Williams' aim he has succeeded admirably. Much of the picturesque detail chronicled by Tobit Evans is omitted, and much is made of the penumbra of private revenge which is always associated with such events. Again, an Irish historian who sought to belittle the events of 1916 because they gave a cover for criminal activity would receive short shrift. There was a healthy nationalist character about Rebecca which was noticed in detail by the contemporary hostile English press, but Professor Williams ignores much of this and writes the rest of it off as mere local grievances. He is silent too about the atrocities committed by English troops. Not so about the weakness of such Welsh leaders as Shoni Sguborfawr and Dai'r Cantwr. Their addiction to drink and loose living, like the Drovers' smell, completely disqualify them from serious consideration! And yet, as the Professor himself has abundantly shown, these were the natural consequences of their conditions. They had the faults of their class and period. They also had its strength. An English historian who wrote off Nelson as an adulterer or Warren Hastings as a speculator would be laughed to scorn. Professor Williams finds it strange that such characters should be 'idealized' by Nonconformists. Was there ever a historian so lacking in history? Nonconformists are so called because at one time, like Rebecca, they refused to conform. Again Professor Williams quotes, as if to confirm a statement made at the time, that 'English' Pembrokeshire and Gower held aloof from the Rising because in some way they did not feel themselves to be part of the Welsh Nation. Yet many incidents occurred in the 'down-below' territory of Pembrokeshire, as he himself chronicles, and the attack on Poundffald took place in 'English' Gower. Perhaps there is nothing sinister in all this, but there are crippling limitations of outlook involved.

There are undeclared limitations to the scheme of the book itself. Incidents occurring outside the main area are noticed summarily, though they could possess illuminating significance if explored. The enigmatic raid as far north as Machynlleth is not noticed at all. The relationship between Rebecca and the Chartists in east Glamorgan is gone into, but not the interesting situation in the Swansea district. Who, for instance, was Walter Anthony, the Socialist, who is only mentioned once? And what of the 'later Rebecca' so abundantly noticed by Tobit Evans, who operated well into the century? It may seem graceless to criticise the product of so much industry. But we judge Welsh historians by the standards of Gweirydd ap Rhys, O.M. Edwards and John Edward Lloyd. Harsh things have recently been said about the treatment of Welsh history in the University of Wales, and it may be that Professor Williams is a victim of circumstances. But, it seems to us, a very willing victim. We have had our suspicions of him ever since his *History of Modern Wales*, an apologia for the status quo, full of out-moded prejudices. Every age must write its own history. The future of Wales demands history written not from the colourless view point of academic time-servers, but conceived in love and pride. Professor Williams has many gifts, and could serve Wales well. But Rebecca and her Daughters still await a chronicler who will do them justice.

The Welsh Republican (April-May 1956)

The Stage Welshman

We are reluctant to criticise the Welsh Region of the BBC, who are labouring under the obvious difficulties inherent in being a mere 'region' of 'Britain'. We are reluctant to plunge into the cultural controversies which are already so well ventilated elsewhere. But as television rapidly supersedes sound broadcasting as the principal medium of mass communication – and, some would say, of mass conditioning – it is not a cultural question in the more rarefied sense that we must consider. As television enters more and more homes, the quality and wider implications of the programmes must be a matter of urgent concern to those who have the welfare of Wales at heart. What, for instance, are we to say of the musical saws and tin whistles which have recently appeared on the Welsh Television hour? It is no good shrugging this rubbish away with Dylan Thomas's unforgettable 'Praise the Lord, we are a musical nation'. Many uninformed people will derive their impressions of 'Welsh Culture' from insulting exhibitions such as these. Wales is a small nation and must offer nothing but the best. What, too, are we to say about the monotonous succession of homely 'Welsh' dramas, served up in English on both sound radio and television, in which writers of little talent, no taste and a complete lack of true Welshness, hold up our people to the amused scorn of a wider audience. The 'stage Welshman', in all his horror, is not only a legitimate object of aesthetic disgust, he has his political side as well, which is equally unpleasant. He has had his counterpart. There was the stage Irishman, until the real Irishmen stood up for themselves. There is the endless caricature of the 'lower orders' in English drama, symptomatic of the deep social and economic malaise of that unhappy country.

The stage Welshman is always a contemptible trivial creature. No hint is ever given that the ordinary Welshman has shown fire and resource that amount to heroism. We cannot imagine the stage-Welshman facing up to the Long Strikes, taking up arms in defence of his rights, possessed with a passion for social justice and the ability to build his ideals into reality. The hacks who pen this muck are even worse traitors to their country, tearfully deny it as they may, than some of our leading politicians – and that is saying a great deal.

Meanwhile the potentialities of television are being unimaginatively ignored. Most people today are accustomed to sitting through a film in, say, French, and following it by superimposed 'sub-titles' in English. What is stopping the Welsh broadcasting authorities from employing the same bilingual methods in Welsh television? There have been some excellent Welsh programmes lately, in sharp contrast to the offerings we have just been condemning. Monoglot non-Welsh speakers have expressed their enjoyment of what they could follow and said, 'What a pity we couldn't know more of what was going on'. Here is a chance to make a modest step forward with the thousands who bitterly regret that they know no Welsh. Here is the answer to those who resent television as inimical to Welsh culture. We present the idea to Park Place. And to Mr David Llewellyn the traditional Welsh version of what Moses said to Pharaoh!

The Welsh Republican (April-May 1957)

Yet Another Aberystwyth Anthology

A Treasury of School Verse?

Professor Gwyn Williams, *Presenting Welsh Poetry*.

Professor Gwyn Williams occupies a lonely eminence as the interpreter of Welsh poetry to those ignorant of the language, and our
debt to him is considerable. His previous anthologies and commen-
taries have given us the impression of a figure shamefully rare in the
modern Welsh scene: a scrupulous and deeply informed scholar with
a genuine poetic sensibility, a dedicated teacher whose sense of
responsibility to his nation is not bounded by the class lists. It is all
the more painful, therefore, to have to record that the present volume
does not measure up to the high standard set by its predecessors. He
has set himself a task so difficult as to be almost impossible in 120
pages: to display a representative selection (in translation) of Welsh
poetry from the earliest times to the present day, and, as if that were
not enough, a selection of English poetry written by Welshmen from
the Tudor period onwards.

The Foreword by Sir Ben Bromide Thomas (estrangements have
been dispersing ... for our delight ... liberal spirit of give and take ...
UNESCO) sets the melancholy standard. The compiler does not help
matters with a rather confused introduction which is a sad contrast to
the lucidity of his former works. What are we to make of such St
David's Day stuff as 'the Welsh invasion of England under the
Tudors', and 'poetry written by Celts from Virgil to the present day'?
There is a tribute to the 'European tendencies' of Mr Saunders Lewis,
a comparison of Welsh alliterative speech with cockney rhyming-slang,
a line of *cynghanedd* salvaged from Shakespeare, and a few surprisingly vague remarks by Mr T.S. Eliot on the question of writers using
a language other than their own, a subject on which, one would have
thought, the last word has been said much more authoritatively by
James Joyce. 'It is difficult,' says Professor Williams, 'not to see some
significance in the associations so many of the seventeenth-century
metaphysical poets had with Wales.' True, but it is also difficult to
say precisely what this significance is. Here is a field in which English
literary scholars could co-operate with Welsh social historians spe-
cializing in the currents of religious thought in the Border country
and among the Anglicized nobility and minor gentry. But at the
moment the whole subject is perilously vague, and best left.

The scheme of the anthology gives equal space to the whole body
of poetry in Welsh over fifteen centuries and to English writing by

Welshmen, a comparatively recent development of nothing like the same significance, qualitatively or quantitatively. This distortion severely limits the value of the work. The two sections are presented separately, where an interleaving could have been illuminating. In the first section (translations from the Welsh) the difficulties are of course enormous. The anthologist must not only choose his poets, he must choose between variant readings in the older texts, he must choose too between the multiplicity of interpretations which the resources of the language (especially in the medieval period) make possible. We are only just beginning to appreciate the fantastic subtlety that underlies the smooth technique of the *cywyddwyr*. As recent studies in *Llên Cymru* have shown, Dafydd ap Gwilym's exploitation of the *gairmwys*, to mention but one device, extends the language to its utmost. There is nothing for it, of course, but to use those translations which convey the spirit rather than the letter. But here are thirty-two pieces of which no less than twenty are translated by Professor Williams himself. This is unfair both to the originals and the translator; and irritatingly so, because Professor Williams has a recognisable voice of his own. It is confusing and monotonous to have this same voice rendering the princely passion of Hywel ap Owain Gwynedd and the scholarly musings of Sir Thomas Parry-Williams. It obscures Professor Williams's genuine achievements. It is no small feat to produce such contrasting triumphs as his spirited version of the tribesman's lullaby, 'Pais Dinogad', and his meticulous translation of Huw Morris's campanological tour-de-force. Like many pioneers, he has tried to do too much. Here is part of his version of Dafydd ap Gwilym's 'Woodland Mass' (where the song-thrush is priest):

> There was here, by the great God,
> Nothing but gold in the altar's canopy.
> I heard in polished language
> A long and faultless chanting,
> An unhesitant reading to the people
> Of a gospel without mumbling.

And here is Nigel Heseltine's prose translation:

> ... by God's will there was nothing but gold covering this altar ... and in his clear notes I heard him declaring the gospel to the whole parish, clearly and exactly, never hurrying.

Heseltine's book is almost impossible to obtain, which is a shame, and something should be done about it, but one feels that Professor

Williams could have saved himself a lot of trouble by making better use of such existing translations. One questions, too, the appropriateness of including Augustan and Victorian verse-translations which must seem to the present age to be out of sympathy with the originals. Gray's rather pretty rendering of the starkness of the *Gododdin*, or his version of Gwalchmai's 'Ode to Owain Gwynedd', for example. This has a certain swinging zest:

> Owen's praise demands my song,
> Owen swift and Owen strong,
> Fairest flower of Roderic's stem,
> Gwyneth's shield and Britain's gem.
> He nor heaps his brooded stores
> Nor on all profusion pours,
> Lord of every regal art
> Liberal hand and open heart.

But here is the grave prose version of Eben Fardd:

> I will extol the generous hero descended from the race of Roderic, the bulwark of his country, a prince eminent for his good qualities, the glory of Britain, Owain the brave and expert in arms, a prince that neither hoardeth nor coveteth riches.

Here, surely is the truer voice of the hieratic bard seated in his chair according to the degrees of precedence, before his prince in the hall. Gray, sympathetic scholar though he was, could not fathom the stature of Welsh poetry of the heroic age. He was tidying it up for the cultivated audience of his day (his Italianization of Tal-y-moelfre to Talymalfra is a give-away). The drunken curate of Llanfair Talhaearn is our surer guide. After all, as Gwenallt has recently assured us, Eben Fardd alive today would have been a lecturer in the University of Wales!

The more recent poets fall rather better into English (in itself a significant fact), none more so than the arch-European Mr Saunders Lewis, and there is less to criticize in the fidelity of his renderings, but the choice of modern poets presented is rather eccentric. The omission of Gwenallt and Waldo Williams can hardly be forgiven. After all, Hugh MacDiarmid manages to translate Gwenallt into Lowland Scots.

On the whole, what we have here is a hit-and-miss presentation of Welsh poetry by an overtaxed translator who has tried to do more than can be reasonably asked of any one man. The crown jewels of our nation demand a better setting than this. The fault, of course, is not that of Professor Williams.

The section presenting English poetry written by Welshmen must of course pose problems but Professor Williams seems to have stumbled into every possible pitfall. This part of the anthology begins, improbably enough, with King Henry VIII, which, as a later Welsh statesman said, is grotesque and absurd, and there are some equally surprising candidates for the big seat in the English cause.

The word 'Welsh' is meaningless enough in many contexts already without further dilution. A treatise on the Anglo-Welsh novel (always assuming that such an entity existed above the catchpenny level) which sought to extend that category to include George Eliot, Meredith (or even Goronwy Rees) would hardly qualify as serious. And sure enough, Meredith turns up here! One is rather surprised that the Welsh origins of the *cynghaneddwr* Shakespeare have been ignored. Professor Williams would have been well advised to adopt the commonsense standards laid down by the editors of *Y Bywgraffiadur* [the *Dictionary of Welsh Biography*] in respect of the putatively or marginally Welsh.

The earlier poems seem to illustrate the social history of Wales rather than any recognizable literary activity and the picture is not made any clearer by Professor Williams's occupational fondness for translations. There are translations into English by Thomas Harvey, an Englishman, of epigrams written by John Owen, a Welshman, in Latin. How European can you get? And a translation by Sir William Jones, a Welshman, of Persian poetry into English. Is UNESCO behind all this?

The seventeenth-century *englynion* make good reading, but the whole point of the *englyn* is its flea-like vitality, and for those to whom Trebor Mai and Gwydderig are a closed book, more modern examples would have given this anthology a dimension which it lacks. Excellent English *englynion* may be culled from *Blodau'r Ffair* (the most delightful contemporary Welsh periodical) and can even be found in the tabernacular pages of the National Eisteddfod's *Cyfansoddiadau a Beirniadaethau.*

If Henry Vaughan is to be considered as the first Welsh-speaking Welshman to make a worthwhile contribution to English literature, then it would be to the point to select those of his poems which show how the English language was handled by a Breconshire man in the seventeenth century, a subject fully discussed and illustrated in Canon Hutchinson's standard work on Vaughan. It is a pity too that the Matchless Orinda does not appear in these pages.

As for the eighteenth century, surely 'Grongar Hill' has been over-anthologized. Relevant passages from the same author's *The Fleece* would have been a welcome change. One doubts too if any reader,

English or Welsh, could not have been spared 'Guide me, O thou great Jehovah', even at the price of leaving Pantycelyn out.

The nineteenth century is sparsely represented by a few unremarkable writers. It is a rewarding field if explored properly. One could mention, as the sort of exciting find that makes the search worthwhile, a grim description of a colliery disaster embedded in, of all unlikely places, Sir Lewis Morris's 'Ode to the Trades Union Congress'. The most dramatic century in the whole of our long history is full of literary echoes of its great movements, but we do not find them here.

An anthologist who ranges over the centuries is always in shallow water when it comes to selecting among the work of his contemporaries, but Professor Williams's choice here may be faulted, not only for his omissions (R.S. Thomas, an authentic voice of rural Wales; Idris Davies, whose admittedly meagre talents mirror with pathetic accuracy the deracinated aspirations of the South-Eastern Valleys), and for some unworthy inclusions (a slab of stale MacNeice from Dannie Abse) but for persistently presenting good writers at their least convincing: David Jones at his most macaronic; Alun Lewis at his most bogus and inflated (in 'The Defeated') trying hard to be 'Welsh' and blowing his gaskets in the process; Vernon Watkins represented by an empty apocalyptic landscape that reminds one of a modist mural in a British Council house of assignation and hardly does justice to this subtle and keen-eyed poet; Dylan Thomas at his most pastoral, aesthetic and withdrawn from the simultaneous rejection and expression of the 'rubber crust of Wales' which is the most dynamic of his work.

English writing by Welshmen is a fascinating but fragmentary field which has only recently amounted to much. The attempt, in this anthology, to present it as an organically evolving process, analogous in nature to the fifteen centuries of Welsh writing is utterly unconvincing, as must be any attempt to invest the Anglicization of Wales with respectability. There is much here that is pleasant, much that is wildly irrelevant, nothing that contradicts the prim thesis recently advanced in *Yr Arloeswr* that Anglo-Welsh writing is a temporary and shallow-rooted growth of only marginal significance.

A Welshman writing in English only acquires significance when he is seen to be inextricably committed to and involved in the predicament of his country. Professor Williams soft-pedals this and his timorous and conformist attitude shows up most plainly in his handling of living voices.

In a healthy nation, the diversity of tasks that Professor Williams has undertaken here would be shared by a proud and eager multitude.

The exasperating failure of this volume to do what it sets out to do, after so many excellent works by the same author, is not really his fault, but a damning indictment of the Welsh literary establishment.

Wales (46, Nov. 1959)

A Year's Garnering

When the editor of the *London Welshman* asked for an article on books of Welsh interest which have appeared since the autumn of last year [1960], the task was undertaken in blithe unawareness of how difficult it would be to assemble the material. In bibliography, as in other matters, Wales has a long way to go. True, the energy of Alun R. Edwards is closing the gap, but the present list makes no pretence to be other than a random but, one hopes, representative selection of writings in this field.

Wales has figured more respectably than usual in fiction this year. Historical novels include *Helen of the Hills* by Gwen Owen (Gee, 8/6), an artless tale of the princely period, recommended for younger readers, and Edison Marshall's *The Pagan King* (Muller, 16/-), a dusty technicolour epic about King Arthur, obviously destined for Hollywood but none the worse for that (not for young readers!). On a higher technical level comes Prudence Andrew's *The Hooded Falcon* (New Authors, 16/-), an evocation of the Glyndŵr period and the first novel of a writer whose progress will be worth watching. Nearer our own day, *The Drover's Highway* by Roy Saunders (Oldbourne, 13/6), is an excellent attempt to portray the colourful aspects of Welsh life before the Railway Age. The same background is treated more melodramatically in *The Hosts of Rebecca* by Alexander Cordell (Gollancz, 16/-), which will need no recommendation to those who enjoyed *Rape of the Fair Country*. The same period in the grimmer background of cholera-ridden Dowlais is presented in John Parker's *Iron in the Valleys* (Ronald, 15/-), which will be of particular interest in the Welsh-Irish community.

Stories of contemporary Welsh life continue to roll from the presses. The newest talent is that of Ron Berry whose *Hunters and Hunted* is lively and more authentic than most, except when he brings in Welsh lit. (New Authors, 16/-). Menna Gallie's second novel, *Man's Desiring* (Gollancz, 13/6) does not quite live up to the promise of *Strike for a Kingdom*, but shows an ebullient feeling for certain contemporary dilemmas.

In a quieter vein, Donald Ford's *Catch of Time* (Bodley Head, 15/-) mirrors the despair often felt by the less fortunate Welsh expatriate, a theme seldom touched on. As a contrast, back to Wales again for *The Learning Lark* (Dent, 15/-), Glyn Jones's wickedly accurate exposure of political corruption in the valleys. It should get Plaid Cymru a few votes next year. Those with a taste for nostalgia will enjoy William Glynne-Jones's *The Childhood Land* (Batsford, 16/-), another of the precise poignant evocations of childhood at which this author excels. Gwyn Thomas is still at it and his fans will appreciate his latest box of verbal fireworks, *Ring Delirium 123* (Gollancz, 16/-).

It would be an unusual anthology that did not start a slanging match and George Ewart Evans's *Welsh Short Stories* (Faber, 15/-) has been no exception, but despite some strange omissions it is worth reading. An exotic exhibit is Ian Niall's *A Tiger Walks* (Heinemann, 16/-). Mr Niall is a welcome rarity among English authors who venture on to the Welsh scene; he describes Welsh village life and types unpatronizingly and without caricature.

Books by Welshmen dealing with life in foreign parts are equally rare. Specially recommended therefore is Carmarthen author Norman Lewis's *Darkness Visible* (Cape, 15/-), a vivid semi-fictional account of the Algerian War. Also dealing with North Africa is Nigel Heseltine's *From Libyan Sands to Chad* (Museum, 27/6). This Montgomeryshire man is a traveller in an adventurous tradition and his account reads more interestingly than much fiction.

Biography occupies a halfway position between imaginative and factual writing, so we may next deal with the recently published lives of Welshmen. Mention must first be made of the latest story of Lloyd George by his son (Muller, 21/-) which is reviewed elsewhere in this issue. A more objective story is E.W. Evans's *Mabon* (U.W.P., 10/6), another giant. Doctrinaires will object that the author assesses his subject too kindly, but the general reader will welcome a rounded and balanced portrayal of a famous figure. It is a pity that Dr Ernest Jones did not live to finish his autobiography *Free Associations* (Hogarth, 25/-), but the Gowerton boy who became Freud's closest associate has a fascinating story to tell as far as he took it – to the early years of this century. The name of Goronwy Rees reminds us of more recent controversies, but no light is thrown upon these in *A Bundle of Sensations* (Chatto, 21/-), the author of which might best be described as an ex-Welshman.

Most readers will turn more readily to the chronicles of less highly placed individuals. There is Joan Harbone's *The World in my House*

(Hurst Blackett, 15/-), a successful genre-piece dealing lightly with the trials of a university landlady, and a remarkable adventure story by Evan Davies and Aled Vaughan, *Beyond the Old Bone Trail* (Cassell, 16/-), an incredible record of pioneering hardship in the wide open spaces, the tale of a humble Welshman not long dead. Our review of biography must close with a reprint of the most enchanting of them all, *Kilvert's Diary* (Cape, 18/-) – rural Radnorshire touched only by the gentler aspects of change: required reading for escapists, historians, country lovers and just about everybody else.

Among the newer books there seems to be less dalliance with rural Wales than usual. There is Gareth Davies's *Bracken Horse* (Lutterworth, 15/-), a vigorous account of horse-breaking in the Welsh hills which will have both a specialist and a wider appeal, while in *Welsh Rural Communities* (U.W.P., 16/-) three learned authors put three widely differing parishes under the measuring rods of the scientific sociologist – with entertaining and instructive results.

Those who yearn for solid facts could consult an H.M.S.O. Publication *Cambrian Forests* (5/-), the sober record of an impressive transformation over much of our land. Industrial Wales offers us E.D. Lewis's authoritative and extensive survey, *The Rhondda Valleys* (Phoenix, 25/-), rightly hailed as a model of its kind, and the *Gelligaer Story* (Gelligaer U.D.C., Hengoed) by a number of hands, less exhaustive in treatment but equally well done. The local authorities who have sponsored publication of these works are particularly deserving of congratulation.

Another subsidised work is *Iron in the Making* (Glamorgan Records Office, 10/6), selections from the Dowlais Iron Company's records over two hundred years which give insights not only into industry but social life, education and politics in a dramatic period. *The Story of Carmarthenshire* (C. Davies, 18/-) is less well written and produced but is a useful survey of Sir Gâr's incomparable history down to the Tudor period. The admirable Oakwood Press comes up with another in its series on Welsh Railways, I.C. Boys' *Festiniog Railway*, tracing the history of 'lein bach 'Stiniog' from the heyday of the slate industry to its revival as a tourist attraction.

As an example of the type of publication which places both specialist and general reader in the debt of a small body of enthusiastic local patriots there is the *History of the Radnorshire Constabulary* published by the Radnorshire Society and at the other end of the scale the lordly British Association, meeting this year at Cardiff, has sponsored a commemorative volume on the Cardiff Region, which contains authoritative accounts of every aspect of knowledge – from geology to literature – over a wide area of south-eastern Wales.

To breathe a less rarefied air for a moment, Welsh sport is not well represented this year, with the exception of rugby. Cultists of the leather egg will doubtless already have devoured the nostalgic banquet of J.B.G. Thomas's *Great Rugger Matches* (S. Paul, 16/-), the more widely ranging *Report on Rugby* by W.J. Morgan and G. Nicholson (Heinemann, 18/-) – some unusual pictures here – as well as V. Jenkins's *Lions Down Under* (Cassell, 18/-) and J.B.G. Thomas's *Lions Courageous* (S. Paul, 16/-), two exhaustive accounts of more recent triumphs and disasters. Mountaineers and rock climbers will appreciate E.C. Pyatt's *Where to climb in the British Isles* (Faber, 20/-), which deals not only with the well-known regions, but many lesser-known districts, in fact everywhere where climbing is at all possible.

To return to more studious exertions, Trefor Owen's *Welsh Folk Customs* (National Museum of Wales, 10/6) deals with an aspect of history that most people find absorbingly interesting – the life pattern of the 'gwerin' who were often our very near and well remembered forebears. A welcome reprint in a related field is *Clock and Watch Makers in Wales* (National Museum of Wales, 6/-), Dr Iorwerth Peate's scholarly survey of a vanished world of country-town craftsmen. Hadfield's *Canals of South Wales and the Border* (Phoenix, U.W.P., 30/-) also deals with a vanished world, a bustle of progress along these waterways today so placid and neglected.

Life and Death in the Bronze Age (Routledge, 15/-) is Sir Cyril Fox's *magnum opus* and as such is perhaps the most authoritative book listed so far. It is not light reading and should not be lightly attempted, but the serious reader will be well rewarded. An historical name often invoked is that of John Penry. The U.W.P. has placed us in its debt by reprinting his *Three Treatises concerning Church Government in Wales* (25/-). Here, in vigorous Elizabethan prose, is a voice immediately recognisable – that of the passionately patriotic Welshman of whom his countrymen took no notice until long after he was dead.

Wales through the Ages, edited by A.J. Roderick and published by C. Davies in two volumes (25/- each), is a reprint of a series of broadcast talks. It takes us, patchily, from the beginning to the present day. It is not very inspiring, but given some of the contributors, could have been a good deal worse. Turning from the past to the future, and the possibility of devolution, it is worth while looking at C.B. Fawcett's *Provinces of England* (Hutchinson, 18/-), for the boundaries of the 'Welsh province'. The author is not quite clear whether this is a part of England or not; but then, who is?

Finally, and in a class on its own, *Teach yourself Welsh*, by J.T.

Bowen and T.J. Jones (E.U.P., 7/6), the runaway success of the year. Sold out within a few days of publication, this excellent volume has achieved a deserved, significant and deeply encouraging triumph.

The London Welshman (December 1960)

Augustus John – Artist and Patriot

The Welsh middle classes on the whole have all the shortcomings of their English counterparts and few of their spacious and creative virtues. Our great men seem to rocket straight up from the 'gwerin' or from an environment so similar as to make little difference. It is in the 'gwerin', since the destruction of our princely order and the national apostasy (with shining exceptions) of our nobility and gentry that the Shaping Spirit has had its abode. Augustus John, with his impeccably bourgeois background, was one of the exceptions which shows that there are great human resources hidden under the pathological conformism of his class, that only await the quickening of liberation to flourish mightily.

He was an artist of such stature that his work has been subject to exhaustive appraisal, to which it would be presumptuous to add more than a personal tribute of gratitude. But even the uninstructed layman is entitled to express such appreciation, for it was John's genius to appeal not only to the technical analyst of colour and form, but directly to the eyes of all men. I have seen a group of Yorkshire colliers stand riveted in admiration before his drawing of a whippet in the Barnsley Art Gallery, and more sophisticated people enormously enjoying the subtle satire implicit in some of his portraits of the socially prominent. I have heard a man of letters declare that his portraits of Yeats tell one more about the poet than volumes of commentary, and his pictures of children and young women, of gipsies and just plain people bring together the untutored public and the scholarly expert in unanimous pleasure. Not only in his art, but in his life and personality he gave this universal satisfaction that transcends distinctions of class and intellect. Both to the general public and to artists themselves he was everything that an artist should be – magnificent and flamboyant, passionately and unashamedly in love with life. In an age when most of our creative spirits seem to have adopted a drab protective colouring he had this value, that he gave us an insight into the true creative nature of man, despite the colourless uniformity of our over-organised society. And to us Welsh, he taught us something about our country and ourselves. He would have been at home among the riotous audiences that flocked to the interludes of Twm o'r Nant, he would have found his place at the camp-fires where the Drovers sung their ballads as readily as he did among the gipsy tents on Kilgetty Common. The poetical pirate of Plas Iolyn would have found him a comrade in arms. The gusto of the early eisteddfodau, before they became respectable, would have been meat and drink to him. He could have caroused with Jac Glan-y-Gors and Goronwy Ddu, concocted the sly mischief of a myth with old Iolo or participated in a colourfully bogus ritual with Dr William Price. If we look back over the centuries for a fellow-spirit for him, where do we find such panache allied to such precision of workmanship, such gay abandon expressed with so much painstaking mastery of a difficult craft? There is only one answer, and to name it is to grace his memory with the proudest tribute that is in our gift. For the name is the name of Dafydd ap Gwilym.

The Wales we have lost – '*yr hen Gymru lawen gynt*' ['merry old Wales of long ago'] – lived again in the person of this solicitor's son, for the spirit bloweth where it listeth, and Georgian Tenby can again be hailed as it was by a poet a thousand years dead:

Addfwyn gaer y sydd ar don nawfed
Addfwyn ei gwerin yn ymwared.

Yet he was no stranger to the shadowed side of life. His brush and pencil lingered most lovingly over the poor and suffering, the disinherited wanderers and hard-tried soldiers, the outcast and the innocent. The truly great he depicted worthily, but those whose only claim to eminence lay in rank and money he flayed like Goya. It is particularly gratifying to remember that one of his most uproariously unacceptable portraits was that of a Lord Mayor of Liverpool! A life like John's cannot be divided into neat compartments, and what the painter depicted, the man believed. He was always on the side of the people against their exploiters. The glittering social world which lay at his feet he spurned for the companionship of those who had no possessions but shared his own zest for living. His instincts led him to espouse the cause of all whom justice had forsaken but kept him free of formal political allegiance – until in his later years he looked on Welsh Nationalism and found it good. His nomadic temperament and the demands of his calling, even his justifiable distaste for the prissier aspects of Welsh life, never estranged him from the nation and people he was proud to call his own. His paintings of Welsh scenery and characters are absolutely authentic, the product of a vision unflawed by preconceptions and untainted by artifice. Wilson had painted Wales as if it were Italy. Innes interpreted our landscape in terms of some private vision, others, like Sutherland, have looked at our land with foreign eyes, but John's Wales is triumphantly Welsh. As the artist, so the man. He was utterly unsentimental, and it is typical that he saw nothing at all wrong with a nuclear power station in Trawsfynydd provided it was well designed – and provided it served Wales. His formal adherence to Plaid Cymru, though an inspiration, was almost unnecessary. He could never have been anything else.

Through him there shone much of our past greatness, and through him we glimpse something of the future that may be ours. Wales has been called a visually illiterate nation, and the private and public taste displayed in some of our architecture and town-planning, and furnishings and much of what passes for art, sadly endorses this judgement. The contrast between the highly developed literary and musical susceptibilities of our people is so shocking as to be almost incredible. Yet there are signs that all this is changing as the new mood of national self-respect and awareness sets in. Indeed, one sometimes feels that there is a future for Wales in this field that is not generally suspected. It has always been paradoxical that such an immensely gifted people should in the main have been tethered to the crudest and most laborious tasks. Not that the Welsh worker has not, in the past, made an art of farming and coal-cutting, of quarrying and the working. But as these callings became less individualistic, it is essential to develop those sectors of the economy which call for skill, craftsmanship, judgement and taste. A grudging installment of this development has already produced some results, but much further expansion is necessary, not only on purely economic grounds, vital as these are, but for social health and the full development of individual talent. A small nation must concentrate on quality rather than quantity. (We should have been ruefully aware of this ever since the bottom dropped out of the Coal Boom). Art and design are not such suspect and cranky subjects as they once were, and a society with a keen concern for the seemly appearance of the manufactures by which it lives is good ground on which imaginative talent may grow. It is true that most 'pure' art today tends to experiment and abstraction. But without being at all philistine one must hope that this represents an extreme swing of the pendulum, and that, when they have returned from their own private explorations, enriched by what they have discovered, our artists will once again be able to communicate to us all as directly and vividly as Augustus John.

Our country offers such scope in the wealth of its scenery, the beauty of its women, and the character of its people, that its worthy and comprehensible interpretation is an enticing prospect. The quality of light in Wales is as distinctive as that of the Netherlands or Tuscany. Our older artists saw our land through foreign eyes. John showed the way to see it through Welsh eyes, and when his lead is followed by the Welsh artists of the future, the eyes of the whole world may be opened in wonder and delight. It may seem presumptuous to speak of our hitherto artistic land in the same breath as the classical homes of painting. Yet to a nation which has produced Augustus John it is not impossible. It may even offer a consolation.

Our literature may perhaps dwindle to a muddy trickle, our music may be overwhelmed by the cacophony of cosmopolis. We may never produce another Dafydd ap Gwilym or T. Gwynn Jones. For all our wealth of song, it is on the cards that we shall never emulate the peasant music-makers of Thuringia and produce another Bach. But we have produced Augustus John, and if this may be done in the midwinter of our nation, what may not the summer bring forth?

Wales more than most nations has never deserved its great men but the inspiration they have given remains nevertheless. Let our memorial to Augustus John be a Wales where the work of men's hands is not an offence against the goodness of God who has given us such a beautiful home, a Wales where the heirs of his genius can develop their powers to the utmost, a Wales where life can be lived in a spirit of adventure and achievement by all, the Wales which in the fullness of his years he recognised to be the prerequisite of all these – Wales Free.

Welsh Nation (August 1962)

Highways and Byways

My grandfather, John Webb of High Pennard, was the last man in Gower, and for all I know, the last man in Wales, to cling to the use of the wheel-less cart – the horse-drawn sled. Why, I don't know. The state of the roads in that part of Pennard parish in those days may have had something to do with it; another factor was undoubtedly sheer conservatism and aversion to change. But, by the twenties of this century, by which time he had achieved a certain local fame for his obstinate adherence to this (literally) prehistoric contraption, I believe that he hung on to it out of sheer crushing contempt for the opinions of other people, a characteristic which it is said, has been transmitted to at least some of his descendants.

He was certainly a man rooted in old ways; 'the Welsh way of life' it would be called today – if any of our family had ever spoken Welsh – and his distrust of innovation extended to the new-fangled invention of photography. The man from the Swansea paper who came down the Gower to take a picture of this respected local agriculturalist and his picturesque means of transport etc had to do so from behind a furze bush and at some risk. As it happened, grandfather got wind of this townee manoeuvre and turned round with a ferocious expression and a far from welcoming gesture just as the shutter clicked. Greeting the future with a scowl is predictable, almost a reflex Welsh reaction, but John Webb must be one of the few men who has been photographed in the very act.

It's not as if the sled had any particular virtue – beyond simplicity of manufacture – or was noticeably efficient. I rode on it a few times, perched on bundles of fern, and even with that most desirable form of suspension it was fiendishly uncomfortable. I suppose I must be one of the few people today who is in a position to appreciate what a great boon the wheel must have seemed when it first caught on.

But if my grandfather personified the old stubborn slow-moving world, my grandmother, after the way of women, wasn't so fussy. It was she who altered the name of the farmhouse from 'The Pit' to 'Sunnyside'; the change from isolated peasantry to an outpost of Swansea suburbia expressed in a word. It was she who pioneered, I suppose you could say, the tourist industry on that part of the coast, by supplementing the income of the cliff-top small-holding with ham-and-egg teas for the few hardy souls – hearty Edwardian walkers – who were beginning to penetrate those age-old solitudes. Indeed, when she retired from the business early in the 'thirties, it was felt as something of a loss, and things wouldn't be the same.

But by now the buses were nosing their way down to the bays and the sprawl of bungalows was beginning to spread out from town, and John Webb lay in Pennard Churchyard and the old sled quietly disintegrated in an outhouse, and when I last went to look for it, with St Fagans vaguely in mind, it had gone. Which is a pity, because this year the Hovercraft service started from Hoylake to Rhyl, and the thousands of years of the dominance of the wheel, and the long eclipse of wheel-less transport are coming to an end. It would have been pleasant to know that the sled had survived to see its very remote descendant turn the tables on the upstart wheel – though I suppose John Webb would have disapproved of Hovercraft even more violently than he disapproved of carts, traps, gambos and other such over-elaborate contrivances.

I often wonder if we today have any cause to laugh at the old gentleman. There is nothing sacrosanct about any particular form of transport. Just move a few miles further along the coast from High Pennard and you come (or came) to the Mumbles railway. To me and to thousands of others, the name is a romantic one and the recollection of this extraordinary carnival of off-beat rolling stock is an enrichment of our childhood memories. (One reason which makes me rather suspect of Dylan Thomas is that he never drew so much as a phrase out of the oddest railway in the world.) There were those double-decked coaches, some of them like tramcars, some of them with open sides and furnished with chapel-looking pews, like nothing on earth; there were the saddle-tank engines which once contrived a memorable collision at the Vivian stream end of the Prom, and the fourth-class accommodation – open trucks with backless benches, and all the ramshackle pageant that came to an end when the huge electric coaches swept with a heavy anapaestic rattle and an inexpressibly nostalgic cry of their warning hooter, out from the Sandfields and round the rocking curve of the bay to Mumbles Pier. Poorer we may be for the passing of all this, poorer visually, poorer in experience, but we get to Mumbles just the same, only a bit smoother.

Every day on my way from Merthyr to Dowlais I pass the spot where Trevithick put the first steam engine on rails. It's a bus garage now and the track has been taken up long ago. And one by one all the stations of Dowlais are threatened with closure. Stesion Tip has gone and Stesion Top is going, and Stesion yr Antelope (Cae-Harris in the timetable) where once the colliers poured out of the 'cwbs' that were their primitive conveyance from the collieries of Cwm-bargoed and Nantyffin in which they argued, fought and sang: 'men with ninety per cent dust hitting Top C as if it never existed', as one of them reminisced the other day. And now they all go by bus. And all over Wales this is happening and if you were to take your stand on some Plynlimmon-pinnacle of the imagination you could see them all going, one by one: the scenic railway over the Beacons, the lyrical lines of the central counties, the poachers' lines of the Border, the rodneys' lines of the Valleys, the 'Cardi Bach' going the way of Crawshay Bailey's engine. And the emotional impact of all the vanishing plumes of steam is overwhelming and governments should be wary. And we do right, we of Plaid Cymru, the local authorities, the farmers, the railway unions, to question these closures severely, in terms of what they will mean in work and wages and amenities and trade – and in terms too, of what moral authority sanctions this disruption in Wales.

But we must do more than protest. We must be careful that we are not moved entirely by much the same sort of motives as my grandfather. After all, there was a time when the coming of the railway was seen as a threat to 'the Welsh way of life' of those days. If the rails brought Ceiriog back to Llanidloes, they brought too, anglicization overnight to Llandovery, and the men of Bristol and Somerset to the wild uplands of the South. And now, paradoxically, the taking up of the rails is seen as an installment of ruin. Undoubtedly this is an intention in the black hearts of our rulers, but they are making a case and we must make a counter-case and one not blindly rooted in history, history which like much which passes for tradition in Wales is recent and imported. Of course you can't move a handsbreath in Wales without floundering into history – that is what makes us Welsh. But it is a fourth dimension that can ensnare as well as liberate. You cannot sink a coalmine without stirring the slumbers of a Silurian prince, you cannot route a power-line without trespassing on the enchanted territory of romance. And you can't take up a railway without protesting ghosts following you along the cuttings and embankments.

But what is happening to our rail towns now is what happened to many of our ports a few generations back. From Chepstow to Portmadoc and beyond, steam was the end of an era for them, as it was the beginning of an era for the shed towns and junction settlements. They failed to adjust and some still slumber behind their deserted quays. In a more urgent day and age we cannot afford that to happen again. It may indeed be that Caerphilly Rail Workshops have served their purpose – like Caerphilly Castle. For me it is enough to know that great things were done in Wales in the railway age: that Trevithick invented the whole business more or less around the corner from where I live now, and that passengers were first conveyed by rail not far from my boyhood home, that locomotives were built at Caernarfon and that the Crumlin viaduct crams a breath-taking wonder into the gorges of Ebbw – and it should be preserved as that dream-like aqueduct at Froncysyllte is preserved, where you can float on a boat in the air hundreds of feet above the green meadows of Maelor – as an amenity and as a monument, that will have meaning in terms of human ingenuity when railways and canals are both long superseded.

Because superseded they will be, and by means of transport that are cutting their teeth now. Hovercraft is the most familiar example, but there are others and it behoves Nationalists of all people to find out what they are, to welcome them and to press further adaptation to Welsh needs – I for one rejoice that we had at least a share in the first Hovercraft run (and isn't it perhaps significant that the Welsh language, without any effort at all, came out with a much neater word

– *Hofren*. Perhaps we could present it to the English). Perhaps we should set our sights towards missing out the age of the motorway altogether (just as some Mediterranean countries went straight from candles to electric light, completely missing paraffin and gas) and jump from the railway age to the new trackless highways of the future. Like many Nationalists I have always felt that the concrete achievement, both practical and imaginative, that would crown our country's independence would be the building of the Great Central Highway from Cardiff to Holyhead; that this would be to us what the Shannon Barrage was to Eire and the Volta Dam to Ghana. And I'm loth to lose that dream.

But Wales has survived so much; has lost her way so many times and found it again in the most odd places. When Sarn Helen of the Legions fell into ruin she found a new road – Ffordd y Pererinion – the way not of Empire but of Faith. And in the long twilight of the Norman ascendancy she went off the roads altogether and found her own way through the forests until she was ready to strike back, and for a long time after that the lights went out and we were indeed benighted and astray and stumbled into marshes after Jack-a-lantern guides, and thought we had discovered whole new territories – which proved to be illusion. It is no wonder we were bewitched with the myth of Madoc or that some of us ended up (heroes for all that) in Patagonia.

But for over a generation now, we have known the way. The way of self-reliance, the way of Nationalism. One of the founding fathers of Plaid Cymru, D.J. Davies, actually worked in the lamp-room of a Carmarthenshire colliery. And the symbolism of that is unmistakable. By the light of the lamps that were lit then, and are held aloft by new generations of Nationalists, we can see the road ahead. But how we travel is our own choice. Protests must go hand in hand with projects. Resentment is natural but not enough. Beeching is not the end of the road for Wales. Let us outsmart him by coming up with something as new as Wales itself.

Welsh Nation (December 1962)

Lloyd George and his Bookplate

Books which have belonged to Welshmen of recent fame are quite easily come by these days, if you feel like laying out the extra shillings that 'association' adds to the cost. Recently I acquired such a volume which, according to the bookplate, has been 'one of the books of David Lloyd George.'

Bookplates are sometimes denounced as an unnecessarily ostentatious way of proclaiming ownership, but they belong to a more solid, self-assured world than that of the throwaway paperback, and must be judged in their context. Moreover, anything connected with Lloyd George is interesting, even a detail like his bookplate.

His contemporaries, like the founders of the Merthyr and Aberdare industrial dynasties, were landed gentry, sure of their position in society; their bookplates consist of ancestral coats-of-arms, nothing more. The champions of an emerging social class had no such established symbolism; they had to invent their own and, in doing so, told us a lot about themselves.

Lloyd George's bookplate is also romantic, and though obviously the work of a skilled artist, does not have much appeal to modern taste. The lettering does not satisfy eyes trained to the calligraphy of Gill and Johnson, and the thin, rather fussy pen lines with which a sentimentalised landscape is depicted have little charm for a generation accustomed to the bold, summary drawing of John and Picasso.

It is the iconography of the composition that is interesting. The upper and lower frames of the design are scrolls carrying the wording; the only significant thing about them is that the wording is in English. The sides of the picture are formed by the leaves and stalks of two composite plants. At the top they blossom out into daffodils, but their lower halves are the bulbs and roots of the leek, the roots curling snakily together and interlacing beneath the lower scroll. The effect is rather disturbing and triffid-like.

Yet it is the scene that these accessories enclose which is the main focus of interest. In the left foreground, bold and conspicuous, is the tower of Big Ben, balanced on the right by two lower and less identifiable pinnacles in roughly the same style and belonging presumably to the same building. The irritating vagueness of the drawing enables one to make only a guess at the time by Big Ben; the not particularly symbolic hour of ten to seven seems to be indicated, too late for farmers, too early for townsmen – perhaps just right for rising politicians.

Behind the towers stretches an unsubstantial landscape, consisting of a wide plain, down whose centre meanders a broad river. The scene is drastically foreshortened, and the deliberate indefiniteness of the drawing adds to its unreal quality. There appears to be a small farm by the riverbank and further back a village on a slight rise, clustering around a thin spire. Further back still broods a large town with conspicuous features; a preternaturally high factory chimney and some dominating square bulk which may be a castle keep or a large industrial building. Back of this again are mountains with bold out-lines, and behind these, the stylised rays and beams of the rising sun fill in the rest of the picture.

The symbolism of the principal features is unmistakable. Large and solid in the foreground, more real than anything else in sight, looms Big Ben, the winning post. Perhaps those other, far less con-spicuous towers are the vanquished House of Lords! Down from the (presumably) Welsh mountains in the background, curves the river.

Apart from the mountains, a decorative background, it is utterly un-Welsh. The broad plain, the nucleated village with its limestone-country spire, the lowering town, all are very English. Perhaps the town is Manchester, the Welsh Wizard's birthplace, and that big building a dark satanic mill. All such scenes have features that don't really make sense. It is not at all clear what happens to the river when it reaches Westminster (the lower scroll gets in the way); presumably it waters the roots of the hybrid leeks. And if we are looking back from Big Ben at the mountains of Wales, that sun behind them is obviously not rising but setting!

You can, I suppose, try to deduce too much from such minor evidence, but its owner obviously intended his bookplate to have a significance that could be interpreted, and this does seem to me to be a chart of his mind, and its incongruities – perhaps even a chart of his fate.

The first generation of peasant geniuses to go forth from the cot-tages of rural Wales really saw things in these roseate terms. For all their involvement in the disenchantment of day-to-day politics, they were romantic adventurers ('freebooting radicals' is surely too unkind a description!) in a slightly unreal landscape. The world was all before them, theirs to choose, and whatever they did to the Establishment was all to the good.

And now it is all over. Their libraries are dispersed, their private symbolism comes up for public scrutiny. The romantic English scene it depicts has vanished, cut up by the motorways, blighted by the pes-ticides of total agriculture. The village is a housing estate and the town has been 'redeveloped' in plaster-board and breezeblock.

Big Ben is still there, of course, and the Welsh mountains, but they are looking at one another in a different light these days, across a scene in which the rivers flow in their proper channels and are not well regarded as examples for the conduct of Welsh representatives. And the sun rises in the east.

Western Mail (1962)

At the Ford of Irfon

Type of the wise, who soar but never roam,
True to the kindred points of heaven and home.

Above us sings the lark, over uplands where all who have lived and will live are contemporaries of one another and of ourselves, bounded in space by three seas and a dyke, but free of time. In a valley of these uplands stands a stone. To this we come, a hard ride over drovers' roads from Ystrad Fflur, to this solar plexus of Wales where the foul blow was struck 'by the old treachery at the ford'.

Outward, as we ride inward, they hasten who cover ever more and more ground to even less and less effect, circling the world between mealtimes only to eat the same tasteless meal everywhere. From this two-dimensional unreality, the shallow and vulgar provincialism of time, we turn to greet those whom we have always known: the garrulous intellectual Giraldus, the gifted neurotic Pantycelyn, the repulsive traitor Gam. The girls pursued by Dafydd ap Gwilym are still to be had, as willing as ever, the sins rebuked by Siôn Cent and Mathews Ewenni still hold sway, and if, at a great crux of the sixteenth century, we encounter an ambiguous politician from Carmarthenshire, we are not surprised to learn that his name is James ap Griffith. For the scene is always the same, its contours and its weather unchanged since nameless hands dug and nameless voices sung '*y beddau a'u wlych y glaw*', and we repeat, on this stage, a circumscribed repertoire of actions, many of them infamous, most of them pointless, some few of them glorious. For we are all, from the beginning to this day, in Leopold Bloom's words, 'the same people in the same place'.

But never precisely in the same circumstances. It was perhaps inevitable that those who placed themselves under the dour patronage of Dewi should at some time embrace the deadly determinism of Calvin and Marx, but Pelagius is of us too, and the synods never really succeeded in extirpating the heresy of free choice. Our environment is so idiosyncratic, so emphatic, the influence of its combined features so penetrating and pervasive, that a degree of geographical determinism may be allowed. But the rise and fall of hill and valley, the drift and drizzle of cloud and rain, the rare glory of our sun, are but the ground rhythm, the grace-notes, the bravura flourishes; the tunes we must make are our own: now a march, now a dirge, now a hymn. And sometimes the themes and moods converge and a moment of our history sings to us in the full choir of all our voices, so that they resound for ever, speaking to every generation in turn, the pentecost which is every man's language in his own ears. Some episodes stand out in isolation; a peninsular people must shape more than its share of dead-ends. Some figures more than others are prisoners of their period, of their vocabulary, almost of their costume, whether that be visible to us in stiff prints and faded photographs, or the less tangible shirts of Nessus acquired second-hand from a neighbouring establishment. But on the banks of the Irfon we encounter a personality who is of no age and all the ages, a story whose ramifications recur as predictably as the floods, and from whose waters all our history sings to us.

The great figures loom like those rock pinnacles in narrow defiles which take on the appearance sometimes of natural objects, sometimes of monuments: the Patron Saint, the National Hero, the Giver of Laws, the Chief of Song. It is to none of these that we turn. It is given to none of these to speak to us and for us at this precise moment of time. These men, all of them, were a culmination and a beginning. Their achievements were based on the accumulated labours and discoveries of previous generations, and they crowned all that had gone before with a perfection that was a model for time to come. The man whom we company had seen the accumulated strength of Wales dispersed, its institutions eroded. After his grandfather, called the Great, he stumbles tirelessly and desperately from shift to shift, to the final blundering anti-climax, and is called the Last. His death is mean and meaningless, in a cause already lost, under squalid and mysterious circumstances of which contradictory versions still circulate. In that, at least, he is one with all the wasted dead of Wales, from Morfa Rhuddlan to Mametz Wood, from the field of Catraeth to the coalface of the Cambrian. It is this perhaps which makes the brawl by the Irfon such a familiar and accepted thing. Villages for miles down the valley are still eager to disclaim any share in it, and as eager to denounce the neighbouring village for the treachery. The very place is known with certainty after seven hundred years, when the sites of historic and fateful battles are a matter for learned conjecture. The first monument was placed there at a time when the Welsh were still putting up statues to bogus benefactors, the second magnificent memorial, perhaps the most striking and imaginative of its kind in our country, is one of the few things which give dignity to our own day. Few men speak so urgently to our time as he. It is a time, now as in the thirteenth century, when so much that has stood for so long seems to be crumbling. The House of Gwynedd, however recent its emergence, however imperfect its pedigree, yet carried the Sovereignty of Wales, an unbroken heritage of independence claimed from the earliest times. The claim was not unchallenged and had constantly to be vindicated, and in such struggles, over centuries, the nation was shaped within its historic frontiers, and according to its own ability to sustain its identity, to assimilate or reject what came to it from the outside. Llywelyn the Great had been among the most vigorous to organise the Welsh polity on lines that offered, in contemporary terms, the greatest modernity and efficiency. He had taken an ancient people into the full current of the life of the day, ruthless with the old institutions, eager to adopt the new ways, ready to sacrifice much that was traditional in order to guard and enrich the essential being of the nation. All this long heritage and all the social and political machinery installed for its maintenance was in the keeping of one man, in times when all the omens were against him. So he fought with every weapon, ransacking all the possibilities and permutations of native and alien political manoeuvre. There were few to help him. At the right hand of Llywelyn Fawr had stood Ednyfed Fychan, Chamberlain of Gwynedd. But it was far other for his grandson. The tedious catalogue of our irremediable vices stretches out to its full, shaming length. Unstable, unreliable, faithless, treasonable, never at hand when they were wanted, performing prodigies of heroism when it was too late, the local and tribal leaders of the thirteenth century are embarrassingly familiar. Stupid, stubborn and perverse in all things except deviousness and fratricidal intrigue, for which they demonstrated an infallible genius, the Welsh were brought down by their own inner rottenness far more than by any external enemy. The date hardly seems to matter. It was seven hundred years ago, but only the water in the Irfon has changed. At the head of such a people, Llywelyn fell, isolated, deserted, betrayed, hardly more so in death than in life. And with him fell Wales; the headless corpse buried in the poorest and remotest abbey of the hill-country, the head, crowned in mockery, paraded before the cockney rabble, the fallen sword rusting in the wet grass. The chroniclers told their slanted stories, the professors of history, from that day to this, with honourable exceptions, proved by science that it was all for the best, the fashionable poets found other patrons and new metres. So it was left to an unfashionable poet, about whom nothing is known, and none of whose other works have survived, to take up the harp for the greatest *marwnad* of all: '*Oer calon dan fron o fraw ...*', the death-song that reaches over the centuries and with particular poignancy into our own. For us, too, the end of Wales, of so much that Wales has meant, of so much that is Wales, seems to be about us. With Gruffydd, Son of the Red Judge, whose words come to us over all the changes in language, we see the sun eclipsed, the stars falling, the sea coming over the land: the ruin of the old community of the countryside, the bleak prospects of long-established industries, the decline of the historic language of the land, the abandonment of religious sanctions and social customs that have given comfort and strength, cultural impoverishment, the failure of political nationalism.

All this and more: a deep malaise arising from the suspicion that the whole of the national experience has at last become irrelevant, that in a drastic revaluation not only the national hoard of junk but the veritable treasures of our inheritance as a people have been declared demonetised and worthless. War, it is said, is the great auditor of societies and institutions, and the last two audits have dealt harshly with us. But it has taken the succeeding generation of mis-management to bring about a position only a hair's breadth from total and irrevocable bankruptcy, the squandered twenty years when every organised force in Wales, not excluding official nationalism, has made every possible false move, has contravened every canon of commonsense, has allowed itself to be distracted by every ideological circus from over the border.

The sky over the hills holds not only the soaring lark but the hov-ering kite, the eye of history. It looks down on the green desert where the tracks and roads converge, from the abandoned defences of the dyke, the grass-grown furnace floors of Dowlais, the cold hearth-stones of Eppynt, the gimcrack towers of the capital, the despoiled shrine of Ystrad Fflur, to the ford of Irfon. Scattered here and there are hard-pressed detachments without supply-lines or a secure base, hidden from one another by mist, often enough mistaking one another's intentions. One of them has scouted ahead already and has stood where Llywelyn fell, and under a long grey sky words have been spoken that, in the queer, muffled weather of December in the hill-country, have been answered by echoes from the great stone. The song of those waters is loud in our ears, and more than perhaps are known are hastening to the banks where the fallen sword lies in the grass for whoever dares to take it up again.

Cilmeri/New Nation (December 1965)

Has Goronwy Rees a Future?

Mr Goronwy Rees's article 'Have the Welsh a future?' which appeared in the March issue of the influential review *Encounter* is an attempt at a serious appraisal of the situation and is worthy of serious comment.

The Welsh, says Mr Rees, are a separate people, but not a different nation, nor, despite Plaid Cymru, do they wish to be, preferring to express their identity in such institutions as the Eisteddfod. Wales is small and beautiful but above all, remote, and the intelligentsia are the slaves of a myth, idealising the Bible-based peasant culture of the past. They resemble the Jews; their religion is tribal, but redeemed by music and poetry. It gave rise to education, which produced radical liberalism which in its turn produced Lloyd George since when everything has gone to hell, and Welsh mental life has stagnated. Rural Wales is dying but industrial Wales has more vitality. But even here, militant socialism is on the way out. The impersonal and alien techniques of the new technology inspire in this people further tension and indulgence in the over-aggressive attitudes of a subject race, which they are not. South Wales proletarian culture owes nothing to the traditional rural culture, and 'official' Welsh culture is impoverished by the dichotomy. The tension between the two societies is sterile because nobody can belong to both. The Welsh language is a divisive factor. The recent Government Report on the language is unrealistic. It is also nationalist propaganda. Nobody who does not speak Welsh can possibly have interest in or concern for the language. National unity does not exist. Lord Raglan is a much maligned man. Language and other controversies are a thing of the past. A new type of Welshman is arising, more like the English, outward-looking and preferring to go to an English university. He lives in Wales not for idealism or tradition but because he likes it, but he emigrates easily and enjoys life. Fears of suburbanisation and uniformity are not exaggerated, but with a release from the past will come a revival of energies, like the regenerative phases of the eighteenth and nineteenth centuries. Acceptance and assimilation will produce a new and living culture.

We believe the above to be a fair summary of Mr Rees's message, and we leave our readers to judge it for themselves. In the original, however, it creates a strange, hallucinatory effect, as if we were listening to a voice from one of those parallel universes beloved of science-fiction writers, where things are almost but not quite the same as they are in this continuum. In Mr Rees's Wales, nuclear power stations are sabotaged by fanatics, everybody at the National Eisteddfod wears fancy dress, the South Wales Miners' Federation continues to exist, but the Miners' Eisteddfod does not exist and could not possibly do so, there is only one Liberal M.P. (we should dearly like to know which one!), Mr Kingsley Amis is a Welshman and neither Mr Saunders Lewis nor Mr David Jones appear to be nationalists. It is a Wales in which, although the Government publishes nationalist propaganda disguised as official reports, Plaid Cymru hardly exists. There is an Iron Curtain along the Brecon Beacons: *nullus nostrum ad illos, neque illorum ad nos pervenire potest.* In the industrial areas (alpha plus) all is affluence. There is no unemployment, no rundown communities haunted by anxiety about their future, no forced emigration. In the rural areas (gamma minus), there is only squalor and religion.

Nowhere are there Welsh-language schools nor parents in anglicised areas making every effort to see that their children shall acquire a possession of which they themselves have been deprived, no campaigns for official status for Welsh or unseemly episodes on Trefechan Bridge, no clamour for the new Welsh television service in areas of poor reception. Glimpses of the history of this para-Wales are revealed to us: Iolo Morganwg was a 'fraudulent antiquary'; instead of a War of Independence, Owain Glyndŵr led a 'savage revolt'. It is doppelganger country in which 'the tension between Wales and her great neighbour has made their union fruitful for both of them.'

Mr Rees's contacts with a more recognisable scheme of things, although intermittent, are rewarding, and he makes some good points. He notes the poor quality of much Welsh writing and the meretricious and infantile character of some over-rated Anglo-Welsh writers. He can unsentimentally dismiss Aneurin Bevan as the relic of a past age. He can make the point that 'the Welsh are educated to the point of over-sophistication. Nowhere in the world is the word more easily taken for the deed.' Grateful as we may be to Mr Rees for such observations, his picture of Wales is nevertheless superficial and complacent, spoilt by out-dated information and ignorance of elementary facts, distorted by such outbursts of downright doctrinaire silliness as: 'The coal miner of South Wales is more akin to a miner in the Ruhr than he is to his rural countryman across the mountain.' He is hard, and rightly so, on various romantic myths of the past, but is himself marooned in a limbo which can be accurately delineated. The piece of nonsense we have just quoted, the animus against religion, the sentimentalisation of the industrial worker, the curious delusion that country life is somehow less 'real' than urban life, the non-involvement in distasteful reality, the confident diagnosis followed by a nebulous prescription, the conformity underlying the iconoclasm, even such a detail as the quotation from Holderlin with which the essay ends, all betray their source in the mental habits and fashions of the English intellectual sub-Marxist Left of the thirties.

Here and elsewhere in his writings, Mr Rees honestly admits that he is still influenced by the 'traumatic shock' caused by the contrast between rural and industrial Wales as experienced early in life. It is pathetic that such a keen intellect should be just as much a prisoner of the past as any embittered old Labour Party bore whose mind stopped working in 1926. And what possible answer can such a one have to those whose personal experience has been otherwise, to whom the encounter with unfamiliar aspects of Wales has been an enrichment and a liberation? It was in any case an unfortunate choice of escape route which led to a milieu whose nagging joyless perfectionism, sterile solipsism, and superior attitudinising, all isolated from reality by dogma, had more in common with the background from which he fled than he seems to have realised. But his escape velocity has not carried him off into outer space. There is a type of alien or alienated mentality with which no contact is possible or desirable or tolerable. But a continued concern for, indeed identification with the country and a belief, however inchoate, in some sort of future for her, suggest that, in this case, a message can get through – though whether it will be understood is another matter.

In one of his better passages, Goronwy Rees says: 'A people cannot live upon its past, and that past itself, however well loved, ceases to have any meaning unless it is continuously transformed and transmitted in the light of the present. This is a task which modern Wales has conspicuously failed to discharge, and the responsibility for this failure falls pre-eminently on those who would claim to be its spiritual and intellectual leaders, who, having little virtue left in themselves, continue to live on the little that is left of the faith and energy of their fathers.' Good strong stuff and Nationalists will endorse every syllable of it. Nay, we would go further, and to these anathematised categories would add those whom, perhaps understandably, Goronwy Rees chooses not to mention: political misleaders. If escapism, retrospection and nostalgia have ravaged the mental life of Wales, it is in the atmosphere of a prison house that such attitudes are bred. And it is the jailers, not the prisoners, who must bear the guilt: the politicians who sold us for petty party advantage, who undermined our self-confidence with their idolatory of London, and our self-respect with their craven conformity masquerading as rebellion. And their allies, the 'treasonable clerks' of Wales, whose preachments besought us to look elsewhere than in our own selves for our salvation, who badgered us into hysteria about every conceivable problem on earth instead of putting the needs of our own people fairly and squarely first, who passionately hawked all the dubious nostrums of Cosmopolis in market places of our credulity and grew sleek on the plunder of our threadbare pockets. It is no wonder we are what we are. And from the depths of our inaction and tedium we can justly reproach our critic for the part he and his generation have played in creating it. *'Tu l'as voulu, Georges Dandin.'*

Savouring Mr Rees's reproaches a little more particularly, we are haunted by a suspicion. Haven't we heard all this before? Not in the same cultured accents, not from the same heights of cosmopolitan omniscience possibly, but somewhere surely, all this about the language, rural Wales, religion .... And then it dawns on us. This is the same message that is snarled and hiccuped out by socialist headmasters in the pothouse Kremlins of our Valleys, is whined and ranted at election time by the seedy and disreputable politicians of a degenerate cause, sad creatures to whom the limitations of their own ignorance are the bounds of human knowledge, to whom the urgings of their own crude lusts are the pulse of the universe. It is all pure coincidence of course. Mr Rees cannot possibly have any contact with the stumble-bums of this particular Skid Row, and it is no part of the function of an intellectually outstanding personality to lend any cogency to the babblings of the most futile bearers of office and responsibility that Europe has seen since the depths of its Merovingian night. Even so, the flaws in Mr Rees's appraisal are made more apparent by this similarity. Is Wales the only country in which there are sterile tensions? The Brahminical devotion, to minutiae of caste and class, the psychopathic obsession with the more arcane manifestations of sex are but two burdens of which Wales is mercifully free but which dominate the society and literature of our neighbours to a point beyond comprehension, let alone beyond tedium. Is Wales the only country that has lost one role and not found another? Or was Dean Acheson talking about somebody else?

So we take courage. Mr Rees mentioned the Jews. It is a pity he did not pursue the comparison. There are (or were) more than one sort of Jew. There were the elegant, assimilated boulevardiers of Cosmopolis; there were the dour pietists of the ghetto. As one might say, the Bloomsbury Welsh and the diaconate of Siloh. But the future of this ancient people was in other hands, that minority to whom Zion was on this earth, not in the clouds, and who fused the brilliance of the assimilated Jew with the tenacity of the ghetto to build a miracle. And it is in the hands of young Welshmen and women like these that our future is entrusted: the sabras of the New Country, who are already among us. It is only the sterile who find sterility, where in fact there is the vibrant tension of creativity. Of course there is more to rural Wales than old farmers dying of Pantycelyn and little girls whose cat has gone to Jesus. As there is more to urban Wales than Mr Rees's favoured breed of mobile hedonists. A country needs, in Toynbee's phrase, its Herodians and its Zealots, its Helenisers and its Maccabees. Wales, which has a future, needs us all. It could even need Goronwy Rees, in which case, he has a future too.

Welsh Nation (April 1964)

Swansea proclaims its Welshness

This was my second National Eisteddfod at Swansea. I can just remember 1926 when I took fright at the sight of the Gorsedd in their regalia, and had to be taken to Brynmill Park to feed the ducks as a consolation, when my mother held me up to see Lloyd George, the wicked man who had disestablished the Church.

From the back of the crowd in Victoria Park, framed in one of the apertures of the Pavilion wall, I remember clearly that tiny white-haired gesticulating figure. I suppose I was enjoined to remember; in any case, I have never forgotten. Today, the Swansea Guildhall stands where the pavilion was raised in Victoria Park, the Druids no longer have power to frighten, and the Wales of Lloyd George is receding rapidly into history.

The Eisteddfod has migrated to Singleton Park, surely the loveliest setting it has ever had, with the smooth springy turf sloping down to the shore, so that even when the rain interrupted the perfect weather that prevailed most of the time, it was never uncomfortable under-foot. There was much about the Eisteddfod this year that suggested a deliberate attempt to live up to the comeliness of its surroundings and the modernity of the University buildings and the Bishop Gore Grammar School that encompassed the 'Maes'.

The Arts and Crafts Exhibition was impressive (in some recent years, best left unidentified, it has been an absolute disgrace) and for once, the Arts Council deserve full marks for sponsoring the support-ing exhibition, four thousand years of Art in Wales, at the Glynn Vivian Gallery in Swansea itself. A prize was offered this year for the best laid out tent on the field, a long overdue innovation. Are we beginning to realise how ghastly most Welsh things look to the outside world?

The tents seemed tidier and more tasteful than usual; the Babell Llên, focus of the literati, well patronised, a healthy trend of the last few years after a long slump, and one which suggests that new blood is coursing in this channel; the crowds seemed younger and better dressed than a few years ago. The old Wales is passing away, and one gets the impression that there is at least the possibility of a future for a people who can adjust to the world as it is.

Closed circuit television screens and transistor sets broadcast the proceedings in the pavilion with an English commentary for those innocent of Welsh; an enterprising but simple use of modern techniques that should completely silence the stupid critics of what is called 'the all-Welsh rule'. It suggests that a widely bilingual Wales is not an old-fashioned anachronism, but something belonging to our super-scientific immediate future.

Glamorgan beat the Australians, the Crown went to Patagonia, and there were only four marks between the three leading choirs in the Chief Male Voice, twenty thousand people turned up for the hymn singing outside the Guildhall, and the minister who tried to anglicize the chapel at Y Friog was reported by a joyful Miss Roberts (whom we met at Llandudno last year) as having been deported to Tasmania.

The *Ddraig Goch* tent on the field and its neighbour, the Welsh Language Society, were full of life and activity. There was a constant demand for the 'illegal' Welsh stamps, and the mis-spelt signposts removed from Tre-fin turned up to be taken away by the police. For once, criticism must fall silent. In many ways, it was a perfect week.

As usual, there were so many Plaid Cymru people prominent as competitors, adjudicators, officials, committee men and prizewinners that it would take a long time to name them all. So let us single out Mrs Gwyneth Morgan, President of the National Eisteddfod for Tuesday. Her work for Welsh schools, which brought her this honour, is but one aspect of her exertions on behalf of the nation, and her address, uncompromising in its statement of national duty, brought dignity to the festival.

A native must record with particular pride that, of all the towns that have housed the National Eisteddfod over the last decade and more, Swansea must take place of honour for its loyalty to the flag. The alien red-white-and-blue was seen here and there, but in the major official and commercial displays, the Red Dragon predominated. And not only in the city centre, but in the suburban shopping precincts there was this exuberant Welshness: demure Brynmor Road festooned with fairy lights from end to end, sedate Uplands a rash of flags.

But it was the backstreets of the Sandfields, where I don't suppose the average visitor penetrated, that were the most moving to me. Vincent Street and Rodney Street were decorated as I have never seen streets decorated, with innumerable strings of flags. And not only flags, but paper chains and other Christmas decorations pinned up in the windows and doorways. Messages welcoming the Eisteddfod were painted on the roadway at street intersections, and at least one pub had translated its name into literal Welsh. Flanking the austere façade of the Tabernacle of the Assemblies of God in Spring Terrace were houses where even the drainpipes had been decorated with greenery of trailing vines.

The casual visitor may be inclined to take a lot of this for granted, but, making every allowance for Eisteddfod week exuberance, I cannot help feeling that somewhere along the line, something has happened since I was at school in Swansea before the war. These were the people who would say 'they weren't really Welsh' because they didn't speak the language or were conscious of a recent immigrant background, or were doing their best to anglicize themselves and get rid of whatever Welsh background and accent they had.

Even now I don't suppose one in a hundred of them went anywhere near Singleton, or once there, would have had much clue, closed circuits notwithstanding. Yet they were eager to welcome a national event, eager to identify themselves with it and proclaim their nationality. These are the people whom Plaid Cymru must win. These are the people who will win Wales.

Welsh Nation (September 1964)

Our National Anthem

A man with a problem on his mind is walking by the bank of a river. He has just received a letter from his brother in America. Because he is a poet, even if only a village weaver-poet, he goes back to the weaving shed, where he keeps slate and chalk beside the loom, and sketches out his thoughts in the free, romantic verse of the period. It is a Sunday afternoon in January. He passes the lyric on to his son who is a harpist and singer, then goes to bed early. The son is strangely stirred by his father's verses. He, in his turn, must walk along the river bank with his thoughts as the short day closes. Then, out of the darkness of the January evening, he bursts excitedly into the house. *'Nhad, dewch lawr yn union!'* ('Father, come down at once.') Half-dressed, the father obeys. The young man's face is alight with excitement. The harp is brought out and hastily tuned. Two weavers, these men now work at weaving music and words. They sing and play the song they are making between them. Then, Mam comes home from chapel! The Sabbath is being profaned and she must have her say. For one moment the spell is broken. But it returns, stronger than ever. *'Mam annwyl,'* the son interrupts her, reminding her that David, King of Israel, had played the harp in the Sanctuary at the direct injunction of God Himself. After that, there is not much that even the most determined Welsh matriarch can say. Harp and voice are tuned far into the night. By Monday's chill dawn a song has been born, and something more than a song.

The ritual expression of political loyalty in music is very ancient, deriving from primitive religious practices as depicted in a well-known episode in the Book of Daniel. In the Laws of Hywel Dda, the Chief Bard is commanded to sing *Unbeniaeth Prydain*, a song of obviously political import, at such psychological moments as the departure of troops for battle and the dividing of spoils. But the continuous history of the familiar and, by now, almost universal modern custom seems to have begun in England at the time of the 1745 Rising. *God Save the King* was originally a popular song which expressed loyalty to George II. It became customary, in a country of doubtful allegiance, to demonstrate this loyalty by accompanying the performance with the marks of respect shown in the King's presence. All stood, men removed their hats, officers saluted. A national anthem thus acted as a surrogate for the person of the sovereign or for the abstract idea of national sovereignty. Such a custom was easily incorporated into the baroque ceremonial surrounding the absolute monarchies of the period. The finest of such anthems is Haydn's stately *Austria*. The French Revolution democratised the practice, just as it democratised the concept of sovereignty. The *Marseillaise* expressed the mood of the early days of the Revolution and the fervour it invoked was itself a factor of historical importance. It became so firmly entrenched in popular affection that, like the tricolour flag, subsequent monarchical and imperial regimes had to put up with it. Most national anthems follow one or the other model. On the one hand, there is the dignified composition commissioned by an established government from a court musician or one of recognised status, which can so easily sound empty or pompous. On the other hand, there is the more popular type of tune, often a folksong or the work of an otherwise unknown man, which often seems incongruous when sung in circumstances far removed from the mood which invoked it. Our own Anthem is one of an interesting minority that falls into neither category. Significantly, the Israeli *Ha Tikvah* is the only other example that springs readily to mind. In the anomalous situation of Wales, a nation but not yet a state, as in the days of 'Palestine' during the British Mandate, the National Anthem has become a 'sensitive area'. Its omission from the musical preliminaries of international sporting events can cause angry emotions to arise in breasts innocent of any suspicion of political Nationalism. Among Nationalists themselves there will be those who are contemptuous of these emotions, which they feel to be superficial and meaningless. The fervent singing of the crowd on the terraces at Cardiff Arms Park they equate with the more decorous but equally facile sentimentality of Saint David's Day speeches at Cymmrodorion dinners. Occasionally, in such circles, one may hear criticism not only of the singers, but of the song. It is too lyrical, not martial and militant enough for the New Wales; it has become compromised, emptied of content. The most extreme critic is the one with most right to speak. Mr Saunders Lewis has called it 'the most lying anthem in Europe'. Somewhere between this austere verdict and the boozy *hwyl* of the rugby fans, there is a feature of our national life that commands scrutiny.

The circumstances of the composition of *Hen Wlad Fy Nhadau* form one of the best-known episodes in our history. There is about them an agreeable hint of kitchen comedy: Dad stumbling downstairs in his nightshirt, Mam coming back from Carmel pat on her cue, the argument, the bit from the Bible, the harp sounding far into the night. A pleasant story, one of many such, but remembered beyond all others because it is so much more. As if, before it had taken wing throughout Wales, even before it was written down, the song was saying something. Already, in the weaver's kitchen, the multiple significances begin to cluster. The negative aspect of religion is pushed on one side, the judaised Sabbath of the time is broken without fear. The mother who tries to rule is reproved by her son. The son speaks for a more virile Wales, for that minority of his countrymen who have never accepted defeat. The Biblical imagery in which his passionate reproach is clothed makes wider claims. To men who used such language, God was again speaking to His people. Weavers and wool merchants, they were yet a poet and a musician and therefore priests and kings, with a divine message on their lips, and the leaders of a people.

Beyond the weaver's kitchen, the significances of time and place fall into pattern. Evan James, the poet Ieuan ap Iago, is from Cardiganshire stock, holding to western forms of speech, so that he will write *bau* in his song where the more general word *fro* might be expected. But he was born at Caerphilly and the girl he married was Elizabeth Stradling, from a family whose name above all others evokes the high romantic history of Glamorgan. It is in the awakening valleys of Glamorgan and Gwent that the family lot is cast. Early in life, we find Ieuan ap Iago at Argoed in the parish of Bedwellty, where he builds his weaving shed by the Ancient Druid Inn, in the valley of Islwyn, long recognised as the greatest poet of nineteenth-century Wales; also the valley of Aneurin Fardd whose influence on the cultural and social life of Gwent was so great that a Tredegar collier, John Bevan, gave the name Aneurin to a son who became a famous politician. Later, Ieuan ap Iago moved to booming Pontypridd, to the 'factory' in Mill Street, the site of which is marked by a simple plaque. At this time, the Taff Vale Railway is bringing the wooded fastnesses of North Glamorgan into a new world. For exactly a century, the bridge built by William Edwards has spanned the Taff in leafy solitude, and now Pontypridd in its turn has become a frontier town, focus of creative tension between the old and the new. A vigorous literary, musical and social life flourishes on the crest of the economic wave and the weaver is part of it. His Gwent-born son, come with his father to the mill by the banks of the Rhondda, is equally prominent as a composer and collector of all sorts of music from hymn tunes to dances, as a good tenor voice, and as a performer on the harp. His delight is to compose settings for his father's verses, all of them, as we hardly need to be told, inspired by love of country.

As in place, so in time. It is 1856. The way ahead for Wales seems clear. The old passions and tumults of the bloody thirties and hungry forties have died. Dic Penderyn lies in his felon's grave. Rebecca has ridden home; of her 'daughters,' Twm Carnabwth has turned preacher, Shoni Sguborfawr eats the bread of exile in Botany Bay, together, on the other side of the world, with the men who led an army on Newport in the name of the People's Charter. It is slack water. The more dour discontents of the Long Strikes and the Tithe Wars belong to the future. The Cwm-bach Co-operative is four years ahead and the soldiers marching up Cwm Cynon. Mabon is still only a boy of fourteen working underground in the Afan Valley. In distant Lanark, a peasant girl is pregnant with the child who will be named James Keir Hardie. At home, the chapels are canalising the energies of the people into a unique network of socio-religious communities. Abroad, the opportunities are opening out, the dazzling deadends. In the years that lie ahead, the Borderers will march to Rorke's Drift, the *Mimosa* will sail from Liverpool docks. The V.C.s will be won and Victoria will crown the colours with a wreath of immortal flowers, while Michael Jones of Bala, homespun prophet of a New Wales, will see his dream brought to its painful birth in the wastes of Patagonia. There are so many ways out of Wales, all profitable, many honourable. Ieuan's brother in the United States is rising in the world. Years hence he will be a member of Garfield's administration and will earn his mention in the widely read pietistic biography of the martyred President,

From Log Cabin to White House. He is anxious to share his good fortune and has written home urging Ieuan to join him. It is a choice which has confronted the Welsh for centuries and still confronts them today. But never more invitingly, perhaps never more justifiably than at that precise moment in their history. The weaver of Pontypridd has to decide: the New World of Opportunity or the Old Country, the Land of his Fathers. So, walking by the river, he goes indoors and writes:

Mae hen wlad fy nhadau yn annwyl i mi.

The original words of the Anthem were a different, more diffuse composition than the ones we sing today. The first version was a short, lyrical ode. But the shaping spirit is at work. Only the familiar three regular stanzas and the chorus will be retained for setting to music. They are a complete statement in themselves. Much criticism of them is based on misunderstanding, perhaps on disappointment. It is felt that the words of the Anthem which means so much to us, which are allied to such a noble tune, should somehow be more charged with meaning, should be more memorable and striking, should be 'stronger'. This view, though understandable, is based on a misconception. When writing a song, or in a lyrical mood, as with most Welsh free-metre poetry of the last century, the poet must exercise a special discipline. He must, of course, pay particular attention to the smooth flow of word and phrase. He must also avoid opacity of expression and complexity of thought. A song is no place for complicated figures of speech or densely woven textures of simile and metaphor. If the poet makes his words a complete artistic expression of his experience, then what he has produced is not a song but a poem, complete in itself, leaving no scope for the composer to play his part. Of course this type of writing has its own skills, lighter in touch than those required for work of a more dramatic or philosophical character, but demanding equal accuracy in their application. Metaphor and all but the simplest simile give place to direct statement, comparisons are made, moods and pictures created by the less striking techniques of association and juxtaposition, emphasis being often a matter of repetition. Thus considered, our Anthem is a very successful piece of writing indeed.

The poem begins with the direct, simple statement:

Mae hen wlad fy nhadau yn annwyl i mi.
The old land of my fathers is dear to me.

This is an avowal in the first person singular, so that we are prepared for what follows:

Gwlad beirdd a chantorion, enwogion o fri.
Land of poets and singers, famous and renowned.

It is a poet and songwriter speaking, so it is natural that his native land is dear to him because it has borne famous poets and singers. Then comes the juxtaposition:

Ei gwrol ryfelwyr, gwladgarwyr tra mad
Her manly warriors, patriots so fine

The virile warriors, lovely in the love of their land, are not directly or explicitly compared with poets and singers. They stand shoulder to shoulder with them. The stanza closes with the simple but tremendous statement:

Dros ryddid collasant eu gwaed.
For freedom they shed their blood.

It is subtly done: the bards and the warriors are one; both have played their part in the battle for freedom. The first stanza begins with a simple, personal declaration, it ends with a panorama of history. The second stanza is descriptive.

Hen Gymru fynyddig, paradwys y bardd,
Old mountainous Wales, paradise of the bard,
Pob dyffryn, pob clogwyn, i'm golwg sydd hardd,
Every valley, every cliff, in my sight is beautiful,
Trwy deimlad gwladgarol mor swynol yw si
Through love of country, enchanting is the murmur
Ei nentydd, afonydd i mi.
Of her brooks and rivers to me.

This is more than a mere scenic picture. The mountains, cliffs and valleys are peopled by the warriors who defended them and the poets draw their creative powers from the land and their devotion to it. None of this is stated explicitly. It is conveyed obliquely. The explicit emphasis in the second stanza lies in the fact that here and here alone in the entire Anthem, is our country invoked by name. It is placed centrally in the poem and flanked by the two adjectives that state the two ultimate truths about her: her survival from generation to generation and the formidable physical character that is basic to her history.

The third stanza is, of course, straight Nationalism:

Os treisiodd y gelyn fy ngwlad dan ei droed,
If the enemy has trampled my country underfoot,

Mae heniaith y Cymry mor fyw ag erioed,
The old language of the Welsh is as alive as ever,
Ni luddiwyd yr awen gan erchyll llaw brad,
Poetry has not been choked by the hideous hand of treason,
Na thelyn berseiniol fy ngwlad.
Nor my country's sweet sounding harp.

This is good strong stuff which speaks for itself. But note the characteristic accuracy of Ieuan ap Iago which names not only the external enemy but also the traitor within the gates, reserving the strong adjective *erchyll* (hideous) for the hand of the latter. Explicit too is the point that with the extinction of political independence, the linguistic and cultural sectors of the national life became more important. Ieuan also chooses to emphasise this last point in the chorus which is sung between the stanzas, ends the Anthem and, in public, is often sung alone:

Gwlad, Gwlad, pleidiol wyf i'm gwlad.

Here we have emphasis by repetition, hammering home the basis of our being what we are: the Land of Wales. It is significant to note that, if the full version of three stanzas and three choruses is sung once through, the word *gwlad*, singly or in compounds, will be repeated no less than fifteen times, while Wales will be mentioned by name only once. The adjective *pleidiol* has been criticised. Literally translated 'I am partial to my country', it is obviously absurd and inadequate. But Welsh, and much of the colloquial English of Wales, shares with Latin a flexible sentence structure, so that the word it is most desired to stress can be placed at the beginning of the sentence. The line could perhaps be rendered as 'I am a partisan of my country', bearing in mind the militant associations that now adhere to the word *partisan*. But Ieuan's unfailing accuracy has led him to make, in one word, yet another profound point. *Pleidiol* is perhaps direct evidence of the circumstances under which the words were written. He is having to choose, whether to go to the United States or stay in Wales. He makes his choice by saying, quite simply:

Pleidol wyf i'm gwlad.

Thus he puts before us all the necessity of making a choice, whether to serve our own country or another. He anticipates those terrible sentences in which Saunders Lewis exposed the shallowness and the rottenness of the 'successful Welsh politicians' of this century: 'Every man must choose ....' To the politically committed Nationalist this line of the Anthem has a special message: that the cause of Wales is a partisan cause, an exclusive obligation freely undertaken as a matter of personal responsibility if you will, a party political issue. *Pleidiol* is the adjective. The noun from which it derives is *plaid*. Furthermore, some old dictionaries give a secondary meaning to *plaid* which can mean not only a party but also a pledge. From this profound line the Anthem's chorus moves to its close:

> *Tra mor yn fur i'r bur hoff bau,*
> *O bydded i'r heniaith barhau.*
> While the sea is a wall to the pure loved place
> May the old language endure.

Land and language are indissolubly linked. But, by the device of juxtaposition, there is more to it than that. As the sea is the frontier on three sides of our country, so is the language a bastion which serves it in the office of a wall or as a moat defensive to a house.

In each stanza the theme has been restated in a slightly different way and now it is taken up again by the chorus. The bards and warriors are alike defenders of the land; creativity can come only from identification with the land and, in turn, must defend the land when other defences have fallen. Ieuan speaks here, in reproof, to the so-called 'exiles' who believe they can 'keep Wales alive in London, Hong Kong and Timbuktu,' as long as they speak Welsh from time to time. He is also speaking to the 'cultural nationalists' to whom the language is an end in itself and not a weapon to be used in defence of the land, for whom it is a private neurosis, not a hard objective political fact, something personal or parochial, rather than the universal heritage of a people. All this Ieuan gives us in three stanzas and a chorus. Yet, if only the first stanza is sung, which is generally the case, that in itself is a sufficient manifesto, for it opens with a personal declaration of devotion and closes with a stirring reminder of the price that has to be paid, while in the second and third lines the flesh and blood figures of committed and embattled patriots are invoked to remind us that the ultimate justification of any cause is the quality of the men and women who uphold it.

What Ieuan contrives to say is quite remarkable. Almost as remarkable is what he manages not to say. It is 1856, remember. The Eisteddfod reigns and the poets are turning out interminable *awdlau* featuring all possible, and some impossible, figures in our history. At a more popular level, the star of the young Ceiriog is in the ascendant. Soon the Welsh will be urged to cultivate *'iaith dy fam, ac wedyn iaith Victoria'*. Soon there will be an outbreak of that sentiment which has moved a *baledwr* of our own day to sing, with tongue in cheek:

Let's be kind to Anglo-Saxons,
To our neighbours let's be nice.
Welshmen, put aside all hatred,
Learn to love the blasted Sais.

On its way also, is the greatest of the century's religious revivals. Dafydd Morgan is already stoking up the fires for 1859. Not only the time, but the place also has its perils. Pontypridd is a centre of the rich delicious nonsense of Druidism, as elaborated by the credulous followers of Iolo Morganwg, lesser men with all the weaknesses and none of the greatness of Iolo. Doctor William Price, flamboyant practitioner of a dozen heresies and eccentricities of conduct and costume, is a friend. Here too is Myfyr Morganwg carrying the secret of wisdom in a blown eggshell and performing strange rites at the Rocking Stone on Pontypridd Common. He is another close acquaintance. His son will marry the girl who gives the first public performance of *Hen Wlad Fy Nhadau* a few weeks later at Maesteg. The great Llangollen Eisteddfod of 1858 is in the offing where the fantasy mongers will have their last fling before being cut down by the cold steel of scientific scholarship wielded by Thomas Stephens from his chemist's shop in Merthyr Tydfil's muddy High Street. It is a near thing, but Ieuan avoids every pitfall. He does not drag the second person of the Trinity in by the scruff of the neck, he spares us the historical waxworks, he has nothing to say about Druids. He avoids royalist flunkeyism and bogus internationalism. He pleads no sectional or sectarian cause. He is unerringly inspired to speak to and for Wales, for Wales Eternal, so that in his own lifetime, he achieves a foretaste of immortality.

Llywelyn Alaw, who was born Thomas Llywelyn, worked underground in the pits of his native Aberdare at eleven years of age. But now he is a musician, harpist to the Bruces of Duffryn and in the household of Aberpergwm. He is collecting material for his entry in the great Llangollen Eisteddfod. What an Eisteddfod that was to be, with everything on a vaster scale than before, and for the first time, special trains bringing the crowds from all parts of Wales. We are recognisably at the beginning of our own times. Not only is Thomas Stephens vindicated in defeat, so that sanity and scholarship triumph over Madoc and other misleading ghosts, not only is Ceiriog crowned, but the prize for a collection of unpublished melodies goes to Llywelyn Alaw. His collection includes the song he knew as *Glan Rhondda*. Iago ap Ieuan is, in every sense of the words, an inspired amateur, whose score leaves something to be desired, though his intentions are clear. Llywelyn Alaw has regularised the notation, perhaps under the impression that he is tidying up a traditional tune.

He keeps the provisional title that Iago had hung carelessly on his song, calling it after the place of its composition, like any hymn tune. The Eisteddfod adjudicator is Owain Alaw, one of the most accomplished and versatile Welsh musicians of his day and the first person of any eminence to encounter the new song. He is strangely taken with *Glan Rhondda* and pays particular attention to it. It seems, says the English musical scholar, Dr Scholes, that Iago ap Ieuan 'never wrote out any harmonisation, simply accompanying his song by ear on his harp'. So Owain Alaw works out the harmonisation and does something more. Again, it is as if a special providence is at work. Just as Ieuan's words were distilled out of a more diffuse original, so the slight changes introduced by Owain Alaw change the tune to make it less the setting of a subjective lyric than a more objective, more public declaration. It was he who set the definitive shape of the tune we all know, he who brought his easy mastery of technique to the harmonisation, he who published it in a collection of Welsh melodies, and because the provisional title of *Glan Rhondda* meant little to him, he christened it *Hen Wlad Fy Nhadau*. In a long and active life of music, Owain Alaw will do nothing more memorable than this. He too is brushed with the wing of the Anthem's immortality.

They do more than offer the composer a basis from which to soar into his own realm. They determine the direction and character of his flight. Vocal music transfigures language but never transcends it. When we say that *La donna e mobile* is Italian or that the *Liebestod* is German we have in mind not merely the vocabulary but a whole world of thought and emotion, a totality of experience which is that people's particular enrichment of our human heritage, expressing something we can all understand independently of our knowledge of the language. So with our National Anthem. In Quaker phrase, 'it speaks to our condition,' however defective our knowledge of Welsh. It is significant that no English translation has ever gained general acceptance. Eben Fardd was the first to try his hand at this work of superogation and was followed by other well-intentioned men. Some of the translations are as adequate as translations ever are. But their very number shows clearly that no one of them has ever abrogated to itself the unchallenged sovereignty of the Welsh original. In the nature of the case, this is impossible. Not even the most vicious enemy of the Welsh language, flourishing the dirty rags of his own ignorance and prejudice as the banner of some dubious crusade, has ever found *Hen Wlad Fy Nhadau* anything but inviolate. Perhaps the most striking illustration of the transcending appeal of the Anthem is that it speaks to others whose condition is like our own, most notably to the Bretons, whose history and experience is so similar to ours. In many matters we have more to learn from our continental cousins than they from us. But during one of our more intolerable phases, towards the end of the last century, we sent the Bretons missionaries to redeem them from the twin evils of popery and drink. By this unlikely channel a greater gift than teetotalism or evangelical dissent found its way overseas. Not without that hint of humorous anticlimax that is so good for the soul of a people given to large utterance. For it was the Reverend William Jenkyn Jones who translated the patriotic sentiments of the Anthem into good Breton. But, under who knows what strange non-alcoholic intoxication, he added new verses in denunciation of the Demon Drink and other exhortations of evangelical piety that must have had little appeal to the hardy fisherfolk of Finisterre. Yet, like a stout ship in a squall off Ushant, the Anthem righted itself and made fair landfall. The new song came to the notice of the young Breton patriot Taldir, who as a veteran leader of his country was to be shamefully persecuted by the French. Besides being a patriot, he was a wine merchant, which perhaps lent him some added incentive to rescue the treasure from its incongruous setting and give it the form in which it has helped ever since to inspire Breton resistance to French dominion. In the year that James James died, *Bro Goz Ma Zhadou* was officially adopted as the national Anthem of Brittany. Its subsequent fortune beyond our borders has included translation into the revived Cornish language and even some talk of its adoption as an Anthem for all the counties of Celtic speech and inheritance.

But, after all, its acceptance in our own country is what is most remarkable, perhaps one of the most remarkable things in our recent history. Wales first heard *Hen Wlad Fy Nhadau* within a few weeks of its composition, when it was sung at Maesteg. Two years later, Llywelyn Alaw, including it in his collection for the Llangollen Eisteddfod, omits the name of the author, perhaps under the impression that it was traditional. Already it is becoming the possession of an entire people. To Owain Alaw, as good a judge of such matters as could then be found, it was definitely traditional and is so published by him just four years after that Sunday walk by the banks of the Rhondda. Performances at the greater Eisteddfodau follow, now being organised as National Eisteddfodau. Already, national recognition has been achieved. Great weight is attached by authoritative writers to a performance at the Bangor National Eisteddfod of 1874. The National Anthem has arrived, as if in a year in which there was nothing to sing about, Wales had discovered itself in a song. It was not commissioned. What authority existed to make such a commission? It was not officially promoted. Who could have done that? It was not associated with any stirring event. 'The Soldier's Song' is the National Anthem of Ireland because it was sung on the steps of the General Post Office in 1916, immediately after Padraic Pearse had read out the immortal Proclamation of the Irish Republic and immediately before the 'terrible beauty' was born in Dublin that Easter Week. As part of the story of the 1916 Rising, 'The Soldier's Song' is inextricably bound up with the birth of the Republic of Ireland. It takes its place, because of that, before songs that were once as familiar as patriotic rallying cries and are, one dares suggest, better music. But no such inspiring events attended the birth of *Hen Wlad Fy Nhadau*. It came out of nowhere. That is what makes the whole story so terrifyingly impressive, as if a great voice had spoken. It was not given to Ceiriog, or Eben Fardd, or Islwyn, to interpret that voice into words, but to a weaver poet whose other verses time has scattered to oblivion. It was not given to Owain Alaw or Joseph Parry or R.S. Hughes to interpret the music of that voice, but to a careless young harpist none of whose other works travelled beyond his own place.

Illustrative of the Welsh tendency to sink to the depths immediately after rising to the heights is the sad story of another song, paradoxically entwined with that of the Anthem. The ostensible reason for seeking a modestly competent man to write *God Bless the Prince of Wales*, a few years later, was the approaching marriage of the current incumbent of that title, Victoria's scrapegrace son. Despite the fact that the true Anthem was being sung with enthusiasm, the 'official' tune was vigorously launched and encouraged by all the predictable elements. But it got off to a bad start and has never caught up in a contest in which it has really stood no chance. Bertie, after all, was not precisely the ideal character to parade before our ancestors during one of the more prim phases of our history. His exploits were such as prompted one Welsh town, which it is kinder to leave nameless, to welcome him with a banner bearing the ambiguously loyal slogan, 'Edward, with all your faults, we love you still'. Such touching loyalty was amply rewarded. The curious in such studies may consult lives of this personage, including the most recent and voluminous, to search in vain for any reference to this limp and sycophantic dirge, justly ignored by the breed at whose behest it was composed. It remains notable chiefly for the variety and extreme impropriety of its parodies, the latest of which is now known as *The Exile's Song*. No one, in the present writer's deplorably comprehensive knowledge of such matters, has ever attempted even the mildest parody of the National Anthem. Nearer to our own day the primacy of *Hen Wlad Fy Nhadau* was emphasised from a more respectable quarter. *Cofia'n*

Gwlad was commissioned to fill a need felt in some circles for a more explicitly devotional type of national hymn. There was some talk of elevating Elfed's fine composition to some sort of parity with the National Anthem. But it came to nothing and the hymn remains a welcome and worthy addition to the repertory, nothing more.

Well before the end of the last century there was not the slightest question as to the status of *Hen Wlad Fy Nhadau*. But as the imperfectly recorded circumstances of its composition and the swift rise to recognition began to fade in men's memories, contradictory accounts began to circulate. One of these, for instance, states that James James first composed the tune and then asked his father to write words for it, but this sequence never found general acceptance because it was considered inherently improbable. The story is further complicated by the following version which was published by Gweirydd ap Rhys in his *Hanes y Brytaniad a'r Cymry* (1874), Volume II, page 300:

Mae hen wlad fy nhadau yn annwyl i mi;
Gwlad beirdd a cherddorion enwogion o fri:
Ei gwrol ryfelwyr, gwladgarwyr tra mad,
Dros rhyddid collasant eu gwaed:
  Gwlad, gwlad! pleidol wyf i'm gwlad;
  Tra mor yn fur i'r bur hoff bau,
  O bydded i'r hen iaith barhau.

Os nad yw hen Gymru, fu unwaith mewn bri,
  Yn awr yn mwynhau ei holl freintiau;
Arafwch ychydig! dywedwch i mi,
Pa wlad sydd dan haul heb ei beiau?
  Fy ngwlad, O fy ngwlad
  Rhof iti fawrhad,
Dy enw sydd dra chysegredig:
  O! rhowch i mi fwth,
  A thelyn neu grwth,
Yn rhywle yng Nghymru fynyddig.

The relationship of this version to the more familiar and final form of the poem, which may at first seem puzzling, is really clarified by our knowledge of the exact circumstances under which the poem was written. Moving forward to our own day we encounter a firm and consistent tradition surviving among various descendants of the James family, that the words of *Hen Wlad Fy Nhadau* were written as Evan James's response to his brother's invitation to join him in America. The present writer is indebted to Dr Phil Williams of Bargoed, now an astronomical physicist at Cambridge, for the story as it is told in his branch of the family. An identical version of the events of 1856 is reported from other descendants living in the valleys of Gwent. This point is not mentioned in the printed sources that are available and it is offered here as an original contribution to the written history of our Anthem. Perhaps it is a point that may seem to have possessed little importance till now, but in the climate of the present period, many may feel that it provides a background which possibly deepens the significance of the Anthem and the urgency of its message. Together with the 'loss' of the last ten lines of the less familiar version, it also helps to clarify the sequence of composition which seems to be as follows. Evan James, in response to his brother's letter from America, writes the short lyric poem as published by Gweirydd ap Rhys. He gives it to his son who seizes on the first seven lines as suitable for musical setting as verse and chorus. James James discards the rest of the poem and asks his father to write two more verses on the pattern of its first four lines, to fit the music already composed. If this sequence is accepted, it offers us a remarkable glimpse of the Anthem literally composing itself. The words inspire the music which inspires more words. To some it may suggest a striking analogy with the processes of weaving. It will confirm the detail offered in some accounts that the work of writing and composing was spread over more than one day, a natural enough necessity in an age of long hours and scant leisure. More to the point, it could explain the repetitive nature of the second and third verses. Effective and artistically valid as they are, they offer no development of the theme of the first verse, but are subtle variations on it. Moreover, Gweirydd ap Rhys was a healthily patriotic historian for his day and it is significant that he quotes the poem in a long coda to that passage of his history which deals with the achievement of our national hero, Owain Glyndwr. The 'lost' ten lines are much more explicitly political than anything that was retained but they contain also a hint of culturalist escapism and acquiescence. Their elimination, therefore, must count as one of the uncovenanted inspirations that have gone to the making of the Anthem.

In the years that followed the death of James James active measures were taken to commemorate the men whose work had enriched the nation. Delayed by the hardships which beset the industrial valleys for two generations, the plan was realised in 1930 when the memorial was unveiled in Ynys Angharad Park at Pontypridd. The work of Sir Goscombe John, the statue is one of the better public monuments of Wales, altogether worthy of the men and the music it commemorates. At its unveiling, Taliesin, son of James James, played his father's melody on the harp, and Archdruid Pedrog, a far different figure from those crazy old rascals of Pontypridd's frontier days, dedicated it to the Welsh Nation. The memorial's setting is delightful, an invitation to pilgrimage and homage. Since then, the stirrings of renewed national pride have found the harp of Iago ap Ieuan ever ready to vibrate in sympathy. In 1953, as the result of representations made by the London branch of Plaid Cymru, the Welsh transmitters of the B.B.C. began the custom of playing *Hen Wlad Fy Nhadau* at the end of the evening's programmes. In 1956, the centenary of the Anthem's composition, coinciding happily with the bicentenary of William Edwards's bridge over the Taff, was marked by an ebullient outburst of celebration in Pontypridd, and by commemorations throughout the country. Iago ap Ieuan's harp passed from the possession of his son Taliesin to the venerable patriot, still happily with us, who was the first woman member of Plaid Cymru, Mrs Griffith John Williams. When the Welsh Schools Movement had advanced to the stage at which secondary education in the Welsh language was demanded, it was appropriate that the first such secondary school in southern Wales should be established at Rhydfelen, near Pontypridd, where Iago ap Ieuan had lived for a time, and more appropriate that the children of Rhydfelen should be given the use of the harp on which the Anthem was composed. There are, of course, areas insensitive to such vulgar emotions as mere patriotism, however perfectly expressed. You may, for instance, traverse the deserts of Welsh academic scholarship and among the serried ranks in the indexes of standard and prescribed tomes, among the rollcall of minutely noticed and exhaustively appraised mediocrities, you will search in vain for the name of Ieuan ap Iago. But let us return to the mainstream of our national life. 'The most lying anthem in Europe'? We must disagree with Mr Saunders Lewis. Our greatest teacher brings to his task gifts of organised and orderly thought that are an invaluable corrective to our native exuberance, but which here seem to have misled him. In terms of strict logic he may have a point. But there are, fortunately, limits to logic. The mind is not a computer to be fed punched cards and then produce the right answers. It would go ill with the human race were that so. The sinister philosophies of determinism would hold sway, Calvin and Marx would be right. Of course, not everyone who sings our Anthem understands what he is singing, or if he does understand it, has much intention of doing anything about it. Hence the hopelessly confused and hypocritical habit of playing both *Hen Wlad Fy Nhadau* and the English anthem on public occasions. But it performs, nevertheless, a function that no other agency can perform. At the simplest level, it is one of the few effective, generally recognised and respected public expressions of national loyalty. As such, its worth is incalculable. But there is much more to it than that. Who knows in how many individual cases it has become an inner focus, a summoning of the attention, the crystallising of determination, one of those private experiences with public consequences, a turning point in thought and life? Every such turning is a liberation, the inner decision that must precede the outward act. Having made it, we are already free in ourselves. The alien power does not rule in our hearts or in our homes and the day is that much nearer when it shall cease to rule in Wales, our country.

The swelling wave of song rises into the grey sky over a vast arena or into the smug roof over a cultural festival. Meaningless, emotional, lying? But here and there the message hits home. Wales is a nation and *Hen Wlad Fy Nhadau* is our National Anthem. There is no other. After that, everything else follows.

Our National Anthem (The Triskel Press, 1964)

Some New Anglo-Welsh Poets

Yeats, whom it would be improper to ignore just now, said that 'passive suffering is no theme for poetry'. That being so, it is a wonder that Wales has produced any poetry at all in any language for the last few generations. Certainly the high hopes that were once entertained for an indigenous Anglo-Welsh literature to take the place of an older tradition that was visibly eroding are now being called into question.

But just as the Welsh language somehow manages to outlive all its obituarists so the newer tradition is more flourishing than some of its detractors would have us believe.

We are sometimes asked to look back to a golden age of Anglo-Welsh writing, bursting out of the cocoon of Lewis Morris, heralded by A.G. Prys-Jones, sponsored by Keidrych Rhys and Professor Gwyn Jones and carried to popular acceptance and critical acclaim by Dylan Thomas, Vernon Watkins, Glyn Jones, David Jones and Idris Davies.

Many will be found to suggest that the whole movement was a good idea which started well but got nowhere. Retrospect, however, is a notorious glamouriser. Looking at the scene in the late '40s the American critic Kenneth Rexroth in his anthology *Modern British Poetry*, spoke of the Welshmen writing in English as assuming collectively an importance which they did not sustain when scrutinised as individuals. He also held it against them that they had succumbed heavily to what currently passed as modernism. A generation later we can see them as representatives of a community which was only just finding itself in English. They wallowed in the new medium while remaining – to us at any rate – recognisably Welsh in their attitudes.

Dylan Thomas, in all his aspects, can only have escaped the dissenting pulpit by a few years, or Idris Davies the poets' corner of some vernacular weekly. Even the technical virtuosity of Vernon Watkins relates to the approach of some practitioner of the four and twenty measures; Glyn Jones is a *cyfarwydd*, elaborately eloquent in prose as in verse, while with David Jones we are clearly among the *brudwyr*, the seers. Then came R.S. Thomas, the country clergyman poet, and T.H. Jones, the archetypal *Cymro ar wasgar*, two whose circumstances and experience between them embrace the totality of our condition – rootedness and exile.

Recently, there have been initiatives which suggest the arrival of a new generation which will have to be accepted in its own right. Bryn Griffiths has formed the Welsh Writers' Guild in London and in Wales Meic Stephens has started to publish a 'little magazine', *Poetry Wales*, some of the same names prominent in both.

There is no sign of any prodigy or giant among them yet. What we note is the establishment of a tradition which can accommodate and sustain a variety of voices. They are not so self-conscious or so emphatic in their use of English as the writers collected by Keidrych Rhys in *Modern Welsh Poetry* in the '40s; they do not follow current English or American fashions so closely.

To this extent they may be thought provincial, but to this extent also they are true to the experience of the nation. They are at ease in English and in the acceptance of the limitations of their nationality, and the acceptance of limitations is the beginning of all good art.

They explore facets of individual and national and sometimes intensely local experience, and therein lies the guarantee of their integrity, for the universal may only be reached through the particular.

The poet who attempts directly to address the whole world can only bawl megaphone commonplaces, the poet who sings for his own parish may find the world listening over his shoulder, and, if not, nobody has been deafened or bored.

After the pyrotechnics and virtuosity of earlier decades (with the inevitable nemesis, the academic sterility of the Thomas industry and the meaningless vulgarity implicit in such manifestations as 'Bob Dylan') it could be that the most abiding influence will be found in R.S. Thomas.

Even when they speak from experience far removed from that of the country priest the current writers seem to carry some echo of his voice. However urban and industrial their background, whatever their own emotional climate, their diction tends to be spare, their rhythms restrained; they are not interested in technique for its own sake.

Their tone is ironic, they are involved, in anger and pity, with their community and environment; most of them have come to terms with nationalism (not necessarily Nationalism).

They are thus fulfilling the function that our Welsh society has decreed for its poets from the earliest times. Like that of Welsh poets their work is full of echoes, reminiscences, quotations, cross-references, people, places and history. They must thus write primarily for an audience which has some knowledge of these things, for their own people. But this in no way leads to sameness.

There is the unashamedly personal, often untidy gusto of Bryn Griffiths, the educated sensibility of Peter Griffiths (noted in some quarters as the man most likely to succeed): intelligent observations of Sally Roberts, the lyrical vignettes of Alun Rees, both with a luminous quality that enhances common experience.

We may respectfully note the technical range of Meic Stephens, from syllabics to pothouse ballads (some of which are actually sung in pothouses), and that of Anthony Conran, whose translations from Welsh are eagerly awaited. Nor must we overlook Charles Jones who has achieved the unusual recognition of municipal sponsorship.

Many more may be mentioned, all worth reading. All of them tend to be un-self-critical, and to go on for too long; they are all too solemn (but perhaps most of them are young) and short on badly needed satire and humour. But perhaps it takes a more self-assured tradition to sustain these genres, which do not seem to have flourished on Welsh soil in the 1,000 years of the anterior tradition, and perhaps we should not expect too much too soon. Enough for now that the graft has taken.

Western Mail (6 July 1965)

Owain Glyndŵr: Profligate Rebel or National Hero?

When, in 1915, a Swansea librarian, Rhys Phillips, signalled the fifth century of Owain Glyndŵr's presumed death by compiling a bibliography, which, incidentally, he dedicated to the leading Home Rule spokesman of the day, E.T. John, he could say, 'No other Welsh Prince has been so extensively noticed in literature.'

But for centuries after the fall of the Welsh state his reputation went underground. When he died the bards were silent. They had been silent in any case for fifteen years. Significantly, tradition assigns 1400, the year of Owain's rising, as the year of Dafydd ap Gwilym's death.

The world of Morfudd and Dyddgu was to give way to a sterner order; the society beauties and their playboy pursuers who frolic through the *cywyddau* were to bear the brunt of war. And when it was all over the traumatic shock of defeat gave a strange turn to the national mind, duly reflected in our fifteenth-century literature, full of confused prophecies.

In Mr Anthony Conran's memorable phrase, 'the messianic Cadwaladr-mongers prepared the way for the Tudors.' A lad who had carried a spear for Glyndŵr could live into old age and see a Welshman on the English throne (at least as Welsh as President Kennedy was Irish).

The case was altered. Obviously the way to get the best of the English was not the way of Owain Glyndŵr but of Owen Tudor, not by the sword but in bed. At best, as in the Tudor fable of Owain's meeting early in the morning with the Abbot of Glyn-y-Groes, he could be accused of rising too early.

At worst, his name was used as an object lesson of overweening ambition, of the consequences of treason, of the moral turpitude of being un-English. Even patriotic men like Edward Llwyd, greatest of scholars, and Dr David Powel, the historian, dismissed Owain with such phrases as 'most profligate rebel' and 'seditious seducer'. And this is the general tone of reference to Glyndŵr until well into the eighteenth century. There is one important exception.

Shakespeare was almost a public relations man for the House of Tudor. But when, in *King Henry IV, Part I*, he came to deal with their embarrassing forebear, something happened. The 'irregular and wild Glendower' of the opening lines of the play becomes the uncannily impressive figure of the Third Act, the ironic courtier, pulling Hotspur's leg and playing on the superstitions of the age, the shrewd negotiator, the brisk soldier, absolutely dominant, slightly superhuman.

Shakespeare's kindness to his Welsh characters is well known. One feels it is prompted by something more than his obligations to the Tudors. But however shrewdly observed, they are still tame Taffies, talking funny.

Not so with 'Owen Glendower'. He speaks Welsh to his daughter and perfect English to Hotspur – better than Hotspur's. Shakespeare's intentions have usually been ignored and the scene played not for its courtly irony but for the low dialect comedy of a crazy magician.

Not only is 'Glendower' at variance with the stage tradition of the comic Welshman, it is at variance with almost every reference to Glyndŵr for centuries on either side of it. There were Welsh actors in the company; the praise which Mortimer bestows on his father-in-law is faintly but unmistakably reminiscent of the *cywyddau* which the bards had sung to Owain in Sycharth two hundred years previously.

It is almost impossible to resist the suspicion that Shakespeare may have known a different story from that put out by English chronicles and Welsh arrivistes. It was a story which was not to come fully to light for nearly two hundred years after his time, until in the late eighteenth century the wandering squire Thomas Pennant rode through Wales 'rescuing' in Sir John Lloyd's words 'the genuine lineaments of a great national hero, whom literature had agreed to belittle, but whom folk memory had never forgotten.'

For four hundred incredible years the tradition had gone underground, handed down in the huts and cottages of an illiterate peasantry, through the chaos of the Wars of the Roses, the Tudor honeymoon, the Civil War and the collapse of the Bardic Order, the ferment of the literary revival and the fervour of Methodism, until quieter times offered an opportunity for battles long ago to be sympathetically recalled with no thought of their relevance to the Age of Reason. The tone of references to Owain changed.

To Theophilus Evans, historian of Breconshire, he was 'a bold and enterprising chieftain.' To Sir Samuel Rush Meyrick, the historian of Cardiganshire, he was 'that astonishing hero'. In the age of Sir Walter Scott and his imitators he began to figure in imaginative literature.

Appropriately enough, in view of his foreign policy, his first fictional appearance is in French. *La Belle Sorcière de Glan Llyn*, published in Paris in 1821, seems to have been a ripe specimen of the historical novel of the period, featuring, as contemporaries of Owain, Dafydd ap Gwilym and Twm Shon Catti!

The conception of the warrior-magician continues to have its appeal, most conspicuously exemplified by John Cowper Powys's enormous novel. It is chastening to reflect that this aspect of Owain's reputation is largely due to his luck with our impossible weather.

There were not wanting attempts to see a more serious significance in this great figure from the past. He fitted in well with the endemic tumults of what has been called our fighting century. When the ragged Chartists marched from the valleys of Gwent, the radical John Frost called on the name of Glyndŵr to inspire them.

These rebels who had forged their pikes in the caves of Llangyndir Mountain were the direct descendants of the spearmen of Craig y Dorth; they were treading the same ground and in the same spirit as their forebears; it was an appropriate invocation.

Fifty years later the spell was as strong as ever. In 1894 O.M. Edwards could write of the Glyndŵr rising as 'the extension of the Labour movement to Wales' and Owen Rhoscomyl could analyse the episode in social and economic as well as purely political and military terms. Keir Hardie had not yet come to Merthyr Tydfil to proclaim the absolute identity of the ideals of social justice and national independence, and the grassroots Syndicalists of *The Miners' Next Step* had not yet come to the coalface of Rhondda, but the Owain Glyndŵr of the romantic radicals facilitated the emergence of such ideas.

Indeed the Cymru Fydd movement made such play with Glyndŵr that they have been accused of inventing him. They certainly spoke at times as if he were O.M. Edwards on a horse. To the Liberal nonconformists it was Glyndŵr the domestic legislator who appealed, the sponsor of the Pennal programme with its reformed church, its universities and its priority for the Welsh language. O.M. Edwards collaborated with Dr Joseph Parry in a cantata, *Cambria,* in which a personified Cambria (soprano) joins with Glyndŵr (baritone) in depicting the glorious future of Wales which bears a suspicious resemblance to the then current programme of the Liberal Party.

Then there was a stage piece by Beriah Gwynfe Evans, variously put on as straight drama, music drama and pageant. Its performance at the Investiture at Caernarfon in 1911 did not, unfortunately, save it from oblivion. In another piece of the same period the Welsh characters spoke eisteddfodic Welsh and the English characters pseudo-Shakespearean English. It was successfully acted at Birkenhead and Bootle.

More objective treatment was to follow. The beginning of this century saw A.G. Bradley's sympathetic and still immensely readable history, followed in the thirties by Sir John Edward Lloyd's minor masterpiece in which the prince of Welsh historians sums up all that is known for certain about the national hero. It is a short book, the authentic facts are few. The apocrypha of Glyndŵr extends into folklore.

Trees and conspicuous stones, old buildings and hilltop camps bear his name, testimony to a reputation that transcended facts. But there are few formal monuments or tangible relics. O.M. Edwards campaigned for a memorial to be erected at Sycharth, but, considering the taste of the period, it is just as well that nothing came of it.

Glyndŵr parades with other notable figures in white marble in Cardiff's City Hall, and there is the pleasantly restored Parliament

House at Machynlleth, which, the local guidebook admits with grudging candour, 'stands as a worthy memorial to Lord Davies as well'. The figure of Glyndŵr in the murals in the reading room is said to resemble Lord Davies rather strongly, but few would deny this small compliment to the sponsor of such an attractive restoration, even if its authenticity is dubious.

All official treatment of Glyndŵr is hedged with caution. His title of Prince of Wales is circumspectly placed in inverted commas in the *Dictionary of Welsh Biography* and that excellent work proffers a qualified estimate of him as the most important character in Welsh history before the Methodist Revival. It gives more space to Thomas Charles. Ships called Caradoc and Llewelyn have seen active service but HMS Glendower was a stone frigate at Pwllheli and is now Butlin's Holiday Camp. Only an insignificant street on the outskirts of our capital bears his name.

In this year of centenaries no one has thought of belittling *Magna Carta* or the first English Parliament by slandering the characters of the leading personalities involved. But Owain can still get full treatment.

It is all rather a giveaway. Of recent years groups have taken to keeping September 6, the day of Owain's proclamation, as a festival. It seems that the monkish chronicler was right who, five hundred and fifty years ago entered in his annals: 'In this year Owain Glyndŵr disappeared. Many say he died. The prophets say he did not.'

Western Mail (7 September 1965)

A Poetic Evening

Poetry is a social activity and poets are gregarious and convivial creatures. Not all of them, of course, and not all the time. But mooning after Cynara, wandering lonely as a cloud, and gazing through magic casements are only incidental and untypical aspects of the trade.

When 'Omer smote 'is blooming lyre, when Taillefer rode ahead of the Norman chivalry up the hill at Hastings, when the mead-horn circled in Mathrafal, a more robust strain was heard, and the growing complexities of a literate and industrial society have not, on the whole, been able to silence it.

Public poetry, of course, will have its detractors. One does not have to be a hypocritical purist to doubt whether the appreciation of William Blake's highly idiosyncratic symbolism is really furthered by his verses being sung in the Albert Hall by 10,000 people wearing funny hats.

One can only hope that here and there the astonishing imagery of 'Jerusalem' penetrates a mind hitherto unaware. And this is all that the most earnest and dedicated teacher could expect to achieve by more orthodox methods. And if dead poets can win a following in the fervour of a mass audience, the living may also stimulate and be stimulated.

The poetry conferences at the Edinburgh Festival have seen some right set-to's, with Hugh MacDiarmid, somehow or other, as the inevitable protagonist. It is in the best tradition that the greatest living poet in this island should also be the most belligerent.

And now there is to be a Poetry Conference in Cardiff, part of the Commonwealth Arts Festival. It remains to be seen whether the Reardon Smith Theatre will be the arena for such fiery encounters. Even the most officially-sponsored delegates can sometimes get quite worked up, and we live in hope.

Those Welshmen who choose to write in English are not unmindful of their role as representatives of the host country. Whatever happens at the Reardon Smith, the Guild of Welsh Writers are staging their own evening, to which they invite everyone interested, whether from overseas, across the border or at home. The voice of Wales will, of course, be heard at the official conference, but, when that is over, there will be an informal evening of readings and discussion, at which there will be an opportunity to hear some of the most interesting of the younger men as well as some established names.

The chairman will be the eminent non-poet Mr Tudor David, who in reality is a power in the field of educational journalism, but whose efforts to establish the *London Welshman* as a serious English-language monthly dedicated to Welsh affairs probably bring him more satisfaction.

The Guild of Welsh Writers is, of course, largely, but not exclusively, London-based, a fact which the Guild itself is the first to deplore, and this will be their first major attempt to do something worthwhile in Wales.

The details of the evening were planned at one of their sessions in Covent Garden, with the ghosts of Goronwy Ddu and Jac Glan-y-Gors bestowing their approval, and high hopes are entertained of a worthwhile contribution to the festival scene. If you are one of the dwindling minority who still think that people who write poetry are weedy and weirdy, drop in at the Park Hotel, in Cardiff, on Saturday and you will have the surprise of your life.

Western Mail (14 September 1965)

Ten per cent Poetry

A critical evaluation of the Poetry Conference of the Cardiff Commonwealth Arts Festival

Clutching pieces of paper which proved that they were poets, a few natives, not quite sure whether they were a delegation or a chance contingent, made that first contact with the organised poetry-conference world at a reception where one of the organisers, the attractive Mrs Harpe, wife of the Arts Festival organiser, Mr Bill Harpe, briskly informed them that the Welsh language was dead.

The Poetry Conference hand-out had promised 'the first two days of discussion will centre around the problems of writing in English, particularly in the context of countries where English is not the only language ... This is a problem which will be most appropriately discussed in Wales.' If anybody came to the conference with this admirable aim in mind, it must be frankly said that they were decoyed there under false pretences. The same must be stated on behalf of those who may have been attracted by the promised discussion on 'a Commonwealth culture'.

If all poetry conferences are like this, we'd be all better employed staying home writing the stuff. Monday's discussion started with a statement about hotel bills, and went on to discuss what we should discuss.

Then world peace reared its ugly head, and for a long time the conference appeared to have confused its functions with those of the United Nations and the Vatican Council. There was a period fragrance about it all, of the dear dead days of Stephen Spender and the Left Book Club, and one member of the public was moved to ask when we were going to hear about poetry.

Some interesting suggestions were put forward, but little coherence emerged, either then or at any time until late in the week. What we got was a programme of meandering monologues, loosely intertwined, a Chekhovian inconsequence increasingly dominated by the conference-wise peripatetics.

The Afro-Asians were nowhere, except for a few outstandingly successful set pieces, which, however well-received, were never allowed to enter into the main stream of the discussion.

Some of these readings were heard under appalling acoustic conditions on Monday afternoon at the Students' Union. That evening the Welsh Theatre Company took the stage with a triumphant vindication of our own culture. Even some of the visiting firemen were impressed.

But by Tuesday morning we were back to the windy wastes of

high-flown universalism. The conference, which was supposed to be discussing the role of the poet in society, seemed swathed in soggy back-numbers of *Peace News*. A film show in the afternoon was a disaster; Wednesday was the nadir.

The joint meeting of poets and journalists (who, in real life, are so often the same people) got acrimoniously nowhere, and by the afternoon rival readings to minimum audiences were being organised and 'manifestos' circulated.

Thursday dawned ominously, the conference opening with another discussion of hotel bills, but by now some sort of order was emerging from chaos. James MacAuley, of Australia, was in the chair, and the talk was about poetry with some effective readings. But it was a noticeably Anglo-American session.

An 'action novel' planned for the afternoon does not seem to have (to coin a word) 'happened,' and a poorly attended reading of the evening, organised by Alex Trocchi, was largely by and for beats.

Alison Bielski, one of the few Welsh writers to last it all out, was only grudgingly included in this programme when she was able to inform the organiser that her work had been recognised in the United States by the important Borestone Mountain Poetry Award.

Friday's session, with the witty and incisive Canadian, John Colombo, in the chair, got down to discussion of the role of English as a 'universal' language, and its relation to indigenous languages.

Africans and West Indians were heard, and, towards the end of the morning, one of the few remaining members of the public, not by his speech a Welshman, deplored the fact that, as the conference was in Wales, no Welsh language poet had been invited to speak.

He mentioned Saunders Lewis, and, with vivid memories of the most distinguished Welshman of our time in the high pulpit of a Newtown chapel, holding his audience spellbound last month at the National Eisteddfod, one could not but wonder at the ignorance which had squandered the opportunity for an encounter that could not but have been fructifying.

The conference ended where it should have begun.

One gathers that the list of eminent personalities who were invited but did not come stretches all the way from Hugh MacDiarmid to John Lennon. But there can be no possible excuse for the parochial Anglo-American character of the proceedings. This does not mean that the beats and hipsters were not enjoyable and did not have something to say.

On the contrary, the zest and zing of Adrian Henri was a delight. Jeff Nuttall and Brian Patten are genuinely lyrical, though perhaps in a more naive, old-fashioned way than they would like to think.

Rosemary Tonks gave an interesting recital. But the poetry-and-jazz equation does not really work out. Jazz, however vital and enjoyable, is a minor art, incapable of development beyond a point soon reached, quickly ossifying into commercial clichés.

At a deeper level, Dan Ritcher, and even the impossible Mr Lionni had some serious things to say about the increasingly totalitarian character of Anglo-American society, all the more insidious because it is implicit in the techniques of social organisation rather than in the easily identifiable slogans of extremists.

But Saunders Lewis said all this twenty years ago. And much of the protest itself can be faulted, not only because so much of its expression is second-hand and immature but because of its fundamental inconsistency.

You cannot denounce an over-mechanised civilisation when that same order of things has mass-educated even the most feeble talents, provided them with cheap methods of graphic reproduction, recruited a more or less literate audience avid for any distraction and novelty, and transported the practitioners of these arts by jet plane from continent to continent, where they may pose as Savonarolas calling the world to repentance while Mr Gulbenkian pays the hotel bills.

Some of these people were advocates of a supra-national world culture, but had themselves not succeeded in assimilating anything outside the limits of English literature. MacDiarmid was mentioned by a Scottish speaker, but the implications of his mighty achievement did not fit into the pattern of chat. I do not think Quasimodo, Rilke or Apollinaire were mentioned at all. Obviously the great world culture will be, by a fortunate coincidence for these advocates, merely Anglo-American writ large.

One does not begrudge some of these birds of passage such crumbs as they may pick up. Most of them have something to say, and they have only a little time before their audiences tire of them, but the dominating part they played in the conference stopped so much else being discussed that would have been more worthwhile.

As proceedings petered out in that nonsense of an organised 'happening', consciousness of the wasted opportunities became oppressive. The public audiences dwindled, and one felt that the major item on the credit side was the personal contacts that would otherwise have been impossible to make; with the Canadians John Colombo and Earle Birney, the Australians James MacAuley, Les Murray and Harry Heseltlige (from whom, incidentally, it was interesting to hear news of T.H. Jones in his last phase). These groups must be specifically excepted from the strictures incurred by the Anglo-Americans.

Then there were the non-Europeans; the dignified representative of Guiana, the gentle Gunasingh from Ceylon, the lively exponent of negritudes, Gaston Williams, the Caribbean representatives, Professor Pereira and Louise Bennet, whose readings were impressive.

It was these, really, that one wanted to hear and hear from. They had something to say in common with and something to say to a Welsh audience and Welshmen writing in English.

As for the Welsh contribution itself, we were, as usual, disorganised, but one cannot help feeling that Giraldus was right, and that had we been inseparable then had we been insuperable; the competition was not impressive.

As it was, some clear young voices from Wales came over well, Gareth Griffiths and Andrew Hornung notably. Cynan, who was present, was largely ignored and, although he has said kind things about this conference, made one of the heretical Anglo-Welsh set down his opinion that one of the most disgraceful features of this whole business was the scant respect accorded to the representative of the historic language and literature of the land in which this gabfest was staged at the expense not only of the Gulbenkian Foundation but of the public funds of our capital city.

It has been an interesting and instructive lesson in the techniques and politics of these things, and some of us will feel less inclined to harsh judgements on indigenous institutions after seeing one of the alternatives the great world has to offer. I promise never to speak scornfully of the Babell Lên again! And perhaps, one day, with the Anglo-American circus out of the way, a Welsh audience and Welsh writers in whatever language will have an unspoilt chance to listen and learn from the fascinating voices of Africa and Asia.

Western Mail (2 October 1965)

Babylon has the Edge on Zion

The Mabinogi of Branwen the daughter of Llŷr is a tale of western seaboards and the Celtic Sea.

The armies move between Wales and Ireland, the magic birds sing at Harlech, the seven knights ride down from Menai to Pembroke, and the door that must not be opened looks towards Cornwall. But the talisman head of Brân must be buried in London under the White Hill.

This break in the geographical unity of the story is not so much an artistic flaw as the entrance to one of the great enigmas of the

Welsh mind, that ambivalent relationship with our only neighbours, and the even more special role of London.

As soon as our history emerges from myth (if it ever has done) the chronicles echo the Mabinogi and speak not of the King of England but the King of London.

English historians, dedicated to the concept of national homogeneity, minimise the particularism of their capital as of any other region. More detached and realistic, the Welsh knew better.

The nearer and more familiar English counties and towns have been to us mere market places. The great border cities and ports, for all their military and economic impact, have never been absorbed into the national imagination.

English, not Welsh, poetry familiarises us with Ludlow, Wenlock and Clun. The emigrants are either short-range, never really leaving home, or, in every sense, got lost.

Does anyone know or care how all those Welsh surnames came to be on the shopfronts of Burford in the heart of the Cotswolds? Or what happened to 'Banastre's Welshmen', a considerable medieval exodus to Lancashire?

True, the Welsh clergymen of the West Riding irrupt on to the scene with important educational proposals in the nineteenth century, but they seem visitants from a limbo of Saint David's Day dinners scattered to no purpose over the broad alien acres.

How otherwise with the Welsh of London! Their continuous history goes back far further than their most successful exemplar (Welshman for King. Pembroke boy makes good), back at least to the *Petit Waleis* that clustered around the Tower, that very White Hill of the Mabinogi, in the days when the Princes of Gwynedd were still defying its ruler.

By a weird appropriateness, the site is now a forum for those tame agitators beloved of our English friends.

Our best poets, the late medieval *cywyddwyr*, do not scruple to draw similes from London life. Dafydd ap Gwilym is familiar with the shops of Cheapside and the cloisters of Westminster, and unhesitatingly weaves them into his praise of a man whose immorality rests on his hostility to the commercial and political policies they embodied.

And if the Act of Union had its genesis in a memorandum drawn up in Brecon, its genocidal intentions were largely nullified by the deliberations at Lambeth which sponsored Bishop Morgan's Bible. And for the next three hundred years London was the only place where a sufficient number of influential Welshmen could gather to take important decisions.

The bijou societies of our market towns could not compete, could only breed imitative pretensions. And the first urban centre of any importance in Wales itself was the mining camp, Merthyr Tydfil, until Cardiff came up in the 1860's, one of the younger capitals therefore, and to be forgiven some of its youthful inadequacies.

London, the market of our herds, attracted not only drovers, but, as the Court, called to all those 'impatient of labour and overmuch boasting of the Nobilitye of their stocke, applying themselves rather to the service of noblemen than giving themselves to the learning of handicraftes', as Humphrey Lloyd puts it in a comment which, *mutatis mutandis*, has an oddly contemporary ring.

The dichotomy of tribal, agrarian Wales is thus early established, part retreating ever deeper into defensive emphasis on everything that differentiated it from the outside world (eventually to nurture a cross-grained puritanism utterly at odds with every characteristic that made us a people) and part of it reaching out to embrace commercial and political advancement in a spirit of shallow and pliant opportunism which brought its own nemesis; so Sir Hugh Middleton sank the fortune of his Cardiganshire mines in the New River scheme, which beggared him.

To this day, Ludgate Circus is cluttered with a paltry obelisk commemorating a Montgomeryshire worthy who had made his pile; offered in desperation by the City to his native place, it was refused.

But such acid anecdotes are not the whole story. The Cymmrodorion have, in their day, deserved well of Wales: the attorneys of Tavie's Inn, depicted by Hogarth, the radicals who foregathered with Jac Glan-y-Gors and Iolo Morganwg, the drapers and milkmen, pillars of Jewin and King's Cross.

The recent death of Sir John Cecil-Williams brought to an end a recognisable period, and poses a fundamental question: Is there still a role for the London-based Cymmrodorion? Or should they now seek a home in the Welsh Capital?

It is a question of legitimate interest far outside the confines of the Honourable Society, and of some historical significance.

But there has always been a wider spectrum of London-Welsh than the official and self-conscious element. The Depression may have filled the East End with blue-scarred postmen and chuckers-out, and the purlieus of Paddington with girls who never let on to mam, but this was no new thing.

> *O na bawn i fel colomen*
> *Ar ben Saint Pauls ynghanol Llundain*
> *Er gael gweled merched Cymru*
> *Ar eu cluniau'n chwynnu'r gerddi.*

The country poet who wrote this *pennill* (still quoted in West

Wales pubs), lusting for the pretty knees of the girls who had gone as migrant labour to weed the gardens of London, illuminates a whole unofficial history.

The existence of this great mart of opportunity on the doorstep of a conservative-minded hill country has had consequences which have never really been calculated.

Life in Wales is easy-going, democratic, neighbourly. Or it is slow, inefficient and claustrophobic. If the latter, the escape route is at hand.

Economic necessity, after all, cannot possibly account for the volume and character of our emigration, especially when you consider the number of English people who have to be brought in to keep the country going. The fact is that Babylon has always got the edge on Zion.

The Welsh (or ex-Welsh) community in London embraces a wider spectrum than anything in Wales itself, from Tony Armstrong-Jones who married a princess to Timothy Evans who was hanged by mistake, from Bronwen Pugh who became Lady Astor to Betty Jones who became a gunman's moll.

It took an English writer whose sensibilities had been sharpened by living in Wales, Mr Kingsley Amis, to point out that the most tangible internal frontier in this island is the one surrounding London.

Now that the world no longer thinks tomorrow what Manchester thinks today, the great industrial centres of provincial England have lost their importance like their predecessors, the landed magnates of the shires. Of the old ruling class only the Crown has retained any significance. And from the centuries of industrial growth London has emerged as the only effective centre of influence.

It is not rash to prophesy that decentralisation and regional autonomy will offer very little corrective. If anything, London will expand at England's expense, and its ethos and standards will extend their frontiers over new territories of the land and of the mind.

Already its outposts are only a county away from Offa's Dyke. Bristol may lurk just over the Severn Bridge, but the launching-pad in respect of which the distant-early-warnings are already sounding is the Chiswick flyover.

The city that made its own treaty with the Conqueror, the wool wharf of the Hanse almost as much a city state as any in the League, whose mobs survived policy and whose prentice bands brought down the monarchy, the northern Venice Canaletto saw, the foggy liberal refuge of expatriate visionaries, the hub of Empire, the front-line capital, is facing change with a confidence not born of wealth alone.

Sprouting skyscrapers marketing now not only its old wares but the tertiary products of the contemporary scene – the fashions and the trends – it outlives its Empire like Byzantium, to become one of only a few such centres in the world, cosmopolitan in the literal sense of the word, a market and a magnet for the increasing proportion of the world's population who have the means of mobility, the desire for diversion, the tastes to enjoy and the incomes to afford lavish amenities.

And, even by British Rail on a good day, less than three hours from a country where livestock roam in the streets, business never seems to get started before mid-morning, and any activity after 9 p.m. is regarded as night-life. No wonder there is so much out-way traffic.

Not all the emigrants are a loss to us. Mr Morgan buys a ticket at Swansea High Street, he disappears en route, and Mr Morton gets off the train at Paddington. We have more than our share of people who cannot live with their own identity.

Recently a Welsh lady beat with her umbrella an African speaker at Hyde Park Corner who suggested that people should stay in their own country including the Welsh in Wales.

Not only was the unfortunate blackamoor belaboured with our dreaded national weapon, he was fined for a breach of the peace, for it is important to our expatriates and their hosts that this escape route be kept open.

It must often seem to be delusive escape – into a dead-end ghetto which has been called Tregaron-on-Thames, an incredibly old-fashioned community, walled in by the busy indifference of a great city to the private lives of individuals.

But even this tranquil back-water is feeling the wind of change. The once-a-year Welshman, the long-distance patriots of the Eisteddfod field and the capricious benefactors are greeted not with the respect of yore, but with something like contempt.

Elfed could achieve a personal ascendancy in Wales, part of which was based on the very fact of his long years at King's Cross. Wales today would not accept as national patriarch one so largely representative of the diaspora.

The grotesque 'new national flag', which was invented in London, has died the same death as the even more grotesque idea of staging the National Eisteddfod in the concrete and claustrophobic halls and galleries of Earl's Court.

The social bases in Wales, from which this retrovert colony is mostly recruited, are themselves either eroding or evolving.

The most aware members of it are consciously seeking a new formula for Welsh life in London.

One interesting by-product is the emergence of *The London Welshman*, under the editorship of Mr Tudor David, as an English-language monthly seriously commenting on Welsh affairs – currently the only such.

But it is the Welsh in Wales who must give the effective answer, if they can, to the dilemma of living in the same world with such formidable competition.

Whatever one's assortment of political nationalism, it is obviously only a partial contribution to the problem of maintaining the national identity of a country, naturally conservative, whose most active elements have such an attractive alternative so easily available.

Paradoxically, the proximity of London has reinforced the conformism and suspicion of change which are both the strength and the weakness of highland zone societies, and a thorough-going revision of all our attitudes, in every sector of our national life, is the only hope for the survival of the nation.

Sentimental longing for a Wales which never was, or is deservedly dead, will not save us. The Mabinogi is over. The head of Brân is buried under Tower Hill.

Western Mail (6 November 1965)

A Festival Souvenir

P.L. Brent (ed.), *Young Commonwealth Poets.*

The publication of this anthology coincided with the outbreak of war between India and Pakistan. Neither event argues very strongly for the Commonwealth idea. The wretched Poetry Conference at the Commonwealth Arts Festival, in Cardiff, last September, did little to rehabilitate it, and although the anthology is not quite such a shambles as the conference, no clear intention or pattern emerges.

One could go through the countries represented and arrive at snap judgements. The Australians and the Welsh seem most involved in national experience, while the Nigerians exploit this involvement with most technical skill. The Canadians and the Pakistanis are most influenced by Eng. Lit. The English are most preoccupied with technique. The Ghanaians, the West Indians and the Scots are the most visually aware. The Indians tend to be diffuse, the Ceylonese lyrical. The New Zealanders are introverted and the 'Northern Irish,' perhaps most understandably, dull.

Malawi, Tanzania, Gambia, and Malaysia are, on this showing, one-poet countries and only in the Sierra Leone contribution, by

Gaston Bart-Williams, do we reach outside the charmed circle of English orthodoxy to make contact with the fascinating phenomenon of Negritude. There is only one poem in non-standard English, by a West Indian called Evan Jones. It is a good one. But does this reflect what is really going on? We are told nothing about the poets, whether they are natives of the countries they represent and, if so, whether they still live there, or their relationships and attitudes to the indigenous languages and cultures. Having heard, despite the futility of the conference proceedings, some of the non-European poets speaking or singing their work, one doubts the 'universal' potentialities of English (rather like late medieval Latin; all universal languages outlive their universality).

Even if the stormy circumstances of this volume's compilation permitted it, would any balanced conspectus be possible? The titles of the poems included contain such words as Mugomo, Basho, Kwela, Nargol, Tapu, Gahini, Baobab, Mzee (and, if it comes to that, Pallau). Is anyone, anywhere, competent to appraise all these poems in relation to their objective correlative? Even computers can only appreciate poems written by other computers. The whole concept of the anthology brilliantly defeats itself.

That brings us to Wales, represented here by thirteen poems, in five of which Wales is actually mentioned by name (in one of these it is also called Cymru, for good measure); there are two poems about Dai, two about legs, two about coal, two about dying. On this showing John Stuart Williams and Bryn Griffiths are better poets than anthologists. ('Dying at Pallau' is, in fact, quite impressive). Sauntering easily away with the honours out of this welter of public clichés, Alison J. Bielski and Sally Roberts, being women, speak with their own voices. There is a splendidly masochistic poem by Andrew Davies which Gaston Bart-Williams, of Sierra Leone, has praised highly as immediately intelligible to any African, but as far as Wales is concerned, this selection is at least ten years out of date.

This doesn't mean to say that it isn't worth the money, or that the enlightened bestowal of public subsidy by Cardiff City Council has been wasted. There are probably more good poems in this book than in most anthologies. But don't look for a pattern. Think of it as a Festival souvenir and you won't be disappointed.

Poetry Wales (1.2, Autumn 1965)

The Writer and his Community

I believe the label 'Anglo-Welsh' was first used in a literary way at some time during the Cymru Fydd period, towards the end of the last century. Like so much else at the time, it was modelled on an Irish analogy. It belonged to the vocabulary of politics and, although for the last forty years or so it has been rarely used in a political sense, there is still a political flavour to it. Its firm use seems to have been established by A.G. Prys-Jones in his anthologizing activities in the first two decades of the present century. But it achieved real significance and vitality in the 1930s and the credit for that belongs to Keidrych Rhys and Dylan Thomas.

The previous history of recognizably 'Anglo-Welsh' writing seems to me more curious than useful. Even such an outstanding interpreter of our national literature as Professor Gwyn Williams came to grief when he tried to give to Welsh writing in English the same status as belonged to writing in the Welsh language over the centuries. There is, I think, something bogus about looking for our antecedents in Henry Vaughan or Thomas Traherne and something quite contemptible about trying to conscript John Donne and George Herbert as specifically Anglo-Welsh poets. After all, nobody thinks of George Eliot, née Mary Ann Evans, as an Anglo-Welsh novelist. The modern Anglo-Welsh position is very recent. It has its roots in stony, recently disturbed ground and it has all the wasted vitality of wild nature. At the overlap of two worlds, the English and the Welsh, it is essentially compromised, impure, and therein lies its mongrel strength.

Gunter Grass, the oracle of modern German literature, has said that after the last war there was only one real victor – the English language. But however dominant English may be, it is worth remembering that its effective ascendancy in Wales is a very recent phenomenon and is by no means complete. Wales shares this situation with many other countries, from an old-established polity like the United States, where a common linguistic and literary inheritance sits uneasily with a total rejection of English attitudes in every other sphere, to the emergent nations of Africa, where English dominion has not lasted even for the lifetime of a man like Jomo Kenyatta. I hesitate to use the French word *anglophone* but it is a handy description of a country such as Wales which, though largely English-speaking, is not and cannot be English in any deeper sense.

I was reared in Swansea which has, on its western side, an English-speaking hinterland where the English language is not a recent growth but an ancient, organic dialect with its own tune and tempo, its own songs and even its own folk-poet in Cyril Gwynne. Perhaps it is because I was nurtured on his verses that it has never seemed to me absurd or treasonable to write in English without being anything but a Welshman. In Swansea, too, which I think was one of the first centres of an Anglo-Welsh tradition, there are certain choices for the young man with literary ambitions. Whether he has any Welsh or not, he can easily go English, as the majority of those now growing up in the city will probably do. They assimilate the broad mass of writing in English taught in the schools and lose themselves in it. On the other hand, the young writer, if circumstances permit, can remain totally Welsh in the sense of not writing in any language other than Welsh. This has been the choice of one of the greatest poets of our own time, namely Waldo Williams, who also comes from an old-established Englishry, that of southern Pembrokeshire. With neither of these choices do I have any quarrel.

But between the 'Anglo' and the 'Welsh' falls the hyphen. It is a tightrope for the agile clowning of Gwyn Thomas, a delicate bi-cultural balancing act for Glyn Jones, a narrow and lofty pulpit for R.S. Thomas. In some hands it is held up like the serpent in the wilderness to guide a people to the Promised Land, while in others it can be a club with which to bash out our enemies' brains. The hyphen represents a synthesis, however uneasy or disputed. For Anglo-Welsh writing does not spring from a mature tradition: its boundaries are in doubt, its standards in chaos, many of its claims bogus. Yet it has its own validity because it represents a genuine attitude to life and to writing. Some observers will dispute this, no doubt. We three poets of the Triad group, you will remember, were carpeted by a reviewer in *The Anglo-Welsh Review* for daring to express a personal involvement in our country's condition and were accused of revelling in a predicament that did not exist. But there is no arguing with such critics, for they are in panic flight into their own hells of solipsism and paranoia. To those whose minds are not yet closed, I can only recommend the discussion, published in *Encounter*, that took place between Alexander Trocchi and Hugh MacDiarmid at the Edinburgh festival a few years ago.

So what then is the sense, the point, the satisfaction, for a Welshman who writes in English? The temptations are numerous and few have avoided them entirely. The biggest source of artistic corruption lies in the availability of a mass-market with an insatiable appetite for the quaint and grotesque. The writer who succumbs at this point will find that he is turning out caricatures, becoming reliant on routine farce. There is also the temptation to write for one of the several minority audiences that abound in English-language publishing. Hardly any of the first generation of Anglo-Welsh writers escaped this fate. In retrospect, writers like Goronwy Rees, Geraint Goodwin, Margiad Evans, Gwyn Jones, and even Glyn Jones at his second best, all seem to have strayed into a faded limbo of 'thirties modishness. As for the poets so painstakingly collected by Keidrych Rhys for his anthology *Modern Welsh Poetry* twenty years ago, they testify more to the compiler's industry than to any real achievement.

Some years ago, at Fishguard, I heard the veteran patriot D.J. Williams utter the memorable words, 'Wales can be a cruel mother to those who love her too well.' So much of what we see around us today offers every inducement to turn away into other worlds: the contemplation of the inane generalities of 'universal truth', all those exquisitely evocative studies of childhood, the escape into pathologically euphoric slapstick (*pace* Gwyn Thomas at his worst), the virtuoso verbalism of even some of our best poets, and so on. The more robust temperaments have piled on the drama and sensationalism of Welsh life, no doubt with one eye on the box-office, while the more fastidious have appealed to the sensibilities of a minority audience. In many cases they have brought considerable gifts to the tasks set them, but one common miscalculation has vitiated the achievement of the best-selling novelist and the slim-volume aesthete alike: their choice of audience. Once a writer has been conned by modish reviewers into believing that the Welsh are a marginal, picturesque people, with special characteristics unknown elsewhere, or with a talent for screamingly funny nicknames, or with a monopoly in dark, strong, tragic suffering, he is on the slippery slope to the Big Sell-out. Two points occur to me here. Much of the best writing about Wales has been the work of writers who are not Welsh. I am thinking of Evelyn Waugh's *Decline and Fall* and the more recent delineations of the local scene as we have them in the novels of Kingsley Amis. So few of our writers have felt confident enough to pull their own legs. There is no *Cold Comfort Farm*, despite the proliferation of our death-dung-and-disaster epics which surely invite such treatment. I remember that Nigel Heseltine once wrote a very funny short story on these lines, but not even Keidrych Rhys dared to print it.

What then is the justification of Anglo-Welsh writing? It involves, I think, a fundamental re-appraisal of the creative writer's function and his relationship with his own community. I am not here suggesting the taking up of any particular viewpoint or commitment, although I have a feeling that this would probably be an inevitable development for the writer who wants to take his function seriously.

What is Welsh about an Anglo-Welsh writer is obviously not the language in which he writes. It is not even any special use of that language, apart from a few colloquialisms carried over from the

Welsh language. These amount to very little and attempts to overdo them, to write an incantatory, pseudo-Welsh sort of English, will bring a speedy nemesis. No, the Anglo-Welsh writer can never have the exotic resources of a Synge or Tutuola. His difference must lie in his function, which is to express a way of living rather than a way of considering life. Above all, he does not have to go out looking for his audience because it is there all around him: he is a social animal. He is what writers in the Welsh language have always been, from the warrior-poet who went to Catraeth twelve hundred years ago to the milkman and minister who collect their book-tokens for winning at the National Eisteddfod. He is no different from his neighbours except in the craft that he plies. He is only marginally more articulate than the people who sit next to him in the bar or bus. He draws his strength from the very narrowness of this margin, so that with a bit of luck, he will hear his own words quoted while he is still alive and young enough to enjoy that reward. This, in terms of pure, personal satisfaction, is what makes writing in English – while taking no notice whatsoever of any audience outside Wales – so completely rewarding. Others may achieve critical acclaim and some may gain financial gratification, but at a cost that does not bear thinking about.

The poet's personal satisfaction, however, is not in itself a complete justification. I have said that the Welsh writer, whichever of our two languages he uses, is involved in the life of his community. This life is not life-in-the-abstract but life in a definite, vivid, concrete context, the life of a community and ultimately the life of a nation. In this respect he is more akin to those writers in the Welsh language whose work perhaps he cannot read than he is to those with whom he shares a common language but who write from a profoundly different standpoint. His ultimate allegiance can be seen in the development of R.S. Thomas as a poet. Almost from the outset, R.S. Thomas's work was recognized by a readership outside Wales. The critics found it easy to categorize him: rural poet (comparison with Andrew Young); clergyman poet (ritual mention of George Herbert); genre poet (mention of Crabbe); and so on. Imagine the baffled disequilibrium of the English reviewers, therefore, when they found that Mr Thomas, although he is all of these, is also something bigger and far more disturbing – a Welsh poet. Reading the reviews of *The Bread of Truth*, it was possible to see the confidently prefabricated reviewers' phrases crumpling under the impact of a man who proudly pro-claimed his devotion to his own country. This, I believe, is the final justification of our position as Welsh writers in English.

Letter to Meic Stephens, 1965

From Maxen Wledig to Lloyd George

We begin with a dream. *The Mabinogi* of Maxen and Elen is perhaps the most enchanting of them all, and when the Emperor comes to Caer Seiont in Arfon to claim his bride, we are there with her brothers, ready to go out with Maxen to conquer the world.

It is not entirely a dream, of course, these things happened, but it is the way they grew in the telling that became for us the truth.

The garrison of Segontium, left over from the wars of Maximus, we glimpse marooned somewhere in the Balkans, and it is tempting to linger by their campfires and listen to their tales.

But in the mouths of the men who returned and in the minds of their listeners, those who had never left home, the tales grew taller than any that have ever been told, so that Welshmen have always believed that they once conquered the world, that the wide lands beyond their borders are theirs by right and offer greater rewards and satisfactions than they can ever find at home. It is a dream we have lived by ever since.

Into the unconquered mountains of a dark-age Montenegro came the irreconcilable refugees, the saints and scholars, the dispossessed, ruling families, enriching our genes and our high opinion of ourselves, but bringing, too, a revanchiste nostalgia whose taint still lingers, all fuel to the dream.

It is there, in the beginning of our literature, in the *Armes Prydain*, that astonishing document which seems unable to conceive of a free Wales without a 'reconquest' of East Britain, lands we never owned, it is there in the rambling prophecies of Merlin, caught up in the historical fiction of Geoffrey of Monmouth, in the prediction that a Welsh prince would wear the Crown of London.

Not even the black humour of the Angevin hangman who crowned the head of Llewelyn II with ivy and paraded it in mockery through Cheapside could quench it. Even Glyndŵr had to fall in with its wilder expressions, the skimble-skamble stuff of which Shakespeare makes Hotspur so justifiably impatient.

All subsequent manipulators of Welsh opinion could reliably cash in on it until its seeming fulfilment in Henry Tudor, who indeed wore the Crown of London, and Wales was at peace, not only with her neighbours, but with herself.

But not, of course, for long. Obviously the dream had still to be pursued. There were surely other worlds to conquer than the Court and the Exchange. So it was revealed that the Welsh had discovered America. Madoc took over from Maxen.

But the Welsh Indians remain undiscovered, the plans for new

Welsh dominions obstinately stayed on paper or were realised in sickly and struggling ventures long since vanished from the map: Cambriol in Newfoundland, New Wales, a name you will find in old atlases north of Hudson's Bay, perhaps most fitting of all, a 'Wales' marooned at the tip of Alaska, almost between the hemispheres, so near the Date Line that it is neither east nor west.

Meanwhile, less strenuous theorisers were extending the dream, not in space, but in time, pushing its frontiers into antiquity, scripture and myth. The Ancient Britons make their appearance (and their uniquely noble priesthood, the Druids), radiant Cymbeline and Sabrina Fair, Hil Gower and Hu Gadarn, all the gorgeous nonsense adumbrated in Spenser, Shakespeare and Milton, to be made definitive for our own educated classes by Theophilus Evans in the eighteenth century, at the very dawn of the Methodist revival.

The nineteenth century was a cauldron (still simmering gently in some corners of the national mind) of allocentric ambitions realised in all the tempting imperial and mercantile and evangelical avenues that seemed to lead to such bright promise.

So, at the precise moment when the Welsh woollen industry needed an outstanding personality to organise and develop it, Robert Owen left Newtown for a lifetime of highflown idealism that ran out in the sands, while his own place sank into a decline.

So Timothy Richards became a Mandarin, and Will Paynter became a Commissar. Henry Richard was hoisted into public life on the shoulders of the most-exploited community in Wales to become the Apostle of Peace, and his legatees have been nagging the world ever since with their messages of goodwill, and their monument is the Temple of Peace, opened just in time for World War II, a building whose cold and empty architectural style makes it a fitting sepulchre for a dead illusion.

But more splendid than any of these was the dream incarnate itself: David Lloyd George. The enigma of his personality and of the hold he exercised has defied analysis.

Even the analytical mind of J.M. Keynes was baffled, and he wrote despairingly of a visitant from the Celtic otherworld. In this he was not far from the truth. For Lloyd George, and Wales with him, united as never before, the whole stage of imperial and world politics was the working out of the old obsessive myth, with the moralistic overtones it had accumulated in more recent centuries.

It was more than a place of influence and authority for despised and neglected sectors of the community, tenant farmers and non-conformist congregations, more than a socio-economic surge forward that gave Lloyd George his dynamic, and his followers their fanatical loyalty and solidarity.

It was the fulfilment of the National Destiny, to be pursued from one thrilling instalment to another of growing prestige as a domestic legislator, as an imperial statesman, to the final ecstasy of intoxication when the attorney from Criccieth strode into the Hall of Mirrors at Versailles, arbiter of the world.

'George ddaeth yn bennaeth y byd' ['George became the ruler of the world'] sang the country poet Dolander Jones, a shrill voice picked out at random from a deafening chorus of unanimous adulation that was not to be interrupted until that day in 1930 when, in Caernarfon Pavilion, crowded to pay homage to an idol, young voices called out *'Beth am Gymru?'* ['What about Wales?']

But the weighty opinion of such an historian as Mr A.J.P. Taylor confirms the gushing claim of the Llandovery bard. At that moment, with the Kaiser in flight, the Danubian monarchy in ruins, Russia in chaos and the pride of the Sublime Porte humbled; with Wilson dying, Clemenceau out-manoeuvred, Orlando and the others a stage army, Lloyd George was indeed the most powerful man in the world.

The map of Europe and the Middle East, that most adult Welshmen grew up with, was a Welshman's creation. There was nothing more to strive for; virtue had triumphed, small nations had been restored, usurping emperors brought down. Jerusalem and Damascus were in his gift: Welsh troops mounted guard at the Holy Sepulchre. The dream of Maxen was fulfilled.

It was a long and bitter trek back to reality. As with all hangovers, there were times when we were not really sure whether we were sobering up or still drunk. Old men still shake their heads ruefully at the memory of how Lloyd George came to the Three Valleys Pavilion at Mountain Ash to confront an audience of militant miners, and how he diverted their hostility, by means they still cannot understand.

And as they worked their way back through the agony of strikes, hunger-marches and dole queues, dust and T.B., the man they most hated worked out *his* agony of rejection, growing raspberries in the Home Counties, waiting for the call that never came.

The dregs of the dream were a long time draining out – they linger to this day. The stylised 'Internationalism', completely unrelated to any real interest in other countries or ability to appreciate other cultures, always seems to come more cozily from Welsh lips than the rest of the second-hand left-wing claptrap, and some of the statements of the Nationalist case, happily less frequent of late, postulate a messianic destiny for the revived Welsh State which one doubts would be widely accepted beyond our borders.

But we are coming to at last. In the harsh dawn of disillusion we can see that the irredentism of Dark Age refugees doesn't automatically underwrite our expatriates' expectations; the glittering romance of Geoffrey is revealed as Plantagenet public relations.

Madoc would never have got launched but for imperial rivalry for title to the New World – even the Druids turn out to be rather far-fetched propaganda for Anglican autonomy – and, whoever benefited from all those brilliant careers in London, it wasn't the ordinary people of Wales.

For Maxen's dream was, after all, somebody else's dream and, while the men who had followed him out of history fetched up in distant exile, the tracts they had abandoned were settled, named and defined by Cunedda and his sons, to become the basis of an enduring people who, in the fullness of time, were to place themselves under the patronal protection of a saint who glorified the common tasks of the day and bade them be mindful of the small things.

Western Mail (4 December 1965)

Our Modern Myths

They blow up at you like yesterday's newspapers around a street corner in a high wind – bits and pieces whirled out of a past that refuses to die.

Often there is an urgent, almost unreal drama in the encounter, and it is none the worse for happening, as it so often does, in a public-house. One of those sad, rambling places, perhaps, that so often neighbour a big railway yard on the coast, where the atmosphere in the bar is moist and gusty, like the weather outside.

The clientele appear to have been there since Brunel's day and the conversation is as likely to be about the Taff Vale Judgement as about Dr Beeching.

A hollow-eyed old man, an elder of the tribe, speaks, 'You try getting into Number Eleven Bay late at night. You go out from here at stop-tap and try it. You'll never get anywhere near. Security men all over the place. Do you know why? Because that's where the bullion train goes from. Dead on midnight. All the money being taken out of Wales up to London.'

Nobody disagrees, they mumble into their beer and half-change that subject. They cannot bring themselves to make articulate the contradiction between what they know to be the facts and what, deep down, they feel to be not.

Trains with hush-hush cargoes undoubtedly leave remote bays in the small hours; security checks operate at odd times; there is just enough plausibility in the maundering tale to hold back an open expression of disbelief.

No one questions that 'all the money being taken out of Wales' goes in the glittering guise of bullion, no one questions the unhallowed timing of the deed. Midnight, mischief and gold.

In the second half of the twentieth century, in one of our large seaboard cities, the materials of fable are still to hand, and the ability to make myth is still strong.

Or go to one of the older communities of the coalfield on the outcrop where opencast mining throws up its ramparts of topsoil and the machines of our age reach easily down into the seams that once had to be burrowed for.

Here the talk will always be of coal. At the least encouragement an old miner will be down on his hands and knees on the bare board floor, squeezing between the cast-iron legs of a marble-topped table, and, with a pint glass for a lamp and a rolled-up *Echo* for a mandril, show you how they did things when mining was an art, and every man had his stall, before the pneumatic pitprops and coal ploughs.

And when the talk turns to the newer ways, more is revealed than the glittering lake-like surface of a seam laid bare from the top. 'When they got down to the old nine foot do you know what they found? They found old workings nobody knew about. Workings so old they weren't on any plans or charts. Then they worked along the seam and they came to a fall. And on the other side of the fall there was a journey of trams all loaded up. And the skeletons of the colliers, and the gaffer-hauliers, and the horse, and a little boy.'

It is a self-adjusting story. You will never be able to disprove it because the opencast men are on piece-rates, working against time. Anything like that would hold them up if it was reported, they'll just go right through it, cover it over, deny there was anything of the sort.

In some versions there are no skeletons but the entire bodies of the ancestors, kneeling staring-eyed in prayer, crumbling to dust before the excavator driver can believe his senses and slam on the brakes.

More pervasive, more persuasive, walks the Wandering German. You will come upon his tracks wherever there is or has been any industrial activity. 'There was a German here,' they will tell you, 'and he took one look at that hill and he said, "If that hill was in Germany we'd be getting millions of pounds a year out of it".'

Like all good myths, the Wandering German blurs at the edges. Sometimes he is a Dutchman, more rarely a returned exile from Canada or Peru, and as often as not it is an exhausted scene that he surveys, of weedgrown tips and abandoned workings.

He has stood on the edge of Crumlin Bog and under the shadow of Twyn y Waun by the ruins of Dowlais. He has been heard of in deepest Powys and furthest Anglesey, a voice crying in the wilderness, vainly calling attention to lost opportunities and hidden wealth.

But in his purer manifestations, his significance is unmistakable. Like Chekhov's Russians, whom we so greatly resemble, we have assigned the Germans a definite role: they are the embodiment of efficiency, the people most adapted to survival and success in the industrial age.

Recent history has done little to shake this assessment. The Wandering German is our judgement on ourselves, on our own inadequacy, our lack of initiative and ordered effort, our incapacity for sustained industry and our inability to run our own country for our own benefit.

We do not believe in secret tunnels and hidden caves of treasure; there is too much knowledge of the practical problems, and too much respect for the rapacity of our forefathers for us to believe that there would be any of it left anyway; only the ghosts are still looking for Queen Catherine's gold at the far end of Gower.

But we believe, and in this we are not wrong, that our land is a treasure-house of which we have got to find the key. The belief is expressed in contemporary terms. For the frontiers of the Kingdom of the Tylwyth Teg receded long ago, and the industrial history of Wales is as colourful and as exciting, as full of unlikely events and impossible people as any other chapter in our story.

It is a vast repository of lore not dissimilar to that rambling repertoire of the rural areas of Welsh-speaking Wales – *y pethe*, a mixture of anecdotes and history, poetry and creative gossip – that is a strong, subtle element in the fabric of the nation.

It is a faculty at least as useful as the capacity to arrive at orderly conclusions based on the observation of random facts, and, because it is a lot rarer, a great deal more valuable. If there is a difference between poetry and science, this is it.

To some it may seem to be in itself a guarantee that we will remain a nation despite everything. Others may be on safer, sadder ground in doubting this.

But at least it means that if we do succeed in remaining a nation, that nation will be worth listening to.

Western Mail (5 February 1966)

Poetry of the Scots

Maurice Lindsay (ed.), *Modern Scottish Poetry,*
an Anthology of the Scottish Renaissance.

Poetry is the most arrogant yet the most democratic of the arts.
Claiming, as no other medium can, direct communication with whatever powers lie beyond the conscious limits, it must yet speak with
the tongue of the market-place.

It is human, and it is essentially national, or nothing (we had some
ripe examples of cosmopolitan non-poetry at the Commonwealth Arts
Festival!). Much to the annoyance of mass-merchandising universalists,
a poet can only speak to and for his own people. For a submerged
nation, its poetry is the reefs that break the surface, reminding the
world of its existence, impeding the commerce of commonplaces.

Scottish poetry is such an affirmation of identity (though Hugh
MacDiarmid is more a volcanic island than a coral reef!) and this
anthology gives a conspectus of a movement which is as much social
and political as literary. The Scottish Renaissance, so named by
Denis Daurat (significantly, not an Englishman) in 1924, had been
in preparation since the beginning of the century, with such forerunners as John Davidson (not included here), and the first publication of Mr Maurice Lindsay's anthology in 1946 was a milestone
marking the end of its first phase.

Since then, as he says, there have been some fadeouts and many
developments. Edwin Muir is dead, W.S. Graham, with *The Night Fishing*
and *The White Threshold,* established a reputation not maintained.

There has been the ebullient controversy about 'Plastic Scots', the
passing of the heyday of MacLellan's as semi-official publishers to
the movement, the rise and fall of *New Saltire,* an excellent literary
periodical, and the inevitable reaction against the supremacy of
MacDiarmid. In the 'poor-old-tired horse' school of Edinburgh.

Whether a re-styled anthology can reflect all this after twenty years
is open to doubt, but Mr Maurice Lindsay has certainly compiled a
most readable collection, welcome for its own sake. Not a poem in it
but shows some flash of sharp, accurate observation and a firm, confident use of language. There are no notable absentees, and, with the
exception of Burns Singer as he presumptuously styled himself, no
unworthy inclusions.

There has been a decline in the impetus to establish Lallans as a
separate literary language. The Scotland of Billy Wolfe is not the
Scotland of John Maclean, but this tendency is more than compensated by the continued vitality of Gaelic, with Derek Thomson now

joining Sorley Maclean and George Campbell Hay.

Even in translation their works are impressive; their effect in the original can only be guessed at; the best of Gwenallt suggests itself as a tentative comparison. While Gaelic produces writers of this stature our colleges of advanced barbarism will have all their work cut out to prove that no language is any good unless it is spoken by a hundred million people.

Mr Lindsay's choice is obviously not towards what an outsider thinks of as typically Scots: immense learning, savage humour, harsh satire, but that he has produced such a good anthology while avoiding so much of the good stuff written in these veins, speaks well for modern Scottish poetry.

Now, what about a re-styled *Modern Welsh Poetry?*

Western Mail (2 April 1966)

Poet and Local Patriot

The Heads of the Valleys Road tunnels through its escarpments and vaults its limestone gorges; for over a century the urban spread of nearby Merthyr Tydfil has been eroding its fields – quarrying has left its scars – but the parish of Vaynor is still recognisably Faenor Gwynwo, a favoured patrimony.

There are still people deeply attached to its soil, its traditions and history. But even among these there are few today who remember Creidiol.

Yet it was in the cosy tavern that nestles by the churchyard wall in the old quiet heart of the parish that I heard the verses quoted that set me on his trail; verses in praise of the place and its people. Creidiol the sturdy temperance man would not have been pleased, but Creidiol the local patriot (and, even in Wales, was there ever one to touch him?) would have gloried in the appropriateness of the setting.

Like all good local patriots he came from somewhere else, but from the time he came there as a young curate in 1879, to the day of his death in 1903, after a generation's service as parish priest and public champion, this son of Gwent identified himself with every aspect of life in the Breconshire foothills on the coalfield's northern crop.

In many ways he was a typical rather than an outstanding man of his time, and therein lies much of his interest. Born Jabez Jenkins, into the working class of the Sirhowy Valley, he made his way in the

99

world by his own efforts, growing up in the Hungry Forties, getting what little education he could from the Sunday School rather than the inadequate day schools, and learning the craft of poetry from its patriarch in Gwent, Aneurin Fardd, the miller of his native village. Among his fellow-pupils was a Tredegar collier, John Bevan, so much under the sway of his teacher and the traditions of our people that he gave the name Aneurin to his son. This was before the seamless robe of the national heritage was parted, before the Welsh were cheated of their language and the *gwerin* ground down to proletariat. This was when a young man whose modest talents were nurtured and sustained by a culture going back to the earliest times could rise to the challenge of the new age.

The 1850s saw the young Jenkins in Pontypridd, part of the westward migration from Gwent to the latest frontier of industry, part of the ferment that produced the wild heresies of Myfyr Morganwg, and the picturesque antics of Dr William Price, the lively literary and musical life of 'Clic y Bont' and whose crowning achievement is the National Anthem.

But this young man who adopted the bardic name of Creidiol walked neither on the heights nor the fringes. His first book, *Egin Awen*, was printed by the local printer, with a list of subscribers in small print at the back, a window on a fascinating world.

Here was the public that supported young, unknown poets, the famous and the unknown names all mixed together: the Bishop of St David's and the stationmaster of Llantwit Faerdref, Lady Llanofer and J. Jones, Cloth Hall, a Fothergill of Hensol and H. Hughes, overman, the names (with their bardic names in brackets) of all the local poets, and among them the name of Islwyn, Dafydd Morganwg, the acknowledged authority of the period of the four-and-twenty measures, writes an introduction, and the dedication is to Lady Llanofer.

In a biographical note the young Creidiol explains that the volume is published to help him to get some education. One senses, behind the reticence, years of discipline and voluntary study after a hard day's labour in the pits.

At the back of the book the local printer and bookseller inserts advertisements for his stock: Welsh translations of Thomas à Kempis and Alexander Pope, a treatise on Firedamp and Matthew Ewenni's best-seller, the life of the colourful farmer-preacher, Siencyn Penhydd. Most characteristic of all perhaps is the advertisement for the Welsh version of Dr Channing's *Self-Education*.

The poet himself advertises a forthcoming work, 'to be published when the author shall have received a sufficient number of subscribers: a poem on David, King of Israel, containing nearly 2,000 lines,' one of the chief subjects of the National Eisteddfod at Aberystwyth in 1865.

This never seems to have appeared, which is perhaps just as well; the high fustian of the Eisteddfod was not for Creidiol, nor the barren literary theories. His simple poetry is alive with observation, his subject is not dead kings but real people.

He wrote encouraging verses to the industrial pioneers of his town, praised the local choir, jousted with his fellow-poets, mourned Abraham Lincoln and celebrated Islwyn's wedding.

He upheld, without narrowness, the claims of the Welsh language and reproved the manners of the age, telling young men given to idly wandering the streets that Martin Luther would never have gone around like this. The first generation of 'shoni-hois' are depicted in his verses as by a candid camera.

In a later, longer poem, *Gwenfron o'r Dyffryn*, he betrays a nostalgia for the old life that was passing, but this idyll, which was immensely popular in its day, although located somewhere in the Rhymni Valley, really belongs to the romantic Glamorgan of Iolo Morganwg. For all its naivety, there are some lovely passages in it which do not deserve oblivion, and a sudden quite irrelevant invocation which is a roll-call of his fellow poets:

> *Emrys, Gwalchmai a Nicander,*
> *A Chaledfryn fawr ei ddawn*
> *Hen Hiraethog, Clwydfardd yntau*
> *A Chynddelw, digrif iawn,*
> *Esyllt, Emlyn, Islwyn, Ceiriog,*
> *Gwilym Pennant, awdur cu,*
> *Hywel Cefni a Glasnys*
> *A Thalhaiarn gyda'r llu ...*

Fifteen of them, and one feels he could have gone on, out of the sheer thrill of being a Welsh poet.

Ordained as a clergyman, Creidiol served in various parishes, among them Llanfihangel Cwmdu, where fifty years previously another patriot had been inducted as vicar, Thomas Price, Carnhuanawc, and then he came to Plwyf y Faenor for the rest of his life. Here he brought his bride to the altar on a day of heavy snow, and here, on another day of heavy snow, he saw her to her grave.

He chronicled the doings of the parish, its history and its characters, and took vigorous part in its life. He served on the local council, and other public bodies, and was prominent in the eisteddfodau of the district. One of the last fights, which has a renewed relevance today, was against the incorporation of parts of his parish into the new borough of Merthyr Tydfil.

Towards the end of his life he turned to English to compile *The Vaynor Guide*, a work which is well worth ferreting out, a rich compilation in the best tradition of *y pethe*. All the famous characters of the parish are recalled, the peasant athletes and homegrown wits, long-lived old women and the last of the Crawshays.

All the local poets are quoted, and it is surprising how many of them there were and how well they still read. It was a society that must have been coming to an end before the First War, and which the inter-war years were to transform out of all recognition.

Creidiol may by some be considered fortunate in his generation. His last poem sums up, in Welsh, the contents of the rambling book he wrote in English: it describes the parish and the virtues of its situation and soil, the methods of farming and the excellence of its crops and flocks, it names lovingly the dead who are buried in the churchyard and leads naturally into an assertion of religion as the centre of life.

He could open his poem with a description of the rivers Taf Fawr and Taf Fechan and end it with echoing reference to the rivers of Eden. He could see his parish as a portion of Paradise, and Wales as part of the Kingdom of God.

Western Mail (9 April 1966)

Over the Sea to Wales

At first, the relations between Wales and her nearest trans-marine neighbour may seem a depressing subject, varying from the non-existent to the sullenly hostile. And summed up – like everything else in the national experience – by the *Mabinogion*, where Brân and his warriors can only see Ireland as a place of wrath.

The remotest mythical pedigrees on either side never acknowledged a common ancestry for the two races, and both countries had quite independent links with the continent until the autonomy of each was eroded. Niall of the Nine Hostages and Macsen Wledig were contemporaries, but neither in history nor legend do their paths cross.

Yet the contacts between two such near neighbours could not have been barren. There was colonisation: Lleyn, and even Gwynedd, are said to be Irish names. There were cultural influences, notably in the sphere of religion, as the migrant saints crossed and recrossed the Irish Sea on tombstones, porpoises and, doubtless, more mundane craft.

There were economic contacts; the Irish workmen who were employed on the Neath Bridge in our own day had their forerunners in the Irish craftsmen who built the nearby oratory of Saint Cadoc a thousand years previously. It is the continuing tale that might be expected: there is a Cardiff Lane in Dublin Docks, and in Cardiff itself, the biggest docks are called Roath, which is the pure Irish *rath*, from one of their old fortified settlements.

Dynastic and military alliances were forged against the growing power of England. The *Armes Prydain,* that apocalyptic propaganda poem of the ninth century, is one of the earliest manifestos calling for a Pan-Celtic front. For generations Ireland was a long-stop in the struggles between Wales and England, the harbour of our fugitive princes.

Various uncomplimentary shades of meaning have been attached to all the Welsh words for their neighbours, and while *Gwyddel* [Irishman] lacks the hiss of *Sais* [Englishman], it has always carried even more depreciating overtones, abundant in our rich medieval literature, whose most apt interpreters in our own day are called Clancy and Conran! (not to speak of one of our best modern poets, John Fitzgerald).

It would be true to say that the Welsh have played a part out of all proportion to their numbers in English aggression against Ireland, from the days of the Anglo-Normans (who should more accurately be called Cambro-Normans) up till the more recent troubles. Strongbow and FitzStephen may have only been recently domiciled among us when they set out on their conquests, but the Flemings of Dyfed went into battle with a war cry of 'Sant Devi!' and it is not for nothing that Walsh is reckoned to be the fourth commonest non-Gaelic surname in Ireland.

The misdeeds of the Welshmen of Tirawley are the subject of a long, rather tedious thirteenth-century Irish ballad, and they were not the last by any means. At a much later period, Welsh troops earned themselves a name in Ireland that is best forgotten. Even in such a complicated swindle as the eighteenth-century plan to debase the Irish currency with 'Wood's ha'pence,' Welsh interests were involved. The Wood dynasty were impeccably English, but it was for the benefit of their Welsh-based industries that the scheme, so memorably denounced by Swift, was promoted. The family's connection with Wales is commemorated in the name of one of the best-known streets of our capital, some of the first Welsh soil to be trodden by Irish immigrants getting off the train from Fishguard.

They brought us the craft of whisky-making, which lingered long after the days when Tenby was dolefully described as 'almost cleane irisshe,' but which we managed, in our usual way, to lose, and we exported to them the secret of rich black beer brewed from roasted barley, which, unlike us, they turned to good advantage.

But these convivial exchanges remained untypical. The transformations of the nineteenth century brought all the nations of the world into closer contact than ever before, and the ambivalence of Welsh-Irish relationships was intensified. On the one hand the alien hordes of cheap labour, crowding into the slums 'with famine in their bellies and fever in their rags,' not to mention what many, in those pre-ecumenical days, felt to be an even less desirable import. But on the other hand, the stirring consciousness of a common dilemma.

Not that this was universally acknowledged. The notorious anti-Irish riots of 1882 at Tredegar were sparked off, not by any local exasperation, but by the Phoenix Park Murders. It is ironic to think of the exploited Welsh workers of the period moved to anger by Irish patriots killing English politicians. And, of course, it was the Welsh Nonconformist conscience that dished Parnell.

But there was another side to the story, as if some old theme were being taken up again after a long time, and the fitful co-operation of past ages finding new channels. Owain Glyndŵr had invoked the prophecies to bring about an Irish alliance with his independent Wales, rebellious Welsh lords could still find a refuge across the sea until the Tudor period, there were strong suspicions of Welsh complicity in the rising of Tyrone, but these all have the flavour of desperate ventures, peripheral possibilities.

It was not until the last century that we actually started learning from one another. Rebecca and her Daughters, staunch Nonconformists all, declared their solidarity with Daniel O'Connell and Catholic Emancipation, and the militant Chartists organised their secret armies on lines so similar to those of the contemporary Irish 'terrorists' as to leave little doubt where they learnt their lessons.

Welsh politicians were to the fore in the disestablishment of the Anglican Church in Ireland, a dummy run for their own big battle, and when it came to Home Rule for Ireland, the Welsh M.P.s were more unanimous in their support than those of Ireland itself! The Cymru Fydd movement was established in close imitation of Young Ireland, and much was made of the rather remote Welsh origins of Thomas Davis (as, later, of the entirely suppositious Welsh ancestry of Arthur Griffith).

Tom Ellis was hailed as 'the Parnell of Wales', which, unfortunately, is exactly what he was not, and, on a more practical level, the leaders of agrarian discontent in Wales brought over Michael Davitt, leader of Ireland's Land League, to advise and inspire the tenant farmers of Gwynedd.

All this was before the great landslide in Anglo-Irish relations precipitated by the romantic poets and fed-up labourers in 1916. No one will ever know how Lloyd George should be judged for his part in the subsequent settlement. To the Irish, or some of them, he is the butcher who threatened them with 'immediate and terrible war' and imposed partition; to the English, he is the political leader who settled the Irish question after 700 years; the whole ambiguity of our relations with Ireland is incarnate in him, as are so many other aspects of our character.

The inter-war period reverberated with the grumbling after-effects. Wales was ground between the upper and nether millstone of an aggressively independent new state and an unforgiving former over-lord, at odds in a trade war. The Irish slogan was 'Burn everything English except their coal', which, of course, was Welsh coal. When England, in its turn, imposed an embargo on Irish cattle, the port that suffered was Holyhead.

And when the heirs of Cymru Fydd idealist nationalism preached the inspiration of the Irish achievement, they aroused practically every unworthy reaction, from ancient prejudice to present envy and shame, of which their countrymen were capable.

The story is not at an end, and probably never will be. We can only deduce an interim, but timely, lesson from the history of Ireland, the words of Conor Cruise O'Brien, patriot and internationalist, which apply so strikingly to Wales:

'The test of Irish patriotism is not language or culture or political attitudes. It is being inextricably involved in the Irish situation, and being mauled by it.'

Western Mail (7 May 1966)

A Literary Tradition

A Letter to Meic Stephens

Garth Newydd,
Merthyr Tydfil.
Hydref 7fed 1966

Annwyl Meic,

Some important points were raised by Mr Raymond Garlick's thought-provoking letter in the last number of *Poetry Wales*. I don't think I have ever read a better definition of the role of the Anglo-Welsh writer today: 'a duty, a vocation almost, of reconciliation, of unity in bilingualism, of trying always to present the one, whole Wales.' To this concept he has devoted many years of labour with the *Anglo-Welsh Review*, the years between the first appearance of a recognizable Anglo-Welsh movement in the 1930s and the present efflorescence. I can't help feeling that his experience may have predisposed him to over-estimate the element of continuity in what seems to me to be a demonstrably discontinuous activity, and to postulate a 'tradition' of which I doubt the existence.

As he has spoken kindly of my own work, I hope I may recapitulate what I wrote some years ago when I had the melancholy task of reviewing in *Wales* an anthology constructed around the same thesis: 'English writing by Welshmen is a fascinating but fragmentary field which has only recently amounted to much. The attempt ... to preserve it as any organically evolving process, analogous in nature to the fifteen centuries of Welsh writing is utterly unconvincing, as must be any attempt to invest the anglicisation of Wales with respectability.'

Mr Garlick, on the other hand, says, 'Whether contemporary Anglo-Welsh poets are in the least aware that they belong to and are extending a distinct literature is as irrelevant as whether contemporary English or American poets are or are not aware of themselves in relation to their literatures.' There may be some vantage point from which we are both seen to be right, but I doubt it.

Welsh literature is of course continuous, from Aneirin to Waldo, but in this it is unique among the post-classical literatures, and even granting the existence of 'four centuries of Anglo-Welsh poetry,' it is not likely to have the same impressive continuity. Mr Saunders Lewis, in discussing this point, contrasts Welsh with English, '*Nid un peth yn tyfu ac yn newid yw llenyddiaeth Saesneg cyn oes Dryden, ond nifer o ffenomenau llenyddol mewn gwahanol ardaloedd yn gwbl annibynnol ar ei gilydd. Ni ellir yn gywir sôn am draddodiad yn llenyddiaeth Lloegr.*' Precisely. '*Nac yn llenyddiaeth Cymru Saesneg, chwaith,*' I would add.

Looked at as 'a number of literary phenomena occurring in different contexts completely independent of one another,' Anglo-Welsh literature in the sense that Mr Garlick defines that vague *faute-de-mieux* term, is an interesting and worthwhile study. I agree that serious knowledge of it is disgracefully rare, but surely such knowledge would in the first instance be most usefully employed in cutting the subject down to size and establishing the limits consistent with a respectable discipline. Such tangential, apocryphal and indeed utterly absurd figures as Donne, Herbert, George Meredith, George Eliot and King Henry the Eighth should, in their capacities as 'Welsh' or 'Anglo-Welsh' writers, be briskly bundled aboard the *Prince Madoc* and sent to dwell among the Welsh Indians. After which we are left, presumably, with Mr Garlick's hundred or so names, and I suspect the vast majority of these are complete nonentities.

If I mention Richard Hall of Brecon it is only because he has been summed up more neatly than most by Professor Gwyn Jones as 'self-confessedly content with the lower slopes of that Parnassus whose peak he deemed Eliza Cooke to have scaled'. There let us leave him and all his kind. Maybe in the fullness of time we shall be deemed to have joined him, but meanwhile we must deny his paternity. Coming back to Mr Garlick's comparison, I doubt if even the most ignorant English or American poet is not aware that he is in some sort of lineage with Eliot, Pound, Frost or Whitman. But the Anglo-Welsh poets? Is it possible to belong to a tradition of which one is totally ignorant, to be influenced by names to which if one has ever heard of them, no significance can be attached? Maybe the University of Wales has let us down, but *wara teg*, if there had been any Anglo-Welsh tradition worth talking about surely somebody would have latched on to it.

As it happens, the two bogus elements in the 'tradition,' the philopietism that lays claim to all sorts of tenuous Taffs, and the uncritical cataloguing of anybody and everybody who has ever set pen to paper, are both enshrined for me in the only literary pro-nouncements I ever heard from Dylan Thomas (I make a free gift of this information to the tireless toilers in the Thomas industry, I am only sorry that it is too late for National Productivity Year). In his workroom at Laugharne he had a picture of an impressive Victorian worthy whom I at first thought must be Karl Marx. 'It's Whitman,' he told me, and then added, as if it really mattered, 'His mother was Welsh, you know.' On another occasion, he referred to Huw Menai as 'the best-known modern Welsh poet'.

Leaving aside the Whitmans and the Huw Menais, the apocryphal and the negligible, I can't see that any Anglo-Welsh tradition could have existed before the present century, not because there weren't Welshmen writing in English, but because there was no audience for them. Their work was directed outward to the general English audi-ence and solicited acceptance on the same terms as any other writing in English. They were either cut off from or contracted out of the tradition, the language and the audience that surrounded them in Wales, and either they assimilated to the status of purely English writers or they remained on its provincial periphery, like the

Matchless Orinda and her circumscribed court of anglicised West Wales squires, or that Powell of Nanteos who wrote minor English verse in complete ignorance of the cultural history of his own house. From both the Welsh and English points of view they were, literally, eccentrics. The study of such successive phenomena over a long period would undoubtedly be able to establish some characteristics in common, but this still does not add up to a tradition.

At the risk of being savaged by all sorts of cognoscenti, I must now state my thesis that, if there is a tradition at all, it begins with Keidrych Rhys. I realise that A.G. Prys-Jones had enterprisingly jumped the gun with an 'Anglo-Welsh' anthology during the First World War, but up until about that time Wales was still fifty per cent Welsh-speaking, and the other fifty per cent were culturally inert – unassimilated immigrants or denaturalised natives. A generation later, assimilation was under way, and there was in existence a large population, Welsh in feeling, but English in language, something totally new in our history. Concurrently, the ebbing influence of religion over our intellectual life led to the emergence of another element, a lay intelligentsia. In the early 'thirties these people spoke and were spoken to for the first time. Like Melchizedek, they had no ancestry, and it is no service to them to try and invent one for them. The point is proved, co-incidentally, by Mr Edwin Morgan's remarks in the same number of *Poetry Wales* on the Scottish Renaissance and MacDiarmid's cry, 'Not Burns – Dunbar!'

A decade later, and considerably influenced by MacDiarmid, Keidrych Rhys could utter no such cry. There was no recent but overdone influence like Burns, or magnificent but remote figure like Dunbar, in the antecedents of Anglo-Welsh writing. There would not have been much point in denouncing Sir Lewis Morris or serving affiliation orders on Henry Vaughan. They had to start from scratch and went to their English and European contemporaries for models, so much so that to Kenneth Rexroth, looking back at them from the late forties, this over-emphatic 'modernism' was their most noticeable characteristic as a group.

The need for antecedents that most, though not all, serious writers feel, could only be satisfied by the older literature of Wales. I find it difficult to document the often expressed accusation that Welshmen who write in English are hostile to Welsh, both as a literary and social medium. All the evidence seems the other way and is not discounted by justified exasperation with some of the less worthy aspects of eisteddfodic culture, however sharply expressed. Some are politely indifferent to Welsh, but there are others, of some stature, who bitterly regret their inability to use it as a creative medium. Translations by

Keidrych Rhys of Williams Parry and Nigel Heseltine's of Dafydd ap Gwilym early established the relationship, Alun Lewis was actively concerned to publish the great Welsh poetry of the best periods and Glyn Jones is deeply influenced, in both style and content, by Welsh models. And if the status of independent creations can be claimed, justly in my view, for Arthur Waley's translations from the Chinese, then the same is true of the impressive body of translations from the Welsh by Gwyn Williams and Anthony Conran. As for the attitude of the poets who fill the pages of *Poetry Wales*, it is surely obvious.

If we have any tradition at all, it is not Anglo-, but unhyphenated Welsh. This may not be equally true of everybody and there are all sorts of overlaps and inherent confusions that someone (not me) can have fun sorting out. The whole shape of this body of literature is Welsh. Most of it is poetry and much of the poetry has a homo-geneity of theme, mood and technique that characterises certain periods of Welsh literature. The subject matter, the social orientation, the intimate relation of the poet to his audience, often an intensely local and sectional audience, the readiness to turn out *vers d'occasion* not intended for critical appraisal, the nationalism of many writers, particularly of the new generation, all this is Welsh. The prose is short-winded, exquisite, verbalistic, over-rich. There are a lot of very good short stories but little achievement in the genres that demand extended construction, drama and the novel. Quite a few biographies, criticism mostly an insult to the intelligence: all this is such a faithful echo of the current Welsh-language situation that one is tempted to deduce some tremendous generalisation, but I forbear.

An enigmatic writer, Caradoc Evans was half in and half out of the present situation. His literary antecedents were Welsh, notably the satirical journalism of a professional angry, David Owen, 'Brutus', whose centenary has passed unobserved this year. But, in the early years of this century, there was hardly any audience in Wales itself for writing in English of this type, so he had to direct himself outwards to the general English market, and his work suffered in consequence. The last of the peripheral eccentrics, he lived to see a public arising in Wales which was not there in his creative heyday. Some time between the wars his books were ceremoniously removed from the Barry Public Library and burnt in the municipal incinerator by an urban district councillor, but now that cooler judgements prevail, an analysis of Caradoc Evans' distinctive but flawed achievement would do much to define our terms. I mention this as the sort of job that needs to be done and I am sure Mr Garlick would concur. In the meantime, caution must be urged in accepting the existence of any meaningful tradition, but I for one, am happy to be associated with Mr Garlick in helping to create one.

Cofion cynnes,

Harri

Poetry Wales (2.3, Winter 1966)

The Little White Rose of Scotland

The Oxford Book of Scottish Verse:
chosen by John MacQueen and Tom Scott.

Sneered at as a hack by the purists, reviled as a butcher by his contributors, sat on as a prodigal by his publisher, the anthologist yet plays for high stakes. A successful anthology is a monument and a manifesto. It has a *gestalt* individuality as a creation in its own right, it may define the taste of a generation and powerfully influence subsequent developments.

To the Oxford books a special pre-eminence has attached ever since Quiller-Couch, St John Lucas and Fitzmaurice-Kelly planned and executed the first imposing Edwardian structures. Attempts at adaptation to accommodate later changes of taste only reveal the strong character of the originals. Yeats' *Oxford Book of Modern Verse* caused a whole counter-anthology, the *Faber Book of Modern Verse*, to be launched; Principal Thomas Parry's volume in the same series is a major landmark even in the long history of Welsh. Anthologies of this stature can accord formal recognition to a whole literature, especially if, as in the present case, its limits, its separate existence even, are in dispute. This volume therefore has a particular importance and makes some points of more than purely Scottish significance.

To a massive alliance of vested interests, Scots is a mere dialect, its literature a quaint peripheral phenomenon, its poets rustic bards, good enough for a Burns Night spree but beneath the level of critical appraisal. Such a judgement proceeds from political and social prejudice. It is true that 'the older Scottish tongue' derives from a group of dialects that were once spoken as far south as Nottingham. But south of Tweed and Cheviot they remained dialects. North of the Border they were refined and enriched into the language of a sovereign nation. The political factor, the different social status, the more favourable psychological climate were all-important, and we can trace in this collection their continued relevance.

Up till the Union of Crowns in 1603, Scots maintained a rich vitality. The seventeenth century saw the same sort of impoverishment that befell Welsh after the Anschluss of 1536. The compilers have rather masked the collapse by filling this period up with ballads, many of which can only be arbitrarily so dated. The Act of Union of 1707 furthered the erosion, with the considerable exceptions of Fergusson and Burns, and fostered a dichotomy of derivative English and vapid vernacular, and a pervasive Scoto-English bilingualism, present in the best of Burns as well as in a minor figure like Beattie who is stone dead in English but alive and vigorous in Scots. By the nineteenth century the situation was acute, but there were also the first confused stirrings that presaged the renewed vitality of our own day.

Nearly half this anthology belongs to poets of the present century and the whole compilation may be seen as an effort to provide with a worthy ancestry a generation extremely conscious of its roots, its place in literary and social history, its role in the revival of a submerged nation. The modern developments, including the publication of the present volume, are part of a political-linguistic movement that has been going on in Europe ever since Dante's *De La Vulgari Eloquentia* at least, and attempts to belittle or ignore this aspect of literature are highly suspect. It is significant that Dante's thesis was bitterly assailed by Machiavelli, the father of *realpolitik,* in his *Dialogo intorno alla Lingua.*

Scottish poetry has always been political and social. Political as we see it here: in Barbour's patriotic epic 'The Bruce', which might conceivably have been heard by Prince Owain Glyndŵr's envoys to his northern allies, with its unforgettable lines on freedom; in Blind Harry's evocation of Wallace; Sir David Lindsay's 'Compleynt of the Comoun Weill of Scotland'; the ballads; Burn's fierce pasquinado –

We're bought and sold for English gold –
Such a parcel of rogues in a nation;

and in Fergusson's

Black be the day that e'er to England's ground
Scotland was eiket by the Union's bound;

and in the poets of our own time, Edwin Muir's sombre 'Scotland 1941' and MacDiarmid's splendid lines

A Scottish poet maun assume

The burden o' his people's doom
And dee to brak' their livin' tomb.

Socially, the poets, who include four kings, speak to and for a people, in satire and in genre piece, in flyting and anti-clerical polemic, in praise of drinking, piping and houghmagaundie.

Turning, after all this, to what Sidney Goodsir Smith calls 'the weeshy-washy London bree,' one must agree with eighteenth century Alexander Geddes' view of the southern tongue,

Bedek't, tis true, an' made fu' smart
Wi mekil learning, pains an' art;
An' taught to baike an' beuge an' bou
As dogs an' dancin' masters do:
Wi fardit cheeks an' pouder't hair,
An' brazen confidential stare.

This, even in its poorer patches, is the virile voice of an articulate, cultured people, not drawing-room drivel. It is still a living tradition, like its Welsh counterpart, unselfconsciously part of social life, just like Pontshân's repertoire.

It is difficult to display great riches. It is not to be held against the compilers of this anthology that, for one fifth of the price, MacDiarmid's *Golden Treasury of Scottish Poetry* includes the Gaelic and Latin strands of Scottish literature as well as the Scots and English, but with so much Gaelic so well translated by MacDiarmid, Douglas Young and others, one misses it here and can only echo the anthologist's civilised hope that a comparable Gaelic collection will not be long delayed.

But in the Scots they have served us well, not shirking extensive extracts and whole long poems: Dunbar's 'Tretis of the Twa Mariit Wemen and the Wedo', Henryson's 'Testament of Cresseid', these are the treasures of a nation. The thinner material of less productive periods is yet full of familiar lyrics and these are set out here in their historical context, though the omission of the lively 'Peblis to the Play' is not easily justified. Fergusson is generously represented, Burns' more urban contemporary, with his 'Hallow Fair' giving an unforgettable glimpse of Edinburgh waking to a holiday,

Upo' the tap o' ilka lum
The sun begun to keek.

There is a balanced selection from Burns, from the delightful idyll 'Corn Riggs', perhaps one of his earlier pieces, to the bite of 'Holy Willie's Prayer' and the robust comedy of 'Tam o'Shanter'. It is easy but unfair to cry for more, 'The Twa Dogs' or 'The Jolly Beggars'; at least we are spared 'The Cotter's Saturday Night'.

A similar problem is posed by MacDiarmid, whose achievement defies the processes of selection. An anthology claiming to include him would be rather like the Welsh hotel of bygone days which advertised 'the celebrated mountain of Plynlimmon is on the premises'. Grateful for what is printed here, one may yet sigh for the great 'Hymns', the 'Cornish Heroic Song' or 'In Memoriam James Joyce'.

Sidney Goodsir Smith is well represented and perhaps it is simply greedy to want more of 'Under the Eildon Tree', but Douglas Young, in his translations at any rate, is a bigger figure than appears here. And Mr Tom Scott has overmodestly excluded himself. In fact the latter pages have not altogether avoided the hazards which beset any selection among contemporaries. Edwin Morgan has done more exciting things than the piece included here, as the dazzling virtuosity of *Message Loud and Clear* recently reminded us. Again, Thurso Berwick (a transparently pseudonymous disguise for Morris Blythman) brings to mind a strong body of rebel and republican verse that demands representation. The exact parity observed between Edwin Muir and MacDiarmid is grossly flattering to the former, a sort of Scottish W.J. Gruffydd who certainly deserves inclusion, but not on a scale which seems dictated by literary politics rather than intrinsic merit.

There are at least half a dozen living names whose presence it is difficult to justify at all. With a fitting canniness the compilers proclaim a policy of giving only token representation to Scottish poets who seem more at home in the English tradition, a subjective criterion which seems to have been abandoned where the moderns are concerned (for example, Kathleen Raine, so why not Ruthven Todd?) and raises the whole question of 'English in a Scots mou'.' How famous they all were, how influential: Thomson's 'Seasons', Blair's 'Grave', Campbell's and Cunningham's imperialist pop-art, all part of the broad highway to the esteem of a wider audience. And how dead most of it is, while the despised and patronised vernacular, even at its less than best, still lives. Among the considerable representation of the stream of writing from the seventeenth century onwards, Falconer's *Shipwreck*, a remarkable handing of the polite Augustan idiom, deserved inclusion, and the modest Victorian virtues of polymathic Andrew Lang and Christopher North's son-in-law Ayton were missed by at least one reader. *Per contra*, the greatest English poet of his day deserved to be included; Kipling's 'M'Andrew's Hymn' is too good to be left out of any Scottish anthology.

The Scots are Europeans and much 'English' influence on the European mainstream has really been Scottish: Macpherson's Ossianic prose-poems, perhaps the most inexplicable omission from this book, and in the next century Scott and Byron, whose Scottishness was pointed out by Eliot; and James Thomson's *City of Dreadful Night*, recently hailed by a French critic as '*le testament d'un Européen ... universel comme le livre de Job*', a judgement which the fragment printed here does not help us to understand.

But despite the scope of their appeal, the breadth of their terms of reference, the great learning of some of them, their integrity, be it that of giants like Burns and MacDiarmid (recognised as such by all the wallidrags, worms and old wobat carles of the swinging city) or lesser men who can yet turn out the occasional unforgettable verse, the integrity of these poets is guaranteed only by their fidelity to the girl in the green mantle who appeared to Rab Mossgiel in the auld clay biggin, the native muse. Their reward, and ours, so lavishly displayed here:

> Only the little white rose of Scotland
> That smells sharp and sweet – and breaks the heart.

Poetry Wales (3.1, Spring 1967)

Radio and Television in the 1970s

Extract from a lecture delivered to the Oxford University Fabian Society and Cymdeithas Dafydd ap Gwilym at Wadham College on November 22nd 1967 on 'Mass Media and Minority Culture'

A society inheriting standards and attitudes from the ancient Celtic civilisation of aristocratic equals, thrown in upon itself over centuries of introversion and eclipse, is full of coiled-up energy, awaiting only the liberating touch of modern technology. It is a society where everybody knows everybody else, and is probably related to everybody else, with a high degree of participation and involvement in all activities. There are hardly any internal barriers. Whatever face we may present to the outside world, among ourselves, there is no equivalent of strangulation by the old school tie. One is tempted to describe our nation as a folk community, even tempted to use the pompous expression *volksemeinschaft*. There is no difficulty in finding participants and audiences of a high degree of ability and receptivity. The institution of the Eisteddfod, for all the merited criticism of which it is the target, has, at its best, extended a people's patronage to singers, poets, musicians and writers in great numbers, and has instructed large audiences in the finer points of musical and literary appreciation. Within its limitations it has done, effortlessly and unselfconsciously, what Arnold Wesker, John Arden and Joan Littlewood were striving so hard to do in England.

Wales is in fact ideal territory for the establishment of open-ended mass media, through which a people communicate among themselves, talk to one another and entertain one another, and, by entertaining, sustain one another, creating a strong national identity, a rich and satisfying way of life that will be worth fighting for. To many of us, Wales even as she is today has already got much of this character, and we feel that it is a legitimate claim on all mass media that they be used to enrich and strengthen that character. What in fact has been the position so far? Here I will find it convenient to quote from a recent survey of the Welsh language, *The Dragon's Tongue* by Mr Gerald Morgan.

> The development of broadcasting [was] negative at first because it was only in the thirties that the BBC was to develop 'regional' broadcasting. The first radio talk in Welsh on the BBC was ... in 1923, but the only regular programmes in Welsh were provided by Radio Eireann, who broadcast weekly in Welsh from Dublin. When 'regional' broadcasting began, the BBC pigheadedly insisted on combining most of Wales with the West of England, a process which they fondly called re-writing the Kingdom of Arthur. Although this imbecile arrangement, as irritating to Arthur's Cornish subjects as to his Welsh, was soon abandoned in sound radio, an identical policy was followed in the establishment of BBC television in Wales in 1952 and of commercial television three years later. These later mistakes were partially remedied during the early 1960s by the establishment of a commercial channel for Wales only (1962-3) and of BBC Wales television in 1964. Between the two, viewers can see ten to twelve hours a week of television in Welsh.

Mr Morgan goes on to summarise a whole history in a few sentences:

> The growth of broadcasting in Wales closely parallels that of education fifty years earlier, a national desire for the service and a national craving for English standards, combined with a national lack of confidence in home produce. The whole being combatted by a small group of talented and influential men determined to secure adequate

115

treatment and reasonable standards for broadcasting in Welsh. The concessions gained are statistically small, but they are vital, especially when compared with the suppression of Breton by Radio Télévision Française or the Anglo-American swamping of Irish television.

To take sound broadcasting first. Here is a good example of the double-edged effect of mass media. To Welsh-speaking Wales, it was an intrusion. Whatever the content of the programme, the medium was English – and the medium was the message. But in anglicised Wales, my own early environment, the wireless was our first introduction to the glories of Welsh choral and congregational singing and the eloquence of Welsh speech. The idiotic 'Kingdom of Arthur' arrangement was defended on technical grounds but Mr Eckersley, the then Chief Engineer of the BBC, later revealed that it was deliberate policy for which technical excuses were then invented. How can one characterise this policy? Is genocide too strong a word? The fight to establish a Welsh Region was long and bitter, and now we are having the same battle all over again in television.

The BBC in Wales has a record of patronage and one feels that it would do more if it were freer and had more money. The first play ever to be written specially for broadcasting was by the Anglo-Welsh author Richard Hughes who, imaginatively exploiting the medium, set his scene in the darkness of a coalmine. Saunders Lewis's *Buchedd Garmon*, one of the modern Welsh classics with lines in it that everybody knows, was commissioned by the BBC in 1936. When a decade later, Louis MacNeice was writing his radio plays, he drew up specifications for success in the medium, every one of which Lewis had anticipated. On a less lofty plane, the long-running light entertainment programme *Noson Lawen* delimited and characterised a whole historical period rather like ITMA in England. (Sam Jones, the inspirer of *Noson Lawen* was in fact a character in the ITMA saga – Sam Ffairfechan.) The ability of Welsh culture, at all levels, to adapt itself to mass media, has never been seriously in doubt.

In television it may appear that with all the channels available: BBC 1, BBC 2, BBC Wales, TWW, not to mention Westward, Granada and Telefis Eire in some areas, Wales is televisually over-privileged. But this is only part of the picture. BBC Wales came late on the scene and the costly business of changing the aerials to receive it was a disincentive which keeps probably the majority of viewers not on piped television tethered to BBC 1 and its regional variant for the South and West of England: the Kingdom of Arthur all over again, as with TWW. The arrangement simply cannot be defended on any ground. TWW's three-way obligation to the West of England, South Wales and the areas of North and West Wales they took over from

Teledu Cymru (the defunct Wales-only commercial channel already referred to) is utterly unwieldy and has compelled them to install, at the cost of £14 million, a three-way control system, one of the most complicated and expensive in the world. One doubts whether the takeover of TWW by the grandiosely named Harlech Consortium will make much difference; the territorial Franchise remains obstinately Arthurian and it looks as if the Welsh element in its directorate is there to provide the showbiz glamour, while Bristol is putting up most of the cash, and will, very properly, call the tune.

If we are to have commercial television, and I suppose it is with us for keeps now, or until the revolution, then like BBC TV it must respect the individuality of Wales, as it does of Scotland. It may seem that the failure of Teledu Cymru is a poor augury for the success of Wales-only commercial tv, but the story of that enterprise is a very complicated one, some might say, a fishy one. Every possible mistake seems to have been made at every stage of the proceedings, not least in the abysmal programmes it put out, and it is unlikely that these mistakes would be repeated, while the amount of risk capital that Teledu Cymru found it possible to raise on what may be called patriotic appeal was pretty substantial. As with radio, tv has to limited degrees been a source of patronage, but, again, one feels that more could be done. It is difficult to be critical of tv programmes without putting oneself in the position of a Superior Person, but I believe that public taste is continually being underrated, and thus debased, by excessive weight given to viewing figures. The TAM people do, in fact, provide two separate services, one to find out how many people have seen a particular programme and another to discover what programmes people have actually liked. The findings of the second service are never published! We must take into account, too, a self-flattering tendency to apply a double standard, and to expect each and every Welsh programme to achieve a standard we would never continually demand from the run of English programmes. Welsh culture has always been self-conscious and self-censoring. The simple popular literature which must have existed from earliest times was never deemed worthy of preservation, and only emerges, in all the naive beauty of the carols and the *hen benillion*, in the seventeenth century, with the eclipse of the classical bardic tradition. The serious tone which pervaded a national revival largely nourished by Nonconformity tends to hide from us the simpler, ruder pleasures of our forebears. But one has only to read the educational essays of Lewis Edwards (a sort of Calvinistic Methodist equivalent of Cardinal Newman) to glean many a hint that the congregations who sat at the feet of the pulpit giants were also susceptible to the attraction of the minstrel shows, the harbinger of American influence on popular entertainment. It is possible, I think, within our context, to be simple, direct and popular, without falling into the morass of mindless commercialised subculture.

Indeed, by now the very voracity of the mass media has stimulated life into the very type of culture they once threatened to erode. There is no need to enlarge on the renewed interest in traditional music of all kinds, and the cross-fertilisation that is going on between trad and pop. This became first apparent in Welsh terms in the context of another of these media: gramophone records. I can remember vainly searching Cardiff in about 1950 for records with some Welsh flavour, and being appalled and repelled by the few old-fashioned items that one could with difficulty dig up. But a few years later, the new flexible plastics, microgroove recording techniques, the replacement of the old steel needles by the stylus, all converged to make gramophone records big business again, and for once, uninhibited by unsympathetic official or commercial policies, Wales was on the ball. The history of the Welsh record industry has not been all plain sailing, but there are several firms on a small scale, and one, Qualiton, on a considerable scale, with tie-ups with the big international companies. One has only got to look at the records displayed in the Cardiff shops now to see what sells, and most homes one visits have these records, LPs of the great choral festivals and *cymanfaoedd canu*, choirs, groups, and individuals taking everything in their stride from *penillion* to pop. There have been some wonderful native discoveries in this field: Dafydd Iwan and Helen Wyn are my favourites, and a group called *Y Blew* (The Hairy Ones) have proved that it is just as possible to scream unintelligibly in Welsh as Anglo-American. One of my minor ambitions is to see Wales independently represented in the Eurovision song contest. I'm sure we'd win it, after all, we recently had a Welsh-speaking Miss World.

Consideration of the sudden changes that took place in the field of gramophone records in such a short time should give us power. We are dealing with the products of a proliferating technology; what is the latest thing today is old hat tomorrow! Wireless all but superseded the gramophone, then came the record-player and the big comeback. Then the transistor revolution dethroned the wireless set as a ritual focus of the domestic scene, about which a poet some time in the 'thirties wrote:

Now twixt Van Gogh and Twig-bedizen'd jar
Thou art enthroned, thyself an objet d'art,

and made it an adjunct of informal living. Soon we shall be having colour television, and after that three-dimensional television, and portable wrist-watch television sets, and perhaps we shouldn't look too far ahead. It is sobering to remember that there must once have been a time when the magic lantern was the latest miracle of modern science and the big breakthrough in popular education and mass communication. Has this subject ever received the attention it obviously deserves?

Recently, for instance, the cumulative effect of transistor sets and microgroove records resulted in Radio Caroline and all her piratical flotilla. Acting with incredible speed, they have now, disc-jockeys and all, been absorbed by the BBC, a decision, which if it had been any-thing to do with Wales, would have taken another ten years at least. Concurrently, the BBC announces plans to set up some two hundred local radio stations over the next few years. Owing to restrictions imposed by international agreements they will only operate on VHF. At present a VHF transistor set costs very much more than an ordinary set (£18-£20) so this seems a case of intelligently anticipating a demand that will only maximise when the price of VHF transistors comes down. How will this new development of local radio affect Wales? Out of two hundred stations, we will, on a population basis, be entitled to about a dozen of them and this seems adequate – if we get them. The different settlement pattern of Wales will have to be borne in mind. There are only a few large centres comparable to Leicester and Sheffield; the pioneer English stations and the claims of regional centres and county towns with modest populations will have to be borne in mind, such as Wrexham, Aberystwyth, and Carmarthen. It seems that here is a very good opportunity for giving people what they want as far as the language content of the programmes is concerned: one can easily see that Caernarfon's programme would have a lot more Welsh in it than Newport's. The interesting thing about these stations is their modest cost. Initial capital outlay estimates vary from £18,000 to £35,000; even the higher of these figures is much less than that of starting a local newspaper. Annual running costs estimates range from £28,000 to £40,000. The BBC's initiative, which is to be welcomed as far as it goes, has obviously been in the nature of a pre-emptive strike, forestalling commercial interests who could have manipulated these new stations in all sorts of ways that do not bear thinking about. Deferring consideration of programme content for a moment, the chief problem connected with them seems to be one of finance. There is talk of local authorities financing them from the rates, or consortiums of local interests putting up the money. Neither of those seems to be a very good idea. This is not the place for me to denounce the rates as a very unsatisfactory method of funding local government and expressing a preference for other systems. But if the expense of local radio were to fall on local authorities in some of our heavily rated and thinly populated areas, then they could be excused for not wanting it, and the inequable rating pattern of Great Britain generally would confine local radio on this basis to affluent South East England. Do we then have to pay more for our licences? I think we should be bold enough to say that even licences should be scrapped. After all, nearly everybody has both wireless and tv today, car radios and transistors, and the cost of enforcing an almost unenforcable licensing system must be staggering and the sensible thing to do is to fund the whole lot, tv and radio, all channels, all stations, by a block grant from the general revenue of the state, as is done for the universities, national museums and galleries, the Arts Council etc. I am not saying that local radio shouldn't recoup some revenue from advertising of a genuinely local nature, providing that it is not allowed to dominate and dictate. This could be a useful supplement (not a competitor) to local newspaper advertising and result in increased publicity for local social and cultural events, employment opportunities and trade and commerce generally. Neither am I suggesting that local radio should exist in a parochial limbo. As far as Wales is concerned the set-up I would like to see is this: an autonomous Welsh Broadcasting Corporation transmitting national and nationally orientated programmes over the present BBC Wales television channel at considerably increased strength, and over the present BBC Welsh Home Service wavelength, together with a chain of perhaps 12-15 local radio stations. The National Service would buy programmes, news services etc from London and abroad. The local stations could in turn buy programmes from the National Service. The National Service would, of course, monitor the local stations and buy any programme that seemed of more than local interest. There would thus be an all-Wales network of programmes and a spectrum of programme content to suit all tastes and cultural and linguistic backgrounds. Facilities would have to be drastically improved. Sound radio studios of a 'lock-up' type for contingent use are already available in some centres, but it is unforgivable that there is no television studio outside of Cardiff. The present BBC Wales have, of course, a lavish mobile television unit but this is hardly a substitute, especially when the spirit in which it is intended to be used was betrayed by the announcement of this unit's inauguration a few years ago with the memorable words 'it will make regular safaris to North Wales'. The Gogs begin at Llanidloes!

As for the programmes this service would put out, I am not going to claim that there should be one channel, sound or tv, totally reserved for transmissions in the Welsh language. Not yet, anyway. In a few years time the ability to sustain such a service may be stronger than it is today. But between the national tv channel, the commercial tv channel, the main sound wavelength and the local stations, it should be possible for the listener or viewer in Wales, at any time of the day to tune in and hear a programme in the Welsh language, or of Welsh interest or originating in Wales. Then, and only then, will the mass media be efficiently serving the Welsh nation. As it is we are bound down to the debilitating tasks of eternal vigilance. There have been some excellent initiatives that have not been followed up – a play like Gwenlyn Parry's *Saer Doliau*, a series like *Byd a Betws*, a popular serial like *Moulded in Earth* which as time goes by seem to stand in isolation. And old attitudes to the Welsh-language programmes seem to die hard. The very good and very popular programme of news and comment *Heddiw* has recently been downgraded from its slot after the 6 o'clock news and is now shown much later, sometimes as late as 11 o'clock. And although the Welsh do the informal chat sort of programme magnificently, there is far too much reliance on the natural gift of spontaneous speech, and on low budget quiz-type programmes, and not half enough money spent on programmes demanding careful production and rehearsal. Welsh broadcasting and television should be able to afford the best. Heaven knows we produce enough of it in Wales at all levels. We should be able to have regular screenings of all our local boys and girls who have made good from Gwyneth Jones and Geraint Evans to Tom Jones and Shirley Bassey. And there are more like them in the pipeline, in the pubs and local eisteddfodau. There are large areas of cultural and social activity that are under-represented in our programmes, either not covered at all or only put out in snippets at odd hours like at night or lunch-time. We should demand pretty full coverage, not only for the National Eisteddfod, which does not come off too badly, or the Llangollen International Eisteddfod, which in any case is a television 'natural', but also for the major local and provincial eisteddfodau such as Anglesey, Powys, Cardigan and Pontrhydfendigaid, and the youth Eisteddfod of Urdd Gobaith Cymru.

We need far more from the other festivals. Those of Swansea and Llandaff are well thought of far outside Wales and there are a dozen others listed by the Arts Council, some, like the one held at the remote village of Llantilio Crossenny, remarkable examples of grassroots cultural activity, others, like those based on the Universities, full of rich trouvailles. For instance, at the Aberystwyth Arts Festival a few years ago, Hugh MacDiarmid and R.S. Thomas were together on the same platform. No one interested in modern literature could fail to be interested in a transcript of that encounter.

We need visits and surveys to the art galleries that dedicated people are establishing in our larger towns, and to exhibitions sponsored by public authorities.

We need more fair play for Welsh sporting events. Heaven help even the biggest of them if it clashes with a big English fixture.

We should have visits to the deliberations of our influential cultural and religious bodies.

We must have a more rational allocation of party political broadcasts and conference coverage.

We need, and would highly enjoy, argument programmes that are not short-winded, scrappy and superficial, that are not knocked on the head just as they are getting interesting with the anaesthetic formula 'Well, there I'm afraid we must leave the discussion for tonight,' accompanied by a hypocritical Anglo-Saxon smirk.

We particularly need a new approach to children's programmes, especially in Welsh. Children today are telecentric (if there is such a word, if not it should be invented), and they identify with the heroes of simple action stories. There are just not enough of these with Welsh dialogue or dubbed into Welsh although this is perfectly feasible. Indeed, the Americans make series of the Western type with just such requirements in mind, suitable for dubbing in any language. A pilot episode was shown some time ago with Welsh dialogue (complete with a Welsh-speaking Red Indian – *Fi cyfaill dyn gwyn. Dyn gwyn, dyn da*) but the initiative was simply not followed up. Robin Hood and D'Artagnan get the full treatment, but Twm Shon Catti and Macsen Wledig languish in limbo, and all the care of Welsh-speaking parents and Welsh schools goes for nothing.

We need news bulletins that are not merely a series of unoriginal comment on 'the main news' and parochial gossip, but world news interpreted from an independent point of view.

We need, indeed, we have an insatiable appetite for as much as they can give us of the Welsh National Opera Company, itself a logical development from the native choral tradition and chiefly famous for its chorus, and for our choirs themselves and for congregational singing, and for our own pop stars. This is not a biased estimate of audience preference. I call upon all those record sales to bear me out. I ask you to drink in any Welsh pub where the telly is a background to the bar talk, and to note which programmes still that talk, as if even to the most heedless, uninstructed and disinherited, there are voices that speak especially. We have not yet lost our souls. No one is suggesting, at least I am not, that we should live on an unrelieved diet of traditional fare, as the Slovaks are said to do with a television service monopolised by a narcissistic obsession with their equivalent of *y pethe*. I think our horizons are wider but the types of programmes are after all easily come by, and need no special measures taken on their behalf.

The commissioning of much of this work would be expensive, but it does not have to fall exclusively on the broadcasting corporation, which should work in association with other organisations in the cultural field, notably the Arts Council, whom I will refer to in this connection in due course. Already a precedent exists in the very sensible arrangement by which the Welsh BBC and the Arts Council together sustain a Welsh Theatre Company. It is not a very Welsh company or a very good company, but the principle is sound. In any case, a vigorous exploration of the cultural resources of Wales would not be unrewarding even in the monetary sense. In our global village the Welsh network would merge with the European and the world networks, and Welsh talent would have a high price on the world markets.

Welsh Dominion (2, 1968)

A Package Tour

Gerald Morgan (ed.), *This World of Wales:
an anthology of Anglo-Welsh poetry
from the seventeenth to the twentieth century.*

The present volume falls oddly into one's hands. The cover and the design (by David Tinker, I imagine, not at his best) are skimpily utilitarian as befits a book for school use. But the printing and layout are luxurious by Welsh standards and the twenty-five shillings asked could well price this book out of its intended market. The publishers seem to have been afflicted by mild delusions of grandeur but this discrepancy between accidents and essence could be simply remedied by a paperback edition at, say, fifteen shillings.

To come to the essence, Gerald Morgan makes no bones about being pragmatic: the poems are there and are worth reading; theories and definitions take second place. The anthology is dedicated, very properly, to Raymond Garlick and influenced by the fruits of his learning. But the dissident view that Welsh writers in English only ring the bell when they write about Wales or for a Welsh audience is not without its influence either. The word 'background' keeps on cropping up and is obvious in the choice of particular poems. The awareness of Welshness, which Gerald Morgan does not think existed before the present day, seems, on his own showing, to be pretty strongly present ever since the English language came in. It is there in the seventeenth century, in Vaughan's 'The Waterfall', which can be read today as a political poem, in Dyer's understandable enthusiasm for Dyffryn Tywi, in Morgan Llwyd's evangelical zeal for his country, and in his anonymous contemporary who denounced 'the guile and softness of the Saxon race'.

It is the duty of the anthologist to anthologise. He is our guide on a package tour and if he points out the well-known monuments he is not to be blamed for lack of originality. So here we have Vaughan, Dyer, Hopkins, W.H. Davies and Edward Thomas all represented by familiar pieces. Before the present century the only newcomer to most readers is likely to be Evan Lloyd, an eighteenth-century wit and follower of Charles Churchill. The unforced excellence of this kind of writing, even at second best, almost makes one regret the impact of *Lyrical Ballads*. Gerald Morgan somewhat confuses us by making a distinction (his only venture at dogma) between natives and tourists, which does not really work. Hopkins is arguably a border-line case, but Davies was a tourist in reverse and Treece at best a day-tripper. Hopkins learnt Welsh and would have qualified for admission under the pragmatic admission rules of the National Eisteddfod and the *Bywgraffiadur*. Was the contemporary of Ceiriog and Islwyn ever becalmed at Caersws Junction? Did he ever chat with the Van Line superintendent? Exactly what were his contacts with the native eisteddfodic culture around him? Did the Jesuit ever venture into the conventicles of Calvinism at its floodtide? I can't get over the feeling that it was Welsh speech patterns, as much as literary techniques, that were important for Hopkins. Try reading 'The Wreck of the Deutschland' aloud and you will see what I mean. Perhaps this is something that the newly-formed Hopkins Society could investigate; it would be a more useful track than most through the deserts of parasitic 'scholarship'. The treatment of W.H. Davies shows the editor at his best; he displays the poet of the sinister and ironic who knows life in the raw, rather than the cosy proto-Georgian of most selections. Among the more recent names David Jones is represented by the great set piece from *In Parenthesis*: the Welsh soldiers going 'over the top' on the Western Front at the orders of their imbecile English generals, and Edward Thomas with them, chronicler of an England that drowned in the mud of Paschendaele, in an idiom learnt from the New England of Robert Frost, the last valid traditional English poet. From these the transition is abrupt to Idris Davies, the contemporary of the hunger-marchers and their exact equivalent in literary terms, perfect illustration of Yeats's dictum that 'passive suffering is no theme for poetry'.

At one point the arrangement of the anthology, by birthdates rather than publication dates, is somewhat misleading. R.S. Thomas appears before Dylan Thomas. I do not propose to add any more pebbles to the cairn of comment that looms over one of these names and is beginning to amass about the other. It is not the work of the poets that we must discuss in this context, but the skill of the anthologist in fairly representing it. With R.S. Thomas, of course, one cannot really go wrong. His work is unified in tone, consistent in excellence. With the other Thomas, a hit-or-miss selection would be equally effective, but I would like to have seen what is perhaps his best, and unquestionably his most essentially Welsh poem here, the confessions of the old ram-rod who was once a windy boy and a bit. I am not so sure about the handling of Glyn Jones. The 'Merthyr' poem of course selects itself, but Jake Hopkins has strayed in from Mr Jones's unforgettable prose portrayals of life in that particular world (I almost wrote underworld), and this sensitive poet has better poems to his credit. As for Vernon Watkins, the work featured here actually misrepresents him as a more consciously Welsh poet than he in fact was, taking his writing as a whole. And his consciously Welsh efforts (with the outstanding exception of 'Returning to Goleufryn' – a gamma to Mr Morgan for leaving it out) are not his best, precisely because there is a noticeable element of effort in them, public gestures (like 'The Collier') from an essentially personal poet. Like R.S. Thomas, he could not help writing well, a Mozart in words, but the reader who is tempted by the poems in this anthology will find better outside it. I can never be sure about Alun Lewis. There are suspicious elements of a contrived cult about his reputation and Mr Morgan does not help a sane assessment by such remarks as 'the greatest loss suffered by English literature in the Second World War' which cannot be proved one way or the other. He wrote no better or no worse about his Valley background than some other young poets of the time and place, Leslie Norris for instance. His war poems seem an echo of Edward Thomas, though caught with uncanny skill, and, seriously, it would take an Indian to judge his Indian poems.

Mr Morgan features some poets at length, and presents others as 'solos'. There is an element of critical appraisal in the distinction, which in its turn must be appraised. It is good to see Lewis Morris here, a robust eighteenth-century voice before Calvinism got us. What a pity Mr Morgan was unable to consult the unprinted (unprintable?) stanzas in the MS, and what a pity 'Cywydd y Pais' is untranslated, surely the best indecent poem in any language. Can we tempt Mr Conran to lift those petticoats for the benefit of the monoglots? Of contemporary writers, I would have promoted T.H. Jones at the expense of Idris Davies and represented Conran by one of his dazzling translations. As it is, our debt to the older literature is represented by a paraphrase of Llywarch Hen by Leslie Norris, whom I would have rather seen here as a poet of modern valley life. Llywarch Hen was a nephew of Saint Tydfil and Leslie Norris, I feel, is more at home with Bopa Tyd. But with that particular scene impressively represented in Meic Stephens' 'Ponies, Twynyrodyn', as well as by Glyn Jones, I suppose we can't have too much Merthyr. A.G. Prys-Jones closes this section with some of his funny pieces, but I think future generations will remember him more for his patriotic verse, notably 'A Ballad of Glyndŵr's Rising', which I would have thought ideal for a school anthology.

Gerald Morgan is a practising schoolmaster and knows what is obscure to his audience and what is not, words like pelf, tetchy and velour, so I pass. But, in his notes, he is surely wrong in saying that 'Grongar Hill' is not a popular poem, even if Dylan Thomas did make fun of it. It is in every anthology where it could possibly figure and is generally regarded as the best of the topographical poems whose vogue was set by Denham's 'Cooper Hill'. Again, in the notes on David Jones, a difficult task well-handled, he tentatively glosses *ventaille* as 'a breath of air'. Actually the word denotes the air-vent of a helmet, which fits the metaphor of airless, oppressive darkness. Also, in Glyn Jones' 'Merthyr', I have always taken 'Daeth yr awr' to be a reference to a hymn rather than directly to the Bible. Finally, Dylan Thomas' 'Do not go gentle into that good night' is explained as an elegy, but I believe that it was his father's blindness, not his death, which is this poem's subject and it seems to me that this explanation makes better sense.

I hope that some of these suggestions will be incorporated into subsequent editions of a book which deserves to have a long run. Gerald Morgan is to be congratulated on doing something that urgently needed doing, and doing it extremely well. The foregoing criticisms, of mere detail, must be read in a context of immense gratitude.

Poetry Wales (4.3, Spring 1969)

Peopling the Welsh Past

A.G. Prys-Jones, *High Heritage.*

It comes as a change to review work by a writer on whom the most obvious influences appear to be Kipling, Chesterton, Walter de la Mare and, incredibly, Sir Lewis Morris. But the poems in this book have been composed over fifty years, and have been heavily influenced in form and content by a long and honourable career in the educational fields. I once saw an anthology for children which came with the depressing recommendation that 'every poem in it is written by a teacher'. It is rather more important to have poetry for children which is written by poets, and however modestly, Mr Prys-Jones is on the right side of the fence. It is of course the easiest thing in the world to dismiss this type of writing with a sneer, but English is, I think, one of the few literatures with a definite tradition of good writing especially for children (even in Welsh, I.D. Hooson occupied a rather isolated eminence), and the main literature is none the poorer for it. There are obvious pitfalls. Mr Prys-Jones in his preface says: 'Identification with the serious malaise of contemporary society has tended to replace sentiment by satire, emotion by cynicism, imagination by bleak or sordid realism and true compassion by cruel irony. Fortunately it is abundantly clear that these characteristics are very rarely to be found in the work of Anglo-Welsh poets who are writing today.' Oh dear! Although we are reviewing Mr Prys-Jones's poetry not his *obiter dicta,* it is obvious that he writes to a theory and a standard, both in art and life. Keidrych Rhys once memorably dismissed Mr Prys-Jones's work as 'Fascist piffle', which is a bit hard, but clearly an excess of *gemutlichkeit* can easily slop over into the *volkische.* (As a piece of information for the curious in these matters, when I went to check the spelling of *volkische* in a standard German-English Dictionary I found it had been omitted from the most recent editions. Irrelevant to the matter in hand possibly, but not without significance.)

But on the whole one can cheerfully recommend placing the present volume in the hands of young readers, both as poetry and as a lively picture of Wales which will perhaps arouse a child's imagination and curiosity about a country which even the most cynical, ironical, satirical and bleakest of us acknowledge as the only place in the world in which we could possibly live.

Not all the poems are equally successful or effective. Our author is not alone in this, of course, but where he does excel he does so in a way especially his own, while his less effective pieces share a lack of force and focus which I find widespread among many of his more ambitious compatriots. His forte lies in being able to convey action and movement. His best poems are about people on the move, Roman soldiers, Morgan's pirates, Glyndŵr's warriors, pilgrims to St David's. There is very little call for this particular gift in modern writing and it is consequently underrated just as, in prose literature, the ability to construct and sustain narrative is not in high repute, with consequent impoverishment. These are the poems of this author which I think will live by their sheer simple extrovert vitality (but I would beg him to derevise – if there is such a word – the 'Ballad of Glyndŵr's Rising'). In his descriptive poems, his portrayal of typical characters, his attempts to convey the historical atmosphere of particular places, he is up against some pretty distinguished competition but even so, if he arouses the interest of the intelligent child who will then come to appreciate subtler and more sensitive handling of these themes he has fulfilled a worthwhile function. In the genre which he has made his own he is by way of being a minor master; it is perhaps significant that though this type of writing may seem easy very few others have ever tried it. Descent into bathos and the commonplace is a pitfall he avoids, except perhaps in the high fustian of 'For Saint David's Day' with its unintelligible message that Wales is 'doubly free' (because it has been conquered?). The old weirdie of Llangunnor seems to have got through on the astral plane here, but it would be ungenerous to make too much of an untypical lapse. In peopling the Welsh past with lively, vigorous characters, Mr Prys-Jones has played his part in helping to build her future.

Poetry Wales (5.1, Summer 1969)

Come Home, Caradoc, All is Forgiven

T.H. Williams, *Caradoc Evans.*

Come home, Caradoc, all is forgiven. Rehabilitation has been discreetly under way for some time. In his indispensable guide *The Dragon Has Two Tongues*, Glyn Jones dealt sympathetically with the personal and cultural predicaments which obviously colour Caradoc's work. Now Trevor Williams carries the process a stage further with an excellent monograph. A study of a short-story writer and novelist, this little book claims review space in *Poetry Wales* not only because

Caradoc's prose was as stylised and cadenced as Ossian's or Rimbaud's and his vision had an intense poetic concentration, but because he is a figure of historic importance, relevant to all Anglo-Welsh writers whatever their medium.

Trevor Williams opens *in media res* by chronicling the public reaction to Caradoc at the height of his notoriety and places him in the context of his age. Against a summary sketch of Welsh Nonconformity, we are given a brief biography of the subject with emphasis on the unhappy features of his life and environment which seem relevant to his art. We are led through his career as a creative writer and controversialist. There are perceptive analyses of his narrative techniques and use of language, and a just and generous appraisal of his contribution to English writing in Wales.

It may be that so winnowed an oeuvre cannot be discussed at much more than monograph length. If so it will be difficult to better the present work. Caradocologists (a numerous underground) who will be tempted to make their own contributions to a rewarding and fascinating subject will for some time to come take this book as a meridian. That Caradoc will continue to attract study and comment is beyond doubt.

First, the artist narrow to the point of obsession, but shaping the obsession into almost tangible artefacts. There is the great mystery of all creation here. Trevor Williams reproduces at length an early sketch of village life, which only feebly foreshadows the more developed work. And this development started at the top. It is almost incredible but we have it on the authority of Professor Gwyn Jones' introduction to the 1953 reprint of *My People* that the first story Caradoc wrote in his fully evolved style was 'Be This Her Memorial', his masterpiece. He never, in the short story, looked back, never did anything better. Once he had somehow (and how one would like to know quite how) hit this vein, it yielded undeviating excellence. The milieu was unpromising, stale controversies (who now reads *The Perfidious Welshman?*), 'popular' magazine stories for the lower middle classes, seedbed of W.W. Jacobs and Pett Ridge, well-turned anecdotes of the pastoralised lower classes, clever but spurious, dead. And after his marriage, the world of tatty theatre and rubbishy novelettes. Yet here is an artist who, we are constantly reminded in the reading, was the contemporary of Firbank, whose elliptic narrative line parallels Virginia Woolf, whose tea-tabling of violence compares with Forster, whose outrageously explicit treatment of sex goes beyond Lawrence, whose bleak vision foreshadows Camus.

His work will live because he is, among other things, very much a writer's writer. Graham Greene's praise is not casually or conventionally bestowed. Dylan Thomas, notoriously a grudging debtor, proclaimed himself a pupil; Evelyn Waugh's ghastly village band in *Decline and Fall* offers even more explicitly the homage of an aspirant to an admired master. In Anglo-Welsh literature all influences tend to be bad and there has been plenty of awful pseudo-Caradoc, but Nigel Heseltine showed what could be done by deliberately adapting much of Caradoc's technique to a neighbouring county and a different social scene (*Tales of the Squirearchy* should be reprinted and a second collection, still lurking in typescript, should see the light of day.)

Then Caradoc the controversialist. Not such a unique figure. All Welsh writers, in either language, are *engagé*. The heirs of Henry Richard proclaimed their Apostle's doctrine that only Nonconformists really counted as Welsh. Caradoc took them at their word and depicted a whole nation as Canting Dissenters. This, as much as the political background of the Lloyd George Disestablishment era, explains his success in England. It was a convention with illustrious antecedents in English literature; it may be relevant to note that a London production of *Twelfth Night* in 1970 portrayed Malvolio with a grating Welsh accent. Caradoc too was among the first fruits of the 1870 Education Act and the 'iobish' language of his characters is the most devastating comment we have on its immediate impact. This great comic invention, more so than the dreadful conduct of his characters, probably explains the reaction to his work among a people who were doing their utmost to kid themselves that they were English. In the process the older stereotype of the Welshman represented by Fluellen and Smollett's Morgan, proud and choleric, completely disappeared, and is only just reappearing in the works of sympathetic English writers.

Finally, to paraphrase Kott's title, Caradoc our Contemporary. True, he could only mirror a society now quite dead, was indifferent to twentieth-century Wales. But how relevant he is. Only a few years older than D.J. Williams, born only a few miles away, they could have passed one another in the lanes, though on different journeys. Ajax and Thersites. The bitter soil of *Capel Sion* is the good earth of *Storiau'r Tir*. Those arguments that are still going on about whether such and such a horrible event in the stories really happened (they nearly always did and can be identified) are the dark side of *y pethe*. The Wales we have inherited is as much Caradoc as D.J. Enemy of Capel, he was yet no friend to squire and parson who often had an old-fashioned national pride. Dr Kenneth Morgan has quoted the strictures of the early Labour movement on precisely the bleak and philistine aspects of religious life that angered Caradoc. It could be held against him (we cannot deny this) that his achievement gave some sanction to the holus-bolus rejection of everything Welsh by, say, Goronwy Rees and his retinue, and is clearly related to the ravings of anglomaniacs in various public spheres. But in the context of his time and place he exposed something which has been permanent in the Welsh pattern, and by exposing it he warns us, and inspires, one hopes, some of us to destroy it. For his unspeakable Big Heads and Respecteds were the heirs of Pantycelyn and Gruffydd Jones, as the jackal politicians are the heirs of Keir Hardie and Noah Ablett. How will they be, the heirs of Gwynfor Evans and Phil Williams? Ask you, people bach.

Poetry Wales (6.2, Autumn 1970)

Some Recent Anthologies

Tom Scott (ed.), *The Penguin Book of Scottish Verse*;
Brendan Kennelly (ed.), *The Penguin Book of Irish Verse*;
Edward Lucie-Smith (ed.), *British Poetry since 1945*.

Mr Tom Scott, a distinguished poet in his own right, was co-editor of *The Oxford Book of Scottish Verse*. Now he is sole editor of the present anthology. It is as if one of the curators of a great collection of national treasures were called upon to mount a display for Expo. There is no point at all in making minute comparisons between the methodology, contents and emphasis of the two anthologies. They perform obviously different functions, and that of the present collection is to give a general conspectus, pointed up by a few acknowledged masterpieces. Mr Scott has done this very well. The reader whose interest is aroused will continue to explore this richly rewarding literature by means of the *Oxford Book* itself and such collections as the *Penguin Book of Ballads, Contemporary Scottish Poetry* and *The Golden Treasury of Scottish Poetry* as well as by seeking out *Akros, Lines, Catalyst, Scottish International* and other magazines which make the Scottish scene so lively.

In addition, Mr Scott contributes a long and valuable introduction. If I knew as much about Scottish literature as Mr Scott does, this is the introduction I would have written myself. He has all the right attitudes and all the right prejudices. One gets some idea from it of *why* modern Scottish poetry is so vigorous. Indeed, perusal of the reviews mentioned above is rather a humbling experience for anyone writing in English in Wales, or would be if one did not take into account how much our national fund of talent expresses itself in Welsh, which plays a much stronger role here than Gaelic does in Scotland. Scottish poetry should be a must for all Anglo-Welsh writers. The present volume does not, cannot, do real justice to the moderns; Mr Scott's main task is to put them in their setting as continuators or revivers of a great tradition, which he displays with some plenitude. But perusal of the anthology in its entirety will help to explain, say, the difference in stature between MacDiarmid and Dylan Thomas.

Mr Kennelly places us equally in his debt, although I must enter one major qualification. His anthology is divided into three parts: Gaelic translated, from the eighth century (St Patrick himself, no less) to Merriman; Anglo-Irish, from Swift to Ledwidge, and a final section called Yeats and After. His laudable (and vindicated) aim is to demonstrate that 'Gaelic and Anglo-Irish combine to create a distinctively Irish tradition.' As he finely says, 'In a nation's tradition poets who have not heard of each other are brothers.' But by his method, Gaelic drops out of sight after Merriman and the impression is inescapably given that one tradition has taken over from the other and displaces it entirely. A few sentences in the Introduction (which is very sound and perceptive on the whole) are not sufficient counterweight. Otherwise, here is another anthology that it is a pleasure to recommend. The editor harvests in rich territory, of course. I doubt if there could ever be finer translations into and from any language than Frank O'Connor's; these, I am sure, rather than his stories, will be his lasting fame. As the editor says, Irish poetry in both languages is vibrant, rhetorical and direct. It is also committed and involved, as such poetry must always be, vibrant often with hatred, lashing out at foreign oppressor and native exploiter. That is why this collection, which spans a thousand years, seems to be not only written by contemporaries of one another but written by our own contemporaries. In the world as it is today, can there be any other valid utterance? Readers who do not know Frank O'Connor and Merriman will boggle with incredulous delight as they make their acquaintance. Those of us who had perhaps dismissed the pre-Yeats Anglo-Irish as minor and peripheral will be pleasantly surprised by the quality displayed here. Mangan comes over as a considerable figure (the editor's comparison of him with Hart Crane is very much to the point) but I would have liked to see more of those two utterly dissimilar poets Darley and Thomas Davis. And is it too frivolous to urge the merits of Percy French?

The post-Yeats poets are all represented by one poem each. The

Scottish anthology also drifted into this despairing tactic in its final pages. It is so obviously unsatisfactory that some explanation is called for. Anthologies are expensive, but economics doesn't seem to be the answer. Perhaps it is that the editors are nice chaps who don't like to leave anybody out, but it is hardly fair on the reader who doesn't know whether the one poem in each case is a representative piece by a good writer or the solitary lucky break of one not so good. Which brings us logically to the third volume under review, which is called *British Poetry Since 1945*. I don't want to start a semantic argument, but what the hell is 'British Poetry'? I fear that this is a mid-atlantic barbarism meaning English poetry written in England. For the definition seems to exclude poetry written in the other languages of Great Britain, but a usage debased in itself is still further debased by the bland annexation of Scotland and Northern Ireland and the non-recognition of Wales. I hope one does not sound too hard on the editor, who may have had little freedom in this matter. But it is an important point and one which must be made. Mr Lucie-Smith's readers and those who have heard him lecture will know that although he writes in the *New Statesman*, he is almost luminously free of the grosser incrustations of snobbery and parochialism that characterise the Thames Valley mandarinate, but I am afraid that this anthology gives exactly the same sort of offence. It is arguable that two of the greatest poets active since 1945 in Great Britain have been Sorley Maclean and Gwenallt Jones. The editor has gone to great pains to give representation to much that few readers or critics have found worthy of such dedicated industry, not excepting contributions from persons who more properly belong to the crummier fringe of show-biz, yet ignores major work which belongs to the geographical area, at least, indicated in the volume's title. This is simply not good enough any more. As Miron Grindea has said (and who is better qualified to say it?), 'Our era of interplanetary collisions and space anchorages needs and – one hopes – breeds a *cosmic* approach to all problems of the spirit, consequently a truly *planetary* literature. Our epoch lacks creative literary giants but the reading public is aware of a process which may ultimately make the whole globe into one country. In this context the notion of 'small' literatures is meaningless, indeed a poem or a novel written by a Finn or a Turk can enrich our quest for meaning as much as a similar work by a Frenchman or an Englishman.'

But let us turn from such un-British sentiments to the work at hand. The editor has worked hard at his unrewarding task. The march past of the British Legion begins, appropriately, with a detachment of Dad's Army, nine elderly poets, all British, but only four

English. Then comes a section called Post-War, and if you ask what sort of a category Post-War Poetry is you won't be any the wiser for reading it here. Then in stately procession come The Movement, The Group, the Expressionists and the Post-Movement, with Influences from Abroad providing a welcome relief from the native diet – supermarket-paella. We make the acquaintance of the Dissenters, though what they have to dissent from will escape most readers, and after a welcome diversion to Scotland, explore the cosmic interplanetary differences of emphasis between Liverpool and Belfast. A read through this British book has all the majestic tedium of a journey by British Rail, and I wish all who read it the best of British Luck.

Poetry Wales (6.3, Winter 1970)

Coming of Age

A Letter to Meic Stephens

Garth Newydd
Merthyr Tydfil

The twenty-first number of *Poetry Wales* is an event to be celebrated, and as one of the original godfathers I am delighted to offer my congratulations at the coming-of-age. The magazine has grown in size and stature, in breadth of coverage and in reputation. It is an achievement you can be proud of. *A vo penn bid bont!*

Part of your original intention, I know, was to steer us away from the boring and irrelevant mainstream of Anglophonia. I hope you will persevere. How rewarding, for instance, was that foray, over two numbers, into modern Breton poetry. Forage further afield for another twenty-one numbers, into the literatures at the growing edge of human consciousness in our time, those that have been revived, those that are struggling, those that are beginning to emerge. These, and not the practitioners of Eng. lit., are our true peers, in their various predicaments, from the Chicanos to the Czechs. 'The frontier of Wales is on the Vistula!' If this means that we have to be less attentive to our immediate neighbours than has been our wont, the best of them will understand.

All this, naturally, will stick in some craws, and I wouldn't be surprised if you have been under pressure to open up your pages to precisely the sort of thing *Poetry Wales* was started to get away from, in other words, under the guise of 'widening one's horizons', to become merely provincial. (There are obvious parallels in other aspects of our national life). Given the requisite backbone – which nobody has ever been able to question in your case – it's obviously not difficult to withstand this sort of pressure. Though, of course, the occasional relevant contribution of a good English poet would always be welcome, as recently with Ted Walker. And it should be comparatively easy (I don't of course, mean less laborious) to extend our consciousness by articles and reviews dealing with many other literatures that are relevant to us all, Welsh and English-speakers alike. The real difficulty, as with everything else in Wales, lies behind our own lines. And this is where the wise godfather finishes the champagne phrases and takes a steely look at the prospects before the young heir.

They are not, neither could they be expected to be, unclouded. As with every inheritance there are parasites, false friends, the patronising settler and native serf with their smooth insinuation of anglocentric aesthetics, the purveyors of bad counsel. There is the temptation that besets every great inheritance, of spreading a board for all-comers, some of them hardly relevant to either word in your title, and a false interpretation of what it should mean. It may be said that there cannot be all that much difference between two communities so near and closely linked in every way. But Wales is either a grey province of England – and its English-language writers must be content to trail behind those who are themselves not conspicuously original – or it is an emergent nation, with problems and possibilities that cannot be discerned or explored from any anglocentric point of view. And from the point of view of one Anglo-Welsh writer at least, most of what emerges from the rest of Anglophonia is irrelevant. Even the apparent similarities are deceptive. I remember Alvarez going on about visiting Auschwitz. When you live, as I do, as you once did, just up the road from Aberfan, such voyeuristic excursions are unnecessary. We don't have to listen to, and can't spare the time for all that fiddle.

In the last number of *Planet*, Ned Thomas says, 'It is probably a necessary stage in the development of Welsh design that we should show that we can be as good as anyone else, even if it means being good in rather similar ways, or with a few emblems of Welsh identification .... But *good* design, that is, creative design, is something else and must derive from creative social movements.' This applies to words as to pictures. The first sentence quoted above adequately covers the claims of some of our illustrious predecessors, the important thing about whom is that they have been dead for some time and had the bad luck to live in the last years of the old Wales, as ours is the good luck to live in the first years of *y chwyldro*. And poets, like designers, will only be any good as they respond or react to that reality.

Ned Thomas goes on to state that creativity in Wales today is largely a matter of protest, that there have been awful lapses but, 'the truth is that people who have some aim in life beyond "good design" are both more likely to make mistakes and more likely to be truly creative'. So with writing. By an inexorable dialectic, the preoccupation with 'good literature' to the exclusion of all else will only produce spurious simulacra, while commitment to a cause which transcends mere literature, the effort, in Lionel Trilling's phrase, 'to raise the shield of Achilles which is the moral consciousness of art' (and which in Wales today carries an unmistakeable inconography) will be suitably rewarded. It would be tedious and unmannerly to go on at length and in more detail, and it is perhaps unreasonable to expect one magazine to try to do too much, though I think well enough of *Poetry Wales* to believe that it should always attempt to do more than most. And I suppose it's only human to complain that there are whole numbers that contain not enough of the stuff one likes and too much of what one doesn't like. But what's become of the young revolutionary poet whose verses are still sung with gusto, the author of 'Let's be kind to Anglo-Saxons', 'The Boys from Gwent', 'The Ballad of Dr Price', 'The Exile's Song' and other hits? Can't we have more of that sort of thing, more satire, more ballads, songs even, with music, always an important part of any live scene, and fewer identikit poems of middle-class *hiraeth* for the old whitewashed *tŷ bach*? (Yes I know, I've written a few myself). More bite, more involvement, less of the genteel suburban piddling. I know you can't make people write good stuff but at least you don't have to print the work of people who pretty obviously don't know what country they're living in. A green desert Wales may be, but let it be a Thebaid, swarming like Prévert's *Sables Mouvantes* with '*démons et merveilles, vents et marées*'.

Poetry Wales (7.3, Winter 1971)

A Far Cry from Milk Wood

A Letter to Meic Stephens

2 Rose Row
Cwmbach
Aberdâr

I was glad to hear that you proposed devoting a whole number of *Poetry Wales* to R.S. Thomas. Not that he stands in need of recognition but because to take stock of his achievement at the beginning of the '70s is to look back over an entire literary generation. It will be, according to Betjeman's foreword to *Song at the Year's Turning*, just twenty years since he secured the favourable notice that brought him to the attention of a wide audience, just six years after the publication of the delightfully produced *Stones of the Field* by Keidrych Rhys which I first remember handling in the upper room above Mr Baughli's chipshop in Lammas Street, opposite the Crimean War memorial. Dylan was the great man then, but he was already going visibly downhill and he died in 1953 at just about the time that R.S. Thomas really began to come to the fore.

It's difficult to imagine two more sharply contrasted figures, both in their poetry and in their personae. So much has been written about the public side of Dylan that it would be boring to add to it, and it is with some relief that one turns to a poet who seems to have no public personality at all, though of course R.S. Thomas is no recluse: he played an active part in the Bryncroes school controversy, but in context, as the local vicar. People I used to meet in England were enthralled by aspects of Dylan that wouldn't have earned him a second glance in any pub in Merthyr. This is a judgement on them, not him. For myself, I found him a very anglicized sort of person, with whom it was difficult to communicate. This, I suppose, is a judgement on me!

Dylan right through his career had the most exceptional *luck*. He had to pay for it in the end, of course, because the gods drive a hard bargain. But look at how he came on the scene in England with gifts that precisely filled the vacuum left by the arid and cerebral offerings of the 'thirties. And in no time at all the war had swept away a whole world which now only exists in his words, giving them not only irresistible nostalgic appeal but also a historical, even a documentary value. And of course he died in the right way that was recognized as very poetic, and at the right time. It is now being incredulously calculated that he'd be fifty-eight if he'd lived, and they ask the same questions about him as they ask about Lorca, Rimbaud and Keats. There's no answer, of course. My wild guess is that he'd have turned to prose and written some gorgeously daft novels that would make Tolkien read like Gissing. Or he could have got chewed up and spat out by the media. And then, as a further bonus, there is the obscurity, tedious and nasty adolescent nonsense most of it, but a boon to the parasites and charlatans who infest his cult. The bombinating solipsism or woozy sexuality of his earlier work give him a ready audience among the young, and his special picture of Wales is irresistibly attractive at a certain level. And this, naturally, is what I am coming to. One has only to compare Llareggub with Spoon River to see the limitations. Nobody seems to work, there are no politics, everybody of all ages is young and easy under the apple boughs. It is curmudgeonly to be over-critical, and, again, I feel that it was his special luck to leave the scene just before Wales itself began to move into a harsher, more demanding phase of its history.

And this, in case you are wondering, is where R.S. Thomas comes in. Only a few months older than Dylan, it is as if he remained silent until the other was almost done. Already I think I may have defined what appeals to me as his special virtues by implication in a negative way in enumerating those of Dylan. In *The Mountains* his prose is appropriately combined with wood-engravings by John Piper, another artist of strong subjective mood. When Piper presented his drawings of Windsor Castle to George VI, the monarch is credited with the sublimely Hanoverian comment, 'You didn't have very good weather, did you?' And this is the weather that R S. Thomas sees and this is the weather of Wales today. So his work acquires a relevance that transcends purely literary merit, in a way that Dylan's never did and never would. In these poems everybody works and indeed seems to do very little else. There is religion, there are even politics of a sort, arguing confusedly under the stars. But not much sex, or at any rate, not much talk about it. This too is true to the facts. The Welsh are an unromantic race and their approach to this side of life is direct and functional, (yes, I know that our greatest poet is a love-poet, but has it ever occurred to anyone that he is also the *only* love poet of any consequence in the whole of Welsh literature?). And the physical beauty of Wales is always presented in ironic contrast to the lives of the people who have to live in it, and to the history of the nation whose home it is. The countryman must work hard and incessantly, the small seaside towns are repellent sucker-traps for seedy tourists, the natives are too harrassed by their daily cares to take any account of their past glories or future possibilities. But for all that they are a dangerous lot. It's a far cry, thank God, from Milk Wood. But both are recognizable scenes, and if the one is too cosy and the other too bleak, we have been fortunate to have two great and dissimilar poets to extend the frontiers of our land in different directions. Dylan gave us a country in which it was lovely to be a child, his successor as *Prifardd* of English-speaking Wales has given us a country in which it is necessary to be a man. I don't think we could ask for better guidance.

Poetry Wales (7.4, Spring 1972)

From Aber Without Love

Goronwy Rees, *A Chapter of Accidents*.

In his public posturings, Mr Goronwy Rees resembles nothing so much as an ageing daughter of the night, blissfully unaware of her faded charms, oblivious of the passing of the Street Offences Act, parading in the pathetic finery of a bygone day on some windy corner long deserted by the traffic of pleasure. The opening chapters of the present volume come therefore as a pleasant surprise. The author writes well, even touchingly, of his childhood and family life, and of his early education. He is shrewd, without being particularly original, about what Robert Graves called 'the long weekend'. But for all his Welsh outsider's detachment he seems to have been well and truly nobbled.

Most of the book is about Guy Burgess, the spy and defector, the physical incarnation, it would seem, of the rottenness of his class and culture, an appalling figure portrayed here with obsessive intensity that makes compelling reading. It is almost impossible to believe that such a character could exist, even in London. Inevitably something of the reek must cling to the narrator of such themes and scenes. When our author goes on television to proclaim that 'Welsh Nationalism is an unmitigated evil', there are those who may well feel entitled to answer, 'Look who's talking'. For Mr Rees loses no opportunity of decrying everything Welsh and has been tireless in advocating the superior values and standards he claims to have found elsewhere. Were his tone less well-bred, one would say that he nagged. Unfortunately for him he keeps it up even while sprawling flat on his back. Here is a man who embraced England for better or for worse, who rose to the high table of All Souls' and was rudely tripped up in the trammels of the gutter press. The exquisite, exemplary irony of this well-remembered *cause célèbre* hardly needs emphasizing. Mr Rees admits the unwisdom, the lunacy even, of his attempt to cash in on his former friendship with Burgess after the latter had attained notoriety by his defection. But it was more than that, it was pure hubris, and the consequences were the classical working out of nemesis. Or is that pitching it too high? For the character self-depicted here is really rather commonplace, typical of the less attractive sons of the Manse as so well categorized by Hugh Ross Williamson, another of them. Burgess he convincingly portrays in Dostoyevskian terms, himself he compares to Köstler's Rubashov but a more apt comparison perhaps would be with some minor character out of Elizabeth Wiskemann, someone, say, like Adam Trott zu Stolz, who played with fire and only had himself to blame for getting burnt, an empty character, with no loyalty or sensibility.

There is a frightening lack of human sympathy in this author, an inability to appreciate ordinary life, that is disturbingly symptomatic of what can happen to so many of our people – *alienation* in the most literal sense. He is scathing about the limitations of Cardiff in his youth, but at that very time it was the city of the young Glyn Jones and the younger Dannie Abse, and a not dissimilar environment was nourishing the imagination of Vernon Watkins and Dylan Thomas. And when the story steers the narrator back to Wales, the pleasant Aberystwyth of the opening pages has become transformed, like the wicked witch's gingerbread cottage, into a place of horror which is simply unrecognizable to any normal person. There is a hilarious example here of Mr Rees's utter lack, not only of sensibility, but almost of decency as he depicts his wife's reactions. One can only hope, for everybody's sake, that the good lady is not such an archetypal burra memsahib as her husband presents her.

It is all very sad. He writes well, but to no particular purpose. He writes about millionaires and Marks & Spencer and lovely, lovely money. He writes about the Great Depression and seems to be still in it, a tedious irrelevant revenant from the dirty 'thirties. His novels have made no great mark. He was, unintentionally, perhaps the last victim of the tireless anti-national intriguing of Tom Jones. He is a bundle of sensations, a chapter of accidents, incensed that the young Welsh of today are beginning to think well of themselves and their country, and are concerned to tackle its problems, miffed that they are not interested in the meretricious trash which has so dazzled his own eyes, offering them nothing but his obsessive chronicles of snobbery, sodomy and treachery.

Planet (11, May 1972)

Memories of the Eisteddfod

My first, traumatic experience of an Eisteddfod was at Swansea in 1926, before I was six years old but clearly recollected because it was so frightening. This was the year Gwenallt won the Chair and Dewi Emrys the Crown, which he pawned in Goat Street in order to buy drinks in the Mackworth, but for us in Catherine Street the really important thing was that our neighbour, Mr Isaac, the lame postman, took part in the ceremonies, blowing the *Corn Gwlad*. He was a musician of repute, as was to be his son George, the cellist, and we were pleased for he was well-liked. We were thus conscious of being part of a great event, albeit rather remotely. The shed-like main pavilion was in Victoria Park, almost at the end of our street where the Guild Hall now stands, and I was held up to watch Lloyd George addressing the crowd. My recollection is of a gentleman with white hair waving his arms about very excitedly and speaking, of course, in a language which none of us understood. Thirty years later, I was to speak on the same platform as his daughter, Megan Lloyd George, at Ebbw Vale. But the real horror was the Gorsedd of Bards, whose ceremonies were held in Singleton Park. The wrinkled faces of those old men, emphasized by their hideous head-dress, were truly frightening, and as this senile company shambled past, terror entered my soul and I had to be carried away in tears.

After this unfortunate introduction to the national festival of Wales, subsequent Eisteddfodau left little mark on my memory. Only the faintest echo reached us in Swansea from the event held in Port Talbot in 1932, when the journalist Hannen Swaffer was received into the magic circle, taking the bardic name *Llais y Werin*. Swaffer was a bit of an Eisteddfod buff and I saw him again at Aberdare in 1956. Then came Neath in 1934, but I don't recall much of it, except that soon afterwards the Bards of the Isle of Britain paraded in their costumes at St Donat's Castle for the entertainment of Randolph Hearst and one of the witty fellows recited an englyn belittling Saunders Lewis. What a shower!

I didn't attend the Eisteddfod at Fishguard in 1936. But a few weeks later, when the little town was still basking in the atmosphere of the event, we went as a family on a Sunday excursion by train that took us through utterly unknown territory, with stops at such places as Clarbeston Road, Whitland, and Llanfallteg West. At Fishguard everything was closed and we had difficulty getting something to eat. We were asked whether we were English and, when we explained we had come from Swansea, they opened up and told us all about the excitement which the Eisteddfod had brought to the place. We went for a decorous walk along a cliff-path and, in a quiet way, thoroughly enjoyed ourselves. In one of the snapshots taken that day I see my mother, just before the onset of her final illness which was to last a long time. I remain grateful to the people of Fishguard and the quiet of that day and their cheerful talk about their Eisteddfod. It was the last of such occasions for a woman who didn't have many such treats.

In 1938 Cardiff was a remote place, officially Welsh but not very much so, and there were other things to think about that year, and in the year following, in the shadow of war. Nigel Heseltine wrote a savage poem about the witholding of both the Crown and Chair and the booing of the assembled bards. After that I went away for a long time, first to Oxford and then into the Navy. After the war, I was working for Keidrych Rhys in Carmarthen and it was from him that I heard about the shambles of the Eisteddfod held in Bridgend in the previous year, the flooded Field, the thieves and vandals which the town has in plenty, and the hostility of Cynan and his cronies to Keidrych and everything he was trying to do. By then I was a member of Plaid Cymru, which was to be closely linked to the Eisteddfod for many years, so that my recollections from now on have to do with the Party's annual conference and Summer School, usually held in the same district as the Eisteddfod happened to be visiting. I was later to play a part in the break-up of this unholy alliance. In 1949, for instance, the Summer School was held in Dyffryn Ardudwy. I remember Eirian Davies, then a fiery young preacher and my first acquaintance among Welsh poets, returning to the school with the news, 'They've chucked out the Republic!' Plaid Cymru had rejected a motion calling upon it to take a more Republican stance. The founding fathers of the Welsh Republican Movement walked out and things were never to be the same again. I had no part in all this, for I was not yet a Republican and, anyway, I had troubles of a more personal nature. By 1950 things were different and were to remain so for the next thirty years.

It was, nevertheless, still axiomatic even among the heretics and scoffers that the Eisteddfod was central to an important aspect of Welsh life, so initiatives had to be planned accordingly. The first number of *The Welsh Republican* appeared in time for Caerphilly and I helped to hawk it around the streets of that town. Of the event itself, although it was the first one for me to attend for a whole week, I have little clear recollection, except that it seemed ill-organized and quarrelsome. The official core of bards wasn't much in evidence and the more raffish fringe of assorted piss-artists hadn't yet emerged. As recently redeemed Republicans we payed little attention to the goings-on of Plaid Cymru. We stuck cheeky Republican slogans on the shiny car of the Lord Mayor of Cardiff and Gwyndaf Evans and Cliff Bere performed the difficult feat of setting fire to a Union Jack on the castle's ramparts so that it flew and burned at the same time. Gwilym Tilsley won the Chair with his '*Moliant i'r Glowr*' and Gwenallt attacked Jim Griffiths in his adjudication. My contribution was a cod letter denouncing the flag-burning which I sent to the *Western Mail* signed I. McHunt, and they printed it!

By the following year the Republicans were in Bargoed, trying to make a success of our bookshop, in a bad position and a bad neighbourhood. One could have said the same about the Eisteddfod of that year, held at Llanrwst, a place of legendary inaccessibility. Our bookshop at Bargoed failed and by the summer of 1952 I was in Cheltenham. There, sitting in a cinema watching a newsreel, I saw the bards in procession on the prom at Aberystwyth. Oddly enough, the English audience seemed rather impressed, and even more oddly, so was I. Then, at long last, I found a job in Wales, and by the Eisteddfod of 1954, at Ystradgynlais, I was working in Dowlais Library. Now I really could go to the Eisteddfod. Unfortunately, the weather was appalling and Wynne Samuel was in charge - a double catastrophe. The festival made a loss for the first time ever and soon only the mud remained in people's memories. Plaid Cymru at this time was also wallowing in the equally glutinous complacency of the Welsh-speaking petty-bourgeoisie. The regulars in the Crown, in Merthyr, were puzzled by my determination to make the journey to Ystradgynlais by bus, but I managed it.

The Eisteddfod of 1956 was an altogether more agreeable event. The venue was Aberdare Park and the consensus was that this was one of the best Eisteddfodau ever held. The weather was kind and the patriarchal presence of S.O. Davies, the M.P. for neighbouring Merthyr, lent the festival some additional lustre. Here I met Dyfnallt, and T. Glynne Davies, who plied me with whisky so liberally that I had to go home the worse for wear in the company of Glynne Jones, who was none too sober himself. It's little wonder that I have no recollection of the open-air singing which was introduced at Aberdare.

From the obscurity of Llangefni in 1957 came the marvellous news of Dyfnallt Morgan's crowning, which made up for the unspeakable failure to honour him for his poem '*Y Llen*' in 1953. In the summer somnolence of Dowlais, a place which wears its leisure uneasily, having been built for work, I scoured the streets to collect signatures for a letter of congratulation to a poet who had been bred in Gwernllwyn Chapel.

It was a crisis year for the Eisteddfod in 1958. The Empire Games in Cardiff had emptied the public coffers and drained the energies of individuals who might have been expected to do their bit. Not a single application was received. But a man called Gwili Lewis, who was Entertainments Clerk to the new Ebbw Vale Council, persuaded the authority to invite the homeless festival to the town. The decision to invite the Eisteddfod was taken on the casting vote of the Council's Chairman. There was such a shortage of local people able to play their part in the preparations for the event that I, as the Librarian of Dowlais, found myself on the Literature Panel, having to travel over to Ebbw Vale long before the Heads of the Valley road, but always finding the journey worthwhile. With the help of a senior man at Richard, Thomas and Baldwin, the local steelworks, we commissioned a small prefabricated pavilion which was to last a long time. At committees I found myself agreeing with Iorwerth Peate. During the ceremonies of the Gorsedd I spotted some of the local Welsh-speakers who had chickened out of the Parliament for Wales campaign.

By 1958 I was in a bad way, frustrated by work in Dowlais and life in Merthyr. That was the year the *Welsh Republican* folded after eight strenuous years and I applied for a post in Australia. It was one of those periods when worthwhile things had come to an end and there seemed (delusively as it turned out) to be no possibility of a new start. For the first time ever I attended Plaid Cymru's Summer School, which was held memorably in Cyfarthfa Castle. But my mood was quarrelsome. Carlo had been proclaimed 'Prince of Wales' at the Empire Games and the folk-dancing fairies who in those days frequented the Summer School were amused. I was not and bawled them out rather savagely, and was reprimanded by Emrys Roberts whom I now met for the first time. He seemed a new sort of Plaid-man. Aneurin Bevan, who was to die two years later, gave an address on the Sunday before the Eisteddfod began in which he said all the right things; it was a serene sunset for him, I suppose. But I got into another fight in Ebbw Vale when some idiot started singing 'God Bless the Prince of Wales' in a pub. Yet I have happy memories of the week. Griffith John Williams gave one of his rare lectures in English, about the Welsh tradition of Gwent, the only time I ever heard him speak. T. Llew Jones won the Crown, the first of his many prizes, with his poem about Caerleon. His pseudonym was 'Emyr' and the poem, which ended ambiguously, was really for his son, then an infant, who was to choose his own path that took him to Tryweryn. Somehow or other I found myself alone with the poet immediately after the ceremony, in one of the many vestries, and I was the first to congratulate him, before the press located him; it remains for me a memorable moment.

By 1959 I was in better spirits, more reconciled to the eventual exhaustion of the Republican Movement and ready to enjoy my first visit to an Eisteddfod in the North (we had, I think, only just started to refer to it as the Gog, more a state of mind than a geographical location). It was a memorable holiday, although the Eisteddfod itself was the occasion rather than the substance, and there was an excellent atmosphere. T. Llew Jones won his second Crown and I walked up Snowdon. The disgraceful shack at the summit and the wretched Gogs ingratiating themselves with the tourists have further enriched my memories of that year. In a reversal of the usual ritual, I removed a stone from the cairn at the mountain's top, and I still have it, one of a collection of symbolic, commemorative and totemic stones which are of no significance to anybody but myself and which eventually will be only stones. Another excursion was in the company of Ceredig Davies and Harri Pritchard Jones, who took me on a tour of Anglesey, visiting Llangefni mart and picking a huge crop of mushrooms, pointed out to us by an utterly unmercenary farmer on whose land their grew. My base, thus provisioned for many days, was the Newborough Hotel in Palace Street in the heart of the old walled town, which was kept by Harris Thomas, an architect from the South, and his blonde wife Stella. There they kept open house for a set which was just then beginning to form, namely *Undeb y Tancwyr*, whose anthem Harris composed. In some ways it was one of the most civilized holidays I had ever spent and it's still fresh in my mind. Hywel Hughes of Bogota was one of the company, an impressively dangerous-looking old man. It was on this occasion that I 'came out' as a poet, after reciting 'Our Budgie' in the bar. At another pub, the Black Boy, Keidrych said to me, in social mood, 'I say, old boy, do go and speak to Siân Phillips's husband, nobody's talking to him,' which I did, although poor Peter O'Toole seemed ill at ease in the effervescent Taffery that afternoon. Only a couple of years later, the lovely Stella dropped dead as she was putting on a pretty dress to go to a dance.

In 1960 the Eisteddfod was held in Cardiff, in Sophia Gardens. There was, as usual in Cardiff, no winner of the Chair, and the whole thing was pretty dull. I remember a young lady playing something by Bach to an unappreciative clientele of a pub now called the Owain Glyndŵr. The presence of royalty inhibited my muse. The Plaid Cymru Conference was held on the campus at Colchester Avenue and was quite an eye-opener. Ever tolerant in such matters, I still found it difficult to credit the open lechery as the gilded flies went to it, only to appear on the Sunday in Capel Heol y Crwys wearing their best hats. It was the year of Fellini's *La Dolce Vita*.

Rhosllannerchrugog in 1961 was something of an *annus mirabilis*. This was the year when the Executive Committee of Plaid Cymru refused to recommend direct action over the issue of Tryweryn. It was on Llangollen Bridge that I met Waldo Williams, as described in my elegy for him, and went with Judy Gurney to the summit of Dinas Bran, where I introduced her to Dai Pritchard whom she later married. I also met two splendid women, Jane Binning and Eiry Palfrey. During the week, in the company of Neil Jenkins, Father Mullins, and Hywel ap Dafydd, who were among those who helped to 'drink the pub dry', I wrote 'The Cross Foxes' and a few squibs about the Old Gang.

In 1962 the Eisteddfod was in Llanelli and the Plaid Summer School at Pontarddulais. Off-stage the Great Train Robbery took place and the suicide of Marilyn Monroe. More to the point, Cymdeithas yr Iaith Gymraeg was founded and Neil Jenkins was expelled from the party. Meic Stephens delivered a stunningly iconoclastic lecture which upset all the right people. I spent a memorable evening with Harri Pritchard Jones and two Irish girls from Gael Linn, and I bought a red *sospan* as a souvenir. At Caernarfon in the year following, the Eisteddfod being held at Llandudno, the sun shone and Helen Wyn and Carys Pugh sang beautifully. The accession of Huw T. Edwards to the ranks of Plaid Cymru was hailed as an event of some importance.

The 1964 Eisteddfod was held once again in Swansea, within sight of Sketty Church. I was still not in touch with my family, so stayed with Ogwen Williams, formerly of Dowlais. Bryn Williams won the Chair with a *cywydd* about Patagonia and Rhydwen Williams the Crown, both worthy winners. Motivated by Meic Stephens, the Anglo-Welsh put on a fringe reading in one of the hotels in which Glyn Jones and I took part in the belief that we were showing solidarity with the cause. In 1965 we were in Newtown and the Plaid Summer School was in Machynlleth. It was a traumatic moment. Elystan Morgan had ratted on Plaid Cymru and gone over to the enemy. I remember how Gwynfor Evans came into a café where I was sitting and told me quietly of the bad news, and that, rather than my own lecture on Owain Glyndŵr, is my most abiding recollection of the Summer School. I stayed with a nice family on the Garth Owen Estate and was very nicely looked after. Perhaps the most notable event was the emergence of Ryan Davies as an entertainer of genius. After one of the best *nosweithiau llawen* ever staged, there was no going back to teach in London for him. Another rich experience was listening to Saunders Lewis in the high pulpit of a huge chapel, declaring his passion for Ann Griffiths.

By the following year everything had changed. In July Gwynfor Evans had won Carmarthen and a triumphalist euphoria prevailed. The Plaid Summer School at Maesteg saw the emergence of an element that was to become the Free Wales Army, a set of lumpen proletarian romantics. Only one of them said nothing as he listened to their hard talk and his name was John Jenkins. At the Eisteddfod the hero of the hour was Twm Jones, recently jailed for his activities in the name of the Cymdeithas. Meic Stephens made an inflammatory speech from a soapbox on the Field, denouncing Leo Abse and Gwyn Thomas, and then we all went off to a poetry reading, on the fringe of the festival. I stayed at a small hotel in Bridgend and was driven back one night by John Davies (Bwlch-y-llan) when I incurred my statutory statistical road-accident, John driving into a bollard on the newly opened motor-way. We were all extricated from our predicament by a group of local lads, experienced accident-spotters to a man, and none of us was any the worse. I met Lennie Peters, the African poet, and Alun Owen, a swaggering bighead then at the height of his brief réclame.

The Bala Eisteddfod held little appeal for me. It was just the wrong place for me, too heavily Calvinist. After that Plaid Cymru tended to hold its Summer School at Aberystwyth, a much more sensible venue. In 1968, when the Eisteddfod visited Barry, I stayed at a small hotel in Cardiff which turned out to be most inconvenient. In its search for non-traditional venues, the Eisteddfod went to Flint in 1969, an utterly unsuitable place. It was the year of the Investiture and there were some ugly scenes, with police harrassment and bar-racking by the scum of Deeside. Ammanford in 1970 offered not much more of the wine of welcome. It has never been a particularly friendly place and on this occasion saw no reason to relax its sour standards. But despite the absence of any general, festive atmosphere, the launching of *Planet* was a memorable event in itself, although it took place in Llandeilo, a much more simpatico town. In 1971 Bangor had other drawbacks, notably the traffic which strangled everything, and the location at Penrhyn Castle left no impression on me at all. Bangor isn't really much of a place, it has its back to Wales somehow. But the most unlikely place of all was Haverfordwest in 1972. My attendance at the Eisteddfod had been so regular since 1950 that my absence started a rumour that I had committed suicide! There was, I was told, a lot of trouble between the local lads and the young visitors. Ruthin in the year following was much more congenial. Brynach Parry arranged accommodation for me in the flat of some-one he knew and I slept there in a hallucinatory décor straight out of a colour-supplement. I had a ticket for a pop-concert but failed to make it, having been beguiled by an assembly in the pub across the road which included Rhydwen Williams and Bryan Martin Davies. It was a session of endless erudition, a real bardic school of the old kind, much more to my taste than pop-singing.

This note brings the story up to 1973, although I shall continue to record my impressions of the Eisteddfod in the diary which I intend keeping this year. *Ah, on a vécu!*

Previously unpublished, found among the author's papers (1974)

The Burning Tree

Gwyn Williams, *Welsh Poems, Sixth Century to 1600.*

Here is a welcome reprint in paperback of Gwyn Williams's *The Burning Tree, Poems from the First Thousand Years of Welsh Verse,* now soberly retitled, with the texts in the original language left out, but with the valuable introduction retained. By typographical virtuosity the entire text is reprinted page for page from the very different format of the original edition, and looking very much at home. Taking the cue, it would be well to look at this as a new publication, offering a different experience from the bilingual parent volume. It is now twenty-one years since this first appeared, a generation before the talents of Joseph Clancy and Anthony Conran had emerged. It was then necessary to break away from what Conran himself rather severely characterised as the 'irresponsibility' of earlier translators, whose habit had been to offer loose paraphrases of Welsh poetry of whatever period in the current or slightly passé English idiom of the day. The situation was not improved by the known preference of major Welsh poets for English versions of their work in distinctly minor English idiom, and their even better-known distaste for the abrupt modernistic versions that appeared in the first floruit of *Wales.*

None of this is irrelevant to the volume in hand. There is an aesthetic of translation as there is of other writing. The best translations must read like independent creations. A poem of permanent appeal may need to be translated every generation or so. The translator will have his own merits as an original writer. An outstanding poem will appeal to more than one translator. What are we looking for? What, I think, Gwyn Williams pioneered, not with *The Burning Tree* but with an unpretentious volume that preceded it by a few years, *The*

Rent that's due to Love. This had a style that was not obviously borrowed from any influential English poet of the day or of a recently past day, a plain, unpretentious style that did not aim for striking effects in its own right, but was good for incidental felicities. Above all, a sound style, that read smoothly, that was obviously not a mere crib or a gloss, yet suggested fidelity to the original text. The average reader, even with a good knowledge of Welsh, is unlikely to be able to assess the scholarly accuracy of the versions, but it is not the least merit of Gwyn Williams that he conveys this, that one takes him on trust as a faithful, scrupulous and scholarly translator. It is, one may say without censure, an impersonal style, and this is particularly appropriate for the main body of Welsh verse which has survived from within the limits which he has wisely set himself in this volume, when the poet was the spokesman for a community and an established set of values, not the individualistic, often socially isolated figure of later times. Gwyn Williams is a poet in his own right, of course, but in his own work he speaks with a very different voice, a totally contemporary figure who can by turns be lively even to jauntiness, yet chilled by all our familiar angsts. This is why I felt that his selection *Presenting Welsh Poetry*, covering a wider period up to modern times, was less successful. Here, the period limitation works in his favour, and the versions read as well as they did twenty-one years ago. He does not attempt to reproduce rhyme, *cynghanedd* or other effects, his adherence in matters of form being basically to the line-length of the original, and as most of this poetry was syllabic this method is effective.

Scholars, according to all the testimony, are pleased with the fidelity of these renderings. The author acknowledges a special obligation to two of the most eminent among them, Professor Idris Foster and Dr Thomas Parry, and for most of us this will be sufficient guarantee. Neither, given the vast field to choose from, can one usefully criticise the translator's choice of material. The big stuff from the *Hengerdd* is here, those voices that speak most urgently to us in our own situation today, many other voices from after ages, but all positive and confident, even in the cosmic despair of Gruffydd ab yr Ynad Coch's great death-chant for Llywelyn the Last. The minor key, though, is almost absent. Like the founder of the Wallace Collection, who only acquired 'such pictures as were pleasing', Gwyn Williams's preferences are healthily eupeptic and his favourite poet is obviously Hywel ab Owain Gwynedd. Nor, happily, is there much religious poetry. This could be reckoned as a major distortion, as I believe that in terms of sheer bulk most of the poetry of the period was religious. (This, in fact, was probably true up till the Second World War!) Literature, in this respect, is not necessarily all that true to life, and

Gwyn Williams is being truer to life than to literature when he leaves it out. Only in the grinding, mechanical morbidities of Siôn Cent do we hear what the great K.B. McFarlane, dealing with Cent's Lollard contemporaries, called 'the premonitory snuffle of post-reformation puritanism'. Here for the most part is a sane sensuality, whether in love or in war or in the presence of death, 'a life of sensation rather than of thought' that Keats expressed a preference for, staggering away from an ultra-cerebral session with Coleridge. It was a *Weltanschauung* maintained by a Celtic society and projected by its poets despite political setback and harrassment from the Church, and it was sustained from the battlefield of Catraeth to the washing-place where a girl scrubbed her man's shirt while the Tudor gentry rode over Cardigan bridge on their way to London and the shadows began to lengthen.

Gwyn Williams's Introduction enhances the value of the book. I have not seen its chief propositions stated so convincingly elsewhere, and even its more arguable assumptions are stimulating. To have brought the feel and flavour of those first thousand years before an age that stands so desperately in need of the stimulus they offer is more than merely a literary feat, splendid though it is. It could be one of the things that will save us yet.

Poetry Wales (9.4, Spring 1974)

Down with the Mandarins!

A Letter to Sam Adams

2 Rose Row
Cwmbach
Aberdare

I read Roland Mathias's letter in the last number of *Poetry Wales* with great interest. Anything he has to say is worth listening to, but I'm not sure that in this instance he carries me with him. I'm afraid that the observations by Philip Pacey which occasioned his remarks have floated out of my memory. I am sure that I was not the only bard-spotter who was disappointed when Philip Pacey, easily one of the most original talents to surface in recent years, left Wales, because I think that if he had stayed he would have written himself into the Welsh experience (as he had begun to do) and would have had something worthwhile to say about it. But his muse called him elsewhere. Even on those who have spent their formative years in this country, exile inflicts its false perspectives. I should like to mention here, as my ideal of the Good Exile, George Ewart Evans, who has written nothing about Wales since he left the Cynon Valley for East Anglia, and has rightly chosen to chronicle the life he sees around him, and has won a high place among its interpreters. Would that others followed his example. Especially today, with the situation changing so rapidly, even a few months puts one out of touch. Always a bother, sometimes a pity, it can also, for a creative writer, be a disaster. It's all right, of course, if he sticks to *hiraeth*, always a seller, or to arcane haruspications, or simplistic cameo-painting, but anyone who has got anything to *say* to, for and about Wales, has got to say it here and nowhere else. *A fortiori*, one cannot expect even the most sympathetic visitor to get it right, and I don't see why he should be chided if he doesn't. St Albans is further from Aberystwyth than Aberystwyth is from Accra. An Afro-English poet, like Lenrie Peters, knows immediately what we are talking about. For nearer neighbours, it's harder. Even Bryan Johnson, the only English *avant-garde* writer of any consequence, and a good friend to Wales, whom we will always miss, didn't get it quite right.

Anyway, and this is my main point, does it matter? Roland, and I hope I don't do him an injustice, seems to think it important that we should gain recognition in London. I don't. I freely concede that writers in other categories may feel that they have no alternative but to seek such recognition. The economics of novel publishing or theatre presentation may mean that London is their only hope. But poetry has no economics, and to be lined up in some publishing conglomerate's prestige loss-leader collection of living and partly-living poets is not my idea of glory. Give me Gomer every time, whose list includes Gwenallt, Euros Bowen and Bryan Martin Davies. I would rather quarrel fiercely with these fellow-countrymen than bask in the patronage of the Thames Valley mandarinate. To pick up a phrase from one of that fraternity's distinguished predecessors, one is just as likely to be poxed by their love as poisoned by their hate. Their embrace didn't do Dylan much good, did it? I believe too they took up R.S. for the wrong reasons, but he has been robust enough to survive.

For all anybody knows, this new attitude to Anglo-Welsh poetry might be just another spasm of the frantic search for exotic novelty that characterizes a decadent and superficial metropolitan culture such as that of modern England. Roland speaks of the 'circus performers' of that poetic stage. Well, Taffy has always been a clown, and the talent scouts are always on the look-out for new turns.

And can we stop attributing some sort of oracular omniscience to the *T.L.S.*, one of the most successful of all English con-jobs. The new editor has noticed that the suckers have been getting restive and has dropped the convention of anonymous reviewing. Yet another false facade gone the way of the Euston Arch. If this minor act of demolition is letting in a little more daylight and revealing a decently conscientious literary magazine, all well and good, but it puts into a different perspective any change of attitude to Anglo-Welsh writers in its pages. One asks again, so what?

Lastly and most awfully, Roland speaks of this changed attitude as part of a new Toleration Act. This really worries me. 'His Highness, therefore, of a singular Zeal, Love and Fervour that he beareth towards his subjects of the said Dominion of Wales ....' Isn't this where we came in? If so, include me out.

Poetry Wales (10.1, Summer 1974)

The Doctor is Unmoved

Two hundred years ago this summer, Doctor Samuel Johnson came to Wales for the first and only time in his life.

The journey was not chronicled by the faithful Boswell, who was at home in Scotland at the time, but we have the Doctor's own diary of the tour, as interesting as much for what it does not say as for what it says.

The occasion of his visit was a change in the fortunes of his benefactress, Mrs Thrale. Although married to a wealthy London brewer, she was a scion of the distinguished Salisbury family of Llewenni in North Wales, with a long and eventful history of public service. When, in 1774, she inherited some ancestral estates in the Llŷn Peninsula she invited her famous protégé to join her and her family on her tour of inspection. On July 28 he records, 'We entered Wales, dined at Mold, and came to Llewenny.'

The country was already being opened up to the tourist. Thomas Gray had popularised its literature with his translations and his dramatic portrayal of the Bard. Mountains, waterfalls and rugged scenery were fashionable. But the Doctor's tastes were rooted in an earlier generation. He was a Londoner and a scholar, urban and rational.

His diary is factual, his observations devoid of rapture. A typical entry reads, 'We went to see a waterfall. I trudged along unwillingly, and was sorry not to find it dry.' He is also neatly sceptical. At Denbigh 'there was a stone in the wall over the doorway, which, it was said, would fall and crush the best scholar in the diocese. One, Price, would not pass under it.' Poor Price.

At Holywell our visitor was more interested in the copper works, of which he gives detailed description, than in St Winifred's Well. He took his manners with him. Dining with Squire Myddleton of Gwaunynog, he poured oyster sauce over the plum pudding, and melted butter from the toast into his chocolate. 'After dinner,' he notes of that occasion, 'the talk was of preserving the Welsh language.' As the subject is still occasionally discussed, it is worth noting that the Doctor was sufficiently interested to 'offer a scheme', though he does not give us the details.

Gray's collaborator, the antiquarian curate Evan Evans, was mentioned, and his addiction to drink was deplored. Johnson recommended Worthington (another learned clergyman, not the cause of Evan Evans's downfall) and advocated the republication of David ap Rhees's Welsh grammar. Modern scholars would not endorse Johnson's choice of this textbook, but his knowledge of it is testimony to the extent and thoroughness of his learning. 'Myddleton,' he comments gloomily, 'is the only man in Wales who has talked to me of literature. I wish he were truly serious.'

Listening to a sermon in Bodfari Church he found that 'the sound of Welsh in a continued discourse is not unpleasant' but he had a poor opinion of Welsh churches in general, and 'mean' is one of his key adjectives.

He was more pleased with the castles. Of Beaumaris he writes, 'This castle corresponds with all the representations of romancing narratives. Here is not wanting the private passage, the dark cavity, the deep dungeon or the lofty tower.' He was impressed, one feels, in spite of himself. Caernarfon was even more striking. 'I did not think there had been such buildings; it surpassed my ideas.'

With his hosts he visited Bodfel, deep into Llŷn, which had happy childhood memories for Mrs Thrale. But the churches of Tudweiliog and Llangwnnadl were in a miserable condition, and the curate could not read the big black-letter old Welsh Bibles in them. Johnson's comment is oblique but shrewd, 'The Methodists are very prevalent here.'

Visiting Snowdon, they sailed in a boat on Llyn Padarn, while a lady sang Welsh songs to the harp, so Mrs Thrale tells us, but the Doctor does not mention what must surely have been a special treat laid on for his benefit. On this day out, they played a game with the Thrales' ten-year-old daughter, who was promised a penny for every mountain goat she could spy. The enterprising child managed to count 149 of the creatures, more numerous then than now. The small fortune in pennies was gravely noted by the sage, a complex character who could be kind and considerate as well as overbearingly rude.

At Conwy, the great fortress 'offered us nothing new'. Over the dangerous rocks of Penmaenmawr and back to the hospitality of Mr Myddleton, who was so pleased with the honour of Johnson's company that he proposed to erect an inscribed urn in his grounds to commemorate the visit. The compliment was not much to the Doctor's taste. 'It looks,' he said, 'like an intention to bury me alive.'

At Ruabon, although he does not tell the tale himself, Mrs Thrale relates in her own reminiscences, 'a Welch parson of mean abilities though a good heart, struck with reverence at the sight of Dr Johnson, whom he had heard of as the greatest man living, could not find any words to answer his enquiries.'

The poor man was so overawed that he could not translate a single Welsh motto on a tombstone, and the Doctor had to do it for him. He was probably more typical than Evans or Dr Worthington. The latter learned cleric was visited at Llanrheadr ym Mochnant. 'In this house,' Johnson notes, 'the translation of the Old Testament into Welsh was made.' Neither the memory of Bishop Morgan nor the beauty of the waterfall moved him to more than a few flat and factual sentences, and on the same day, September 8, they crossed back into England.

From Shrewsbury they made their way through three weeks of hospitality at great houses, and by the end of the month Johnson was back in his beloved London, just in time for the dissolution of Parliament. Immediately he plunged into political controversy, pamphleteering against upstart radicalism and the restless American colonists, within 12 months of claiming their independence. Wales was a long way behind him by now, but he could still pull Boswell's leg about the superiority of its mountains and castles to those of Scotland.

Yet he determined to remain resolutely unimpressed. 'Wales,' he told Boswell, 'is so little different from England that it offers nothing to the speculation of the traveller.' Not everybody was expected to agree with Dr Johnson, even at his most dogmatic. This was one of his judgements from which posterity has emphatically dissented.

Western Mail (31 August 1974)

A Lost Leader

Sometimes, when I stand at my front door in Cwmbach and look across to the deep dark slope of Blaengwawr and up to Foel Penderyn bounding the view to the north beyond St Elvan's spire and the cluster of Aberdare, or in my back garden, looking out at the roofs of Cwmaman shining in the rain and seeming to move, winding their way into the heart of the hills, I wonder how anyone can live in this valley and *not* be a poet. There have certainly been plenty of them. In *Cyfoeth Cwm*, a remarkable compilation by a remarkable man, Jacob Davies could find room for nearly a hundred and fifty names, most of them (though by no means all) of purely local fame, most of them belonging to the last century and the early years of this one, before the collapse of the 1920s, which was as much moral and cultural as economic, nearly all of them, of course, writing in the Welsh language, although there were two Mid-Victorian lady bards who trilled in English as well, the sort of unconvincing ancestry sometimes foisted on modern Anglo-Welsh writers, products of a very different world.

Alun Lewis was in fact the first indigenous English-writing author of any stature the Cynon Valley has produced. This is part of his significance, part of the tragedy. The Cwmaman where his parents set up their home in the early days of the First World War was still a fairly recent community. Despite its origins in the days of Crawshay Bailey, it was largely the creation of Powell Dyffryn. Most of the housing dates from the beginning of the present century. The streets of uncompromising slate and stone are in the same terraced pattern as the older dwellings, but bigger and solider. Whatever their shortcomings, they still have a long way to go before they become slums, and a recent proposal to demolish some of them has provoked a sharp reaction. There are fewer chapels than one might expect, for the place grew up in the long late afternoon of Nonconformity, and fewer pubs too, an effect, one might guess, of improved housing and better schooling, and for reasons only to be guessed at, not many shops. So the streets seem to lack animation. But then, today, so do most streets. The village climbs up a side valley under narrow skies, lacking the ampler vistas of Cwm Cynon itself, burrowing towards the Rhondda, never getting there but getting to look like it. Its identity and its communal spirit are still strong, expressed in a variety of activities from an ambitious operatic society to a colourful and immensely enjoyable carnival. It is still easy to appreciate what it must have been like sixty years ago, with the four pits working in the bad conditions of those days, or ominously silent in the shadows of the interminable industrial troubles. When there was a strike there was starvation. When there was work there was the constant drip of menace. One pit in particular, the nearest to Alun Lewis's childhood home, had a specially bad record, one fall a week. The victims would be brought up and carried on stretchers through the streets to their homes, covered with the rough brattice cloth used underground. If a man's face was covered as well as his body, he was dead, that's how you knew. Alun Lewis grew up knowing, as a child knows, maimed and crippled men, men suffocating with dust, women driven witless by sudden grief, school-fellows without fathers, families without hope, a village living on its nerves, waiting for the hooter. *Ki tant ne set, ne l'ad prod entendut.* One would have to be an absolute swine to grow up in such an environment and not become some sort of rebel. As his unfinished work stands, there is nothing much that relates directly to these formative experiences – the poems about them are not among his best – but they underlie his better writing. The penetration and compassion of his best stories, the acceptance in them of pain and suffering as pervasive and inevitable, these could have been sharpened in other places and in other ways, but in his case they belong to the place he was born in, the place no one can ever really leave.

The uniform streets of Cwmaman proclaim a one-class community, whatever diversity of standards and occupations they may contain. But a land alienated of its aristocracy, without a broad-based self-confident middle class, has evolved its own leadership, and to this Alun Lewis undoubtedly belonged by inheritance and personality. His grandfather was the impressively named Melchisedec Evans, Minister of Aberdare's English-Language Unitarian cause, an enlightened, intellectual denomination with a prestige out of all proportion to its numbers. His mother, a remarkable person, was prominent in the activities needed to keep things going and keep things together in bad times. As the schoolteacher's son he would not go down the pit with a brave swagger and a shining new jack as soon as his schooldays were over, he would not rot on the street-corner with his mates. Not quite *mab y mans* perhaps, but near enough. He was gregarious and conscientious, a good teacher and a good officer. His pupils said he understood them, and his men liked him. And he had to be with them, he was unhappy away from them, he was responsible for them. So he had to go up with the forward detachment, though there was no strict need. That last walk on the Arakan Front had begun in the schoolroom at Glynhafod.

All this could be true of a man who had never published a word of poetry or prose. But we are talking of Alun Lewis, who published many poems and many stories under the most difficult and discouraging circumstances. For it is simply not true, under modern conditions, that war enhances the sensibilities and heightens the imagination, all it does is to inflame the baser lusts and multiply the occasions for their exercise .... It must be said, I suppose, that a man who can be a poet in wartime has at least shown that he can, or could, be an even better poet in better times, but there must always be something suspect about the reputation of a 'war-poet' and I do not choose to think of Alun Lewis in this way. The impact of *Raiders' Dawn* on the reading public in 1942 cannot be questioned, and his death on service two years later magnified it, and created an interest in him as a representative, sacrificial figure, but all this seems to relate to the situation as it was at the time, and although not to be dismissed or despised, is no basis for an enduring reputation. It should be remembered that the English literary world had consistently rejected his work, until it was published at last in the less parochial and incestuous *Dublin Magazine*. Most of the poetry, it must be said, is that of a very young but not startlingly precocious writer (unlike his contemporary, Dylan) still heavily under influence, in this case of Edward Thomas and Yeats. It goes without saying that it does not bear the weight of some recent pretentious critical analysis.

But his stories are something else again, there is no obvious influence here at all. One cannot say, as one so often can with his poems, here he is trying to write like Joyce or Tchekov. There is a plain Tolstoyan directness about the best of them, an unforced fluency (again unlike some of the rhetoric in the poems, he was obviously not a rhetorical sort of person), the accurate observation that is born of compassion and concern, and always some social point to be made, some explicit social criticism. This, too, obviously relates to his background. We know that he dabbled briefly in left-wing politics. His letters are full of what now reads like a naive populism with a dated *Picture Post* flavour to it. But this feeling drove him into the Caseg Broadsheets venture, again in almost impossible times and circumstances, as an attempt to bring art to the people. There seems to be an opinion that it was all rather unimportant, a marginal distraction, but the broadsheets themselves are surprisingly good and perhaps even more surprisingly, they did get through to some of the people. The first one I ever saw was a tattered, treasured possession in an otherwise very ordinary working-class home where it obviously meant something precious outside of daily experience.

Alun Lewis loved Wales, was excited by her rich culture but angry at her sloth. He wanted to wake the Welsh people up. He wanted to write 'a long autobiographical novel about Welsh life'. Well, who doesn't? But he, one feels, could have done it. In 1948 A.L. Rowse wrote, 'I believe he had it in him to write that great work of Welsh life we all look for.' In 1974 we are still looking. Our best novelists, in both languages, have no direct experience of a major sector of that life, the ordinary industrial working class, good as they are about rural and small-town society and the various nuances from the petty-bourgeoisie upwards. The valleys, in particular, have been sentimentalised, and lyricised, or left to the degrading, hate-filled grotesqueries of the *canaille écrivante*. We have been told that it is quite improper to indulge in speculation as to what Alun Lewis would have achieved had he lived: it seems to me to be less improper than to perpetrate inflated gobbledigook about his surviving work and a good deal more natural and creditable. If his best writing was not a literary exercise, it derives its strength from concern and involvement with real people, the attitudes and sensibilities mustered in the streets of Cwmaman. His values transcend mere literature, but he was obviously working towards a mastery of literary technique that could have given these values perhaps their definitive expression. He would have been a wonderful man to have had around in those shameful sodden decades that followed the war, and which are now mercifully only a bad memory.

The valleys are places of irony. No valley in Wales has produced more writers than the Cynon. Yet the best of them emerged after the old cultural pattern had been destroyed, emerged at the very moment of destruction, out of the heart of the trauma. There is a group of streets in Cwmaman called Poets' Corner. The poets are Burns, Byron, Milton, Morris, Spencer, and Wordsworth, built to house an almost totally Welsh-speaking population. Solid, owner-occupied, clean and tidy to this day. Short steep dead-ends, they lead nowhere. It is ironical that the sacrificial figure of English letters in the last war should have come from a community which itself had been martyrised, as if there were to be no end to the demands they made on us. But, as I say, I cannot see Alun Lewis in that role. Looking across from where I live to where he lived, I mourn rather a lost leader.

Poetry Wales (10.3, Winter 1974)

A Welsh Symbolist

Euros Bowen, *Poems.*

In June 1974 the BBC transmitted a remarkable production of *King Oedipus*, in which Oedipus resembled Hussein of Jordan or Gadaffi of Libya, Creon was portrayed as a Greek colonel of more recent vintage, Jocasta wore Dior jewelry and the choric sequences were dissolved into orgiastic *ciné-verité*. It was a long way from Salamis full of the foaming of billows and murmur of bees, rhythmic verse-speaking, Isadora draperies and Olivier with the Elgin marbles in his larynx. I do not suppose I was the only viewer in Wales who followed this outstanding presentation with a copy (the score, so to speak) of Euros Bowen's *Oidipos Frenin*, the felicities of both transcriptions stereoscopically compensating for one's complete ignorance of the original language. No one who did so will regard these remarks as an eccentric or irrelevant introduction to a selection, in English translation, from the main body of Euros Bowen's work. The common factor is the sense of incredulous delight that must always spring from any successful feat of *aggiornomento*, like standing before the fresh colours of a great painting newly restored from the decorous grime of centuries.

How much of this can come across in a volume of Euros Bowen's translations from his own Welsh? Not the whole achievement, nor perhaps very much of it. With Euros, more perhaps than with most, we do not have to be reminded that poetry is what gets lost in the translation, even when the translations are his own. (It's all very well to say he should have got somebody else to do it, but try drawing up a short-list.) For his work, and its value in the context of modern Welsh poetry, must largely be described and evaluated in the technical terms of a complex tradition, and in relation to how matters stood in 1948, and how they stand today after his influence has so strongly pervaded the scene. To digress (apparently) once more: some years ago, Paol Keineg and I collaborated in translating a handful of Maodez Glanndour's poems into our respective *langues véhiculaires*, but we soon gave up, although with regret, because Glanndour's achievement has been to invigorate Breton with English influences, which had long been pervasive in French, and to no good effect. Translating him was like translating him back, almost, into a fairly decent but unenterprising English poet, or a slightly less accomplished English-influenced French poet. The whole question of the relationship between creative writing in such differently circumstanced languages is a fascinating one, and I wish somebody like Bobi Jones or Pennar Davies would go into it in depth. The achievement of poets like

Euros Bowen would make the effort worthwhile.

He has always been an innovator, and first came to public notice as editor of *Y Fflam*, throughout its career which lasted from 1946 to 1952. Those of us who cut our teeth on it will well remember its astringent flavour of uncompromising anti-traditionalism. His Rhondda background relates him to that rather miscellaneous group of poets and writers, Ysgol Cadwgan, with the tutelary figure of Kitchener Davies hovering around: Gareth Alban Davies and J. Gwyn Griffiths with their impressively cosmopolitan range of knowledge and interests, Pennar Davies, a spiritual pilgrim of complex utterance, the colourful individualist Rhydwen Williams, who very nearly refused to accept his Crown at Mountain Ash in 1946, but decided after all not to spoil the show. Something of all of them has rubbed off on Euros, yet he remains greater than the sum of all influences. It is interesting to note, too, that he received part of his education at an Art School, long before this became mandatory among a certain stratum of English poets. It comes out in his poems which deal with the visual arts, always a pitfall unless the poet really knows what he is talking about. Euros does. The nephew of Ben Bowen and Myfyr Hefin, the brother of another crowned bard, Geraint Bowen, it seems odd to hear him state in his endearingly dry, no-nonsense way, that he never really began to write poetry seriously until he was housebound by the great snow of 1947. But there is no evidence to the contrary, and no one who lived through that extraordinary visitation of nature would want to deny that it probably changed many lives. A late beginner then (it was his thirty-second year to heaven) but one who has made up for it since, with six substantial volumes of original poetry and much uncollected work including translations of (and these names are significant) Yeats, Rimbaud, Baudelaire and Virgil.

The first milestone was his crowning at Bridgend in 1948 for the pryddest '*O'r Dwyrain*' (From the East). 'Light breaks where no sun shines' would be a fair comment. For although Euros's poetry is not regarded as among the most immediately intelligible, his example was to illuminate a new path, and to re-invigorate old techniques. The giants of the earlier twentieth century were old men, long unproductive, soon to die. Gwenallt and Waldo were respected, but nothing like the cult-figures they were to become. Formal and thematic experimentation had yet to stake a claim to serious notice. Nobody, not even the best or youngest poets, seemed to be taking things any further. If the Crown at Bridgend went to Euros, the Chair went to the ultra-traditionalist, almost antediluvian Dewi Emrys. The achievement of T. Gwynn Jones, the greatest in terms of sheer technique since Goronwy Owen (some say since Tudur Aled) had not been followed through. By its sheer volume and stature, perhaps it had taken Welsh poetry as far as it could then go. Certainly nobody seemed to be going further. Except Euros. Like all pioneers he has had little thanks. Today it is part of our established cultural faith to worship at the shrine of T. Gwynn Jones, the Lord of Language. Let us turn to the recent biography by David Jenkins, a worthy memorial and a great achievement in its own right, to remind ourselves that it took *eight years* to find a publisher for *Ymadawiad Arthur*! Even in the 1960s, according to Dafydd Elis Thomas, eisteddfod adjudicators were too lazy to try to understand work submitted by Euros Bowen. And if he has been too much for the traditionalists, he is not much to the taste of some of the younger men either, to whom obscurity and compassion and lack of immediate intelligibility do not in themselves present any obstacle to acceptance. It would be unfair to quote verbatim some of their more colourful observations in private conversation, but the burden of their objections is that Euros is too consciously and too self-consciously the literary artist; for the exponents of spontaneity, he is too much a man of letters. I cannot imagine that any of this worries or inhibits the unflappable Euros, either as a man or an artist. A long career as an Anglican clergyman with a minute congregation in one of the sacred heartlands of Nonconformity seems a fitting style for the sort of poet he is. One wonders, for all that, why his Church has not made more obvious use of or given more recognition to his gifts, if only those of learning. Surely he is one of nature's Canons.

He has been compared, among his contemporaries, to Montale, but there is too much Leopardi in Montale for the comparison to stand – there is nothing of Islwyn in Euros. The French symbolists are his most obvious literary ancestors, and as European poetry is only just catching up with Baudelaire, he is as contemporary as anybody else now writing, and still well ahead of the field in Wales. I do not know the extent of his acquaintance with most recent French writers, but, for those who wish to get something of his flavour without being able to follow the original, I suggest a comparison with Guillevic would be helpful. Except that Euros has a much livelier visual imagination than the rather abstract Franco-Breton. It is indeed difficult to characterize Euros, or pin him down. He has retired now from his pastoral labours on the shores of Llyn Tegid and lives on a new estate near Wrexham, where the streets have the names of poets. His address, believe it or not, is Ffordd Cynan. I'm sure he enjoys the joke, and I hope he hasn't retired from writing. I feel he has more surprises for us yet.

Poetry Wales (10.3, Winter 1974)

Webb's Progress (I)

At my nativity, the front of heaven was full of fiery shapes, but whatever flames flared over Warsaw, Amritsar or Cork, the skies above Tŷ Coch were quiet. It was then one of Swansea's newer suburbs, the First World War was just over, and my father had returned from a wandering life, from Gallipoli and the Western Front, to get married and go into rooms, as young working-class couples then almost invariably did. Ours, where I was born, were with a Devonshire family called Brown in Tŷ Coch Road. The upstairs landing window at the back looked out on to a large cemetery. Whenever there was a funeral within earshot – and in those days funerals carried a long way – Mrs Brown, who had obviously gone native, would stand at the window with the lodger's infant in her arms, rocking and weeping to the hymns. I can recollect none of this (though hymns in a minor key still upset me), for before my second birthday we moved into a house of our own in the middle of Swansea, the only home I remember.

A man of quiet temperament and stocky, powerful physique hardened by an upbringing as a farm boy in Gower, and an open-air life in Australia, my father was able to find work soon after his discharge from the Anzac forces. He became a coal-trimmer and then a stoker at the Swansea Corporation's Electric Works, a primitive and dirty place on the once-notorious Strand. When this ancient plant was superseded in the 1930s by the new power station at Tir John North on the edge of Crumlin Bog, he became a boiler operator, exchanging shovel and sweat-rag for a white coat and horn-rimmed glasses but doing basically the same job with equable patience. My mother had learnt her trade as a dressmaker and continued to work at it with a treadle-operated sewing machine situated under the kitchen window to catch the light. The hours she spent at it brought in a useful supplement to my father's moderate but regular wage, and we were never conscious of want or deprivation.

It was a happy, stable, undramatic background. We belonged to that vast invisible section of the community, the un-unemployed, the class nobody has ever heard of or ever heard from, the people who had no ambitions or standards that were beyond their means, who kept a good table, who were neither abstainers nor driven by despair to drink, whose religious observance was one of social custom and good conduct, devoid of rapture, speculation or controversy, who voted when there was an election, but took little interest at other times, who struck no attitudes and minded their own business. Even in Wales, we formed the majority of the population.

The most distinctive thing about living in the middle of Swansea, was that we reckoned ourselves to be Gower people. This both my parents and all my relatives undoubtedly were by birth and upbringing. I was the first of our line to be born in a town. My father was a native of Bishopston, son of a small farmer who later moved to High Pennard, where my grandmother, Elizabeth Rees, made memorable ham-and-egg teas for visitors, and so pioneered the tourist industry which has since engulfed the peninsula. My mother was the youngest of a large family bearing the well-known Gower name of Gibbs. I heard recently that someone is going around genealogising the clan and has traced us back to the Netherlands, an exotic origin that does not really register.

My maternal grandmother was Elizabeth Bowen. There is plenty of room for genealogical speculation about the various Bowens of Gower, but I have never pursued it. On some document I once saw she registered her name with the cross of illiteracy. My mother was born in a little house in the corner of Pennard churchyard. It had some ancient features and was later identified as the old Priest's House. When she died, she was laid to rest a few paces from where she was born. But she spent most of her early years in a whitewashed, thatched cottage on the edge of Fairwood Common. It began to look less picturesque some time in the 1930s, when the thatched roof was replaced by galvanised, and the last time I saw it (it has probably completely disappeared by now) it looked like a disgraceful example of substandard rural housing. But it had sheltered a large and lively brood, always well-fed and well-dressed, high-spirited, quick-tempered, opinionated, talkative, full of self-esteem and usefully employed in the more responsible sort of working-class job.

Between them, my parents provided me with uncles, aunts and cousins beyond counting, and more distant, peripheral and honorary relations and connections in an ever-receding spectrum that seemed to embrace most of Pennard and Ilston parishes, with scattered outposts all over Gower. We spent much time visiting and gossiping. Talking to older relatives, my parents' speech would broaden into the full dialect. To their amusement I soon picked this up and can still speak it if there is anybody left to speak it to. It sometimes occurs to me that I must be one of the last people who could, in the appropriate context, use thee and thou without affectation or archaism.

By the inter-war years, many, though by no means all of the children and grandchildren of farm and cottage had drifted away, not very far geographically, and not at all in any emotional or social sense. Up until the last war, most of my relations were still to be found in Gower, Swansea and the Swansea Valley. (The rare exceptions were spoken of in tones usually reserved for the deceased.)

Their various jobs read like a representative cross-section of a census of occupations: the steelworks, the pit, the line, the land, the Forces, the Trade, the docks, the dead-ends, the dole. The prosperous and the not so prosperous, the country people and the townies, mingled together, visited and gossiped as a family. That was all we talked about, that was all that mattered.

Great Uncle William Webb farmed Ilston Glebe. Every Saturday on his way to market he would detour to our street with his pony and cart, tie the reins to the railings and deliver pale butter of a delicate fragrance (I used to think it smelt of the meadowsweet in Ilston Cwm), eggs each wrapped separately in a page of the *Christian Herald*, and other produce in season. His was one of the places I used to go, to turn the separator in the tiny dairy, drive the small herd of diverse cows down from the moor to the evening milking, carry swill to the sow with the piglets plugged into her huge flank, do odd jobs and earn my reward in milk warm and fresh from the cow, or delicious buttermilk straight from the separator.

A stream ran past the door and down the Cwm to Parkmill. The best way to the farm was through the churchyard and over the stone stile, past the graves of many other Webbs at rest under the huge dark tree that was said in its day to have provided yew-wood for the longbows of even more distant ancestors. A hoard of Roman coins was discovered quite near the Glebe. Lloyd George came and dedicated a memorial to the Baptist pioneers who had once worshipped in these solitudes, among the coltsfoot and cowslips, at a well sacred long before their day, and, I would guess, long before the day of the Trinity to which it had once been dedicated. In the next valley there was a Giant's Grave, and Parc le Breos still retains a name that was part-Norman and a direct link with the crucial manoeuvres for Welsh Independence. Pennard Castle loomed over the dunes. One could well believe the legend that it had been overwhelmed in a night of supernatural vengeance.

As a growing lad, I was taken further afield by my father. Together we roamed all Gower. Unlike my mother's side of the family, he was not a talkative man. He let Gower speak for itself, the castles, the earthworks, the cliffs, the deep limestone valleys, Bacon Hole and Cefn Bryn with their mysterious relics. Rhossili Beacon from which you could see the width of Wales. The ancient parish churches, the mills and kilns of the last century. The quarry above Pwll Du, with its stone sentinel, Davy Dawkin, and the vestiges of the quay beneath, that had shipped the limestone to Devonshire, and the little pub nearby, left over from that vanished trade, and kept by another uncle. The mass-burial trenches at Gravesend on the same stretch of cliffs, dug by the John Webb of his day for the victims of an eighteenth-century shipwreck. Brandy Cove where another John Webb, revenue officer, had an affray with smugglers. John Webb, my grandfather, stern and bearded in his clifftop holding, with his almost legendary reputation as a close-fisted, old-fashioned farmer.

After his time the place was briefly occupied by another great Gower character, the laureate of our community, the poet and raconteur, Cyril Gwynne, also a connection by marriage and I do not know how much of an example and stimulus to my young imagination. I used to have many of his cheerful simple, rhymes, tales and musings by heart – The Giant Mangel-Wurzel, The Hungry Lurcher, What's in a name? Feyther mightn't like it – the titles tell you all about them. I retained a fondness for them throughout the years of Ronsard and Baudelaire and all the other giants, a fondness which unfortunately has outlasted all but a few fragments in my memory. And he established in my mind an image of the poet as essentially a social rather than a solitary character, one, moreover, fortunate in his gifts, however humble, and under something of an obligation to spread them around for the pleasure of the people he belongs to, rather than to hoard them in the dank private cellars of introspection and incomprehension.

Cyril was lively and well-liked. He had many jobs and moved around a lot. Welsh-speakers would recognise in him a mixture of Pontshaen and Wil Parsel, and might marvel that an Englishry could produce such a *deryn*. But this was the special magic of old Gower. It was as Welsh as anywhere in Wales, yet used the English language naturally, without strain or shame or awkwardness or guilt or apology. It is a priceless attitude to have inherited just at this juncture. I speak of all this in the past tense, because I believe that the old, self-contained type of society that I remember in the last decades of its solitude and relative isolation, even from Swansea and 'the Works' in north Gower, has passed away altogether by now, like most such societies. I rarely return there, preferring to keep my memories intact. The Area of Outstanding Natural Beauty which it has since officially become is something else again.

Little of this has found its way into my work, and I sometimes wonder why, though without regret, because it is all very much still there, a massive rock that anchors in position a bobbing buoy whose business it is to offer what guiding light it can in a very stormy sea.

An important aspect of this background was our Church membership. Dissent never struck deep roots in Gower Anglicana, as much, I would guess, for reasons of temperament as of language. Obviously the Church had not failed in its duty here for the latter reason. I was baptised so soon after Disestablishment that the new baptismal certificates were not available; still I consider myself to be among the founder members of the present Church in Wales. I was early enrolled in Sunday School and have still the most clear recollection of being taken there by the hand. It was before I started day school, and it was my first introduction to any society larger than that of my own family.

Saint Faith's, near the Guildhall, long turned over to secular use, was a bright little place with a pretty blue-and-white reredos of vaguely della-Robbian inspiration. There was a succession of cheerful curates serving under a vintage vicar, one of those short, plump, rosy-cheeked West Wales clerics who I sometimes think must be the fruit of a special tree in the palace grounds at Abergwili. He was the only man I have ever heard who could chant the liturgy with the *hwyl* of a chapel minister. The Bishop of St David's had served under him as a curate, and delighted to come back to his first parish, although it was now in the new diocese of Swansea Brecon. My first ambition (after the stage of wanting to drive a fire engine) was to become a bishop, and to resemble that venerable figure in his full vestments. Various factors have prevented this, but there have been more enduring influences from those days.

The first and most fundamental is the Anglican ethos itself: Arminian, Erastian, near enough Pelagian. There is a touch of Calvin's brimstone in the Thirty-Nine Articles, of course, but not very much comes over in practice. Faith, to me, is firmly a matter of good works, good conduct and upright dealing, rather than subjective emotionalism. The Catechism cannot be improved upon as a rule of life. (Like most people, I have, of course, broken most of the rules from time to time.) The love of God is best interpreted in terms of charity, humour, and tolerance. You can't get away from Calvinism, of course, not in Wales, but my portion of this heritage seems to have transferred itself bodily from the spiritual to the political sphere. *There*, I accept cheerfully, even with gusto, that there are individuals damned beyond redemption, and the contemplation of their discomfort in the, I hope, fairly immediate earthly future is going to be a lively augmentation to the pleasures of the redeemed.

Then there is the influence of regular attendance at services with a set liturgy of some magnificence. I don't suppose anybody can be fully literate in Welsh who has not been similarly immersed in the eloquence of the Nonconformist pulpit and the wash of great hymns. Certainly the chances are very much against anyone who has not had an Anglican upbringing being able to write good English. This very point, incidentally, is made by both W.J. Gruffydd and George Orwell, not such an unlikely duo really. The decline in regular attendance at religious services poses problems for the cultures of both languages, which I have been happily spared. Not only the shape of the language, but its sound and presentation, are an integral part of the Church's ministry. I can never read in public without wishing to have in front of me a decent lectern, preferably in the form of the Eagle of the Apocalypse. For the lightest word spoken is an act of pure creation. In all logia is the Logos. To mumble and gobble and make animal noises as some so-called poets do these days, is not merely bad manners, it is a very serious sin, like every other abuse of language.

Next in this tale of origins comes school. There was Church influence here too. Instead of going to any of the nearer places, I was sent to the National School in Oxford Street, not much further away really, but very much a Church school. The headmaster was People's Warden at the town's parish church, and rugby-playing curates came to open each day's education with judiciously-chosen Bible stories of battle and shipwreck. It was a downtown school, cheek by jowl with the market, the Vetch Field, the Gaol, the Grand Theatre and the Empire Music Hall. We were a mixed lot. Some of the boys wore collars and ties, one or two, briefly, came to school barefoot. But mostly it was jerseys and stout boots. The teachers taught and excercised discipline; there was no bullying or bad violence. Billy Meredith's nephew won a cap for football. I was often in trouble, but it was discovered that I could write. At the age of nine or ten I wrote a thrilling adventure story which ended with everybody becoming rich. I've been writing it ever since.

It was a heavily Imperialist school. We saluted the flag on Empire Day, and a huge map showed 'The Empire in red and all the rest grey' (the same one as Chesterton saw, I'm sure) while John Bull stood somewhere south-east of New Zealand with his bulldog holding a Union Jack in its jaws, and one or the other of them saying, 'What I have, I hold.'

Even so, if there is a seed in the air, it will fall to ground somewhere. In Standard One, Miss Lloyd taught a surprisingly healthy and vigorous verson of our own history. In the clear light of later years, I was to read Owen Rhoscomyl's *Flame-Bearers of Welsh History* with becoming detachment. I was to work in Dowlais around the corner from Well Street, where Prytherch, its illustrator, was born, and meet people who had known him, drink in the Church Tavern at Faenor, kept by former servants of the gallant Colonel who had been his model for Prince Llywelyn and Caratacus. It got by, of course, because it ended happily with Henry Tudor winning the Crown of London. Miss Lloyd made us all look out of the classroom window to see the name Tudor on a tailor's shop in Oxford Street – proof indeed.

Catherine Street, where we lived, was at the intersection of many impalpable frontiers. Basically it was respectable working-class, with scrubbed doorsteps and ritually polished brass strips on every threshold. My natural playground was the sweep of the sands. Every summer, we took in regular visitors from the Rhondda. We went to the Grand Theatre most weeks to see sensational thrillers – which never failed to thrill – and rather less gripping intrigues on a different level, involving gentlemen in evening dress and ladies in long frocks. There must have been at least half a dozen cinemas. We lived so near to St Helen's that we could follow the fortunes of the home team by minute fluctuations in the continuous noise from the ground. Evangelists and agitators of every persuasion raised their rostrums on the sands. Holy Joes and other well-known characters walked the streets, creating the atmosphere of a smuch smaller place. Tennyson and Gladstone glowered through the gloom of the Public Library. Later, Thomas Taig inspired some remarkable productions at the Little Theatre. It was a many-faceted town of crowds and encounters, a seaport, a market town, a resort and a place of entertainment. It freed one from narrowness of outlook and from the obsessions of a one-industry economy which even today can infect some quite articulate attitudes to Wales, and prevent many from taking a balanced and optimistic view of the nation as a whole.

Not that the shadows of the Depression were absent, or evidence lacking of the grim price of over-dependence on heavy industry. We lived opposite the Hospital, our house a port of call on visiting days, an ever-open door, and the kettle always on the hob for relatives and their neighbours and workmates, some of them distressed, shocked or bereaved. I never knew who would be sitting down to tea with us when I came home from school on such days, or what stories I would hear. The flame-bearers kindled a spark of anger. This was not what we were born for. On visits up the Swansea Valley, I played with children ruined before birth by their fathers' employment in the spelter works. You could tell the 'leaded' children by their rotten teeth and continuous dribbling, and we romped on a hillside of slag and clinker; the hideously devastated Landore region stretched its ruins beside the poisoned yellow Tawe. In an old encyclopaedia bought from a market stall I read, 'Swansea is the non-ferrous metallurgical metropolis of the world.' And this was all that was left, those children, that place. From the hills around the town, and deep into Gower, you could see at night the sky suddenly lit up by a slow lightning, and you knew then that they were tapping the Bessemers at Dowlais, all those miles away, far inland, a place of power that lit up half Wales. That too, went dark.

In these villages, much Welsh was spoken. There was plenty of it to be heard on the sands during the holiday periods, or in the market and the cinema queues and on big match days, very obviously a living language. Nobody seemed to have any definite attitude to it one way or the other. It was just there, like Kilvey Hill or Mumbles Head. I suppose speakers and non-speakers alike acquiesced in its complete lack of any public recognition or official status. To me, though not understanding more than a few colloquial phrases, it added to the colour and variety of the life around us. The language of home and Church and rural background was English. Welsh excitedly belonged to the industrial places, and crowded streets.

The rewards of the ready verbaliser early came my way. I was destined for 'the scholarship' and passed from the noisy bustle of Oxford Street to a delightful suburban secondary school perched on top of a matchless view of the bay and embowered (a truly appropriate word) in a rose garden, amenities which partly compensated for its rather exiguous housing in wooden buildings left over from the First World War. It was much smaller, and had much less prestige than the other schools, it had no tiresome 'traditions' and was a good place. True, Welsh was not well-taught there in my time, though it improved a lot afterwards, but I learnt enough of the grammar to give me a toehold. French was taught superbly, with a good accent and in a lively manner, stimulating an interest that filled my life for many years and is still among my chiefest pleasures. And, as other and greater Welshmen were finding at that time, acquaintance with Europe's central and seminal culture is in itself a liberation, not least from the hick provincialism that characterizes so many of the claims made for Eng. Lit.

We learnt Spanish too, another window flung open on an unsuspected world, one I could not somehow enter as fully as the other, but providing, as it happened at that time, a more vivid stimulus. Lorca. Not that he was on the syllabus, of course. But the *Romancero Gitano* came into my hands, in a poorly produced commemorative volume brought out soon after his murder. Here now was a poet of my own day, a poet of his own people, killed, as far as I could make out, simply because he was such a poet. His death seemed part of the poetry itself. It meant more to me than anything I had encountered so far in the three literatures with which I was beginning to become acquainted. Later, at Oxford I talked about him with Don Alberto Jimenez. His teacher and mine, a circumstance I still find incredible. *Verde que te quiero verde.*

The Spanish Civil War, of which this was a minor episode, had up till now been a remote, confused business. The burning of Penyberth, which took place on my sixteenth birthday, was equally remote and puzzling. We were not an apolitical generation though. We were in a special position. Hitler had come to power when I was twelve, and all the boys of my age knew, far more clearly than our rulers, that we were the ones who would have to fight him. The thought worried our parents more than it worried us, and they tried to put it out of their heads. For us, it banished all futures.

Ambitious teachers put me on the road to Oxford, frugal parents made the journey possible. In those days one could live reasonably well on remarkably little, if one had it. My time among the dreaming spires was something of a mixture. My first term began just after the Munich betrayal, which jolted me into sudden political awareness, and profoundly influenced my attitude to public morality ever since. My second year began in the early days of the war. Having gone up rather young, I was allowed to stay on and finish my three years, and then I joined the Navy, just in time for Pearl Harbour and the fall of Singapore.

All these years and scenes have been written about by others and my experiences were in no way remarkable. Oxford was a different world in a different country, one I could enjoy without being nobbled by it, unlike some. The war, even if it was full of new experiences, and incidents too stirring to be comfortable, was, on balance, a drag, and has rarely moved my pen. In Cairo, on leave from the Malta convoys, I picked up Aragon's *Le Crève-Coeur*. I knew of him as a surrealist, a Communist, a literary manifesto. Here he suddenly was as a poet of action and feeling, of involvement and immediate communication, a man who loved his country deeply, and was scalded by her shame. It was another revelation of what real poetry was all about. *Je n'oublierai jamais les lilas ni les roses*. In Scotland, on the edge of the Burns Country, I became aware of MacDiarmid, and learnt that *The rose of all the world is not for me*.

I came back to Wales and made up my mind to stay here and slog it out with her enemies, using whatever weapons had been given me. I made a serious effort to learn the language, but could not claim to wear it at all comfortably until I had spent many happy years working in Dowlais and living in that raffish mini-metropolis Merthyr Tydfil, with all its fascinating paradoxes.

My work since the war scarcely needs any further comment or elucidation. Those years have seen significant and encouraging changes in attitude and direction, and I like to think that what I have written has been part of the process. The last decade has been particularly exciting. Now (I write in the summer of 1975) we are in for a less dramatic trudge, while the machinery of devolution is being assembled. Wales is marching backwards into independence, everybody desperately pretending that we are going somewhere else. It is one of those moments of nice irony, with which the story has so often been scripted. But sooner or later the crunch will come, and I hope that what I have written will be of some help to those who will have to take their part in the final confrontation.

Planet (30, January 1976)

Is Wales Really There?

When Edward Gibbon (whose *Decline and Fall of the Roman Empire*, of course, celebrates its bicentenary this year) wished to emphasise the utter insignificance, in a territorial sense, of the land that was the birthplace of Christ and the scene of so many other important events in history, he hammered the message home by pointing out that it was only the same size as Wales. Nearly thirty years later, William Blake urged his fellow-countrymen to build Jerusalem in England's green and pleasant land, and this intention is annually proclaimed in the Royal Albert Hall by thousands of people wearing funny hats and not entirely sober. I often wonder what visiting Israelis must make of it all.

And if any of them ever come to Wales their confusion must be total. They will find themselves in a country which, far from being abashed by Gibbon's comparison, seems to have been manically inspired by it. There are hills which must once have been called something else but have been christened (if that is really the right word) Carmel and Jericho. The great scholar Sir Ifor Williams confesses that he once spent a long time trying to puzzle out the Celtic origin of Golan, the name of a village in North Wales, before suddenly realising that here was yet another Biblical name, and one which has been prominent in the Middle East war news of late. There are signposts pointing to Bethesda, Bethel and Bethania (near Bangor, Caernarfon and Blaenau Ffestiniog respectively) and there was even one place called Sodom, whose location must be tactfully withheld.

Cosiest of all, there is Bethlehem in Carmarthenshire, where a few years ago they made special arrangements to frank Christmas cards from all over. By now, obviously, the whole ploy is seen as fantasy on the level of Santa Claus at a department store, but it was once taken with utter seriousness, as if a damp Atlantic peninsula could

171

really be transformed into a sunburned land of Canaan, complete with prophets and obedient to every last law of Moses, plus a few other taboos we have invented.

This was not the first such act of collective fantasy in Welsh life, although it was much the most impressive. For a long time the Welsh managed to persuade not only themselves but also their notoriously sceptical neighbours that they were the ancient and aboriginal inhabitants not merely of Wales itself (which is probably true) but the rest of Britain as well, not to mention other places further afield. Ceylon, I believe, was the furthest limit of these claims, and in the other direction there was, of course, Prince Madoc who found America, but characteristically, managed to lose it again.

Further back still, a historical novelist called Geoffrey of Monmouth sponsored the alternative and more glamorous theory that we Welsh were all descendants of Homer's Trojans. Virgil had already made this claim in respect of the founders of Rome itself, but a detail like that has never been any obstacle. It never seems to have occurred to anybody that the Trojans were the big losers of all time, and were hardly the most auspicious of people to adopt as ancestors.

As learned in his field as Gibbon, as original a poet as William Blake, was a contemporary of theirs, Edward Williams, the self-educated stonemason from the Vale of Glamorgan, who took the more sonorous name of Iolo Morganwg. A great man in many ways, he had one major disability: he could not distinguish fact from fiction. One of his legacies to posterity was the order of Druids, who materialise every summer at the National Eisteddfod to the wonderment of all beholders. They have about as much to do with the maintenance of Welsh culture as the Beefeaters at the Tower of London have to do with the defence of the realm.

Among their predecessors, clustered most thickly, for some reason, in the rather prosaic town of Pontypridd, were some luminously eccentric personalities who, in the age of Victoria, must have shone like naughty deeds in a good world. The Welsh Jerusalem, as it rose around them, chapel on chapel, was not altogether to their taste, and they concocted a completely new religion, with open-air ceremonies at prehistoric stones and a heady brew of exalted sentiments culled out of every known creed, from Buddhism to the alleged beliefs of the Red Indians, all orchestrated into a cosmology which was, to say the least, ingenious and all-embracing.

One of them, lucky fellow, had discovered the secret of wisdom, and carried it in an eggshell slung around his neck on a piece of string. Another, the most famous of the breed, was the amazing Doctor William Price, pioneer of cremation, nudism and free love –

inter alia. There is something very up-to-date-sounding about their activities, and their obscure publications (obscure in every sense of the word) are in brisk demand at Glastonbury and wherever two or three are gathered together to await the arrival of the next flying saucer.

But the free-wheeler fantasy for which Wales has shown such a gift has always somehow managed to co-exist with sterner and solider values, and that is what, I think, gives life west of Offa's Dyke a character of its own. Iolo has his devout admirers among the sound, patient scholars who have spent years unravelling his fabrications. I know of at least one impeccable historian who still cherishes in a corner of his mind the hope, if not the belief, that Prince Madoc really did discover America, and stayed there for his own good reasons. And the Druids, however unconvincing their ceremonies and hideous their garb, number in their ranks some very good writers.

The generations that dreamed such delirious dreams were also those which, in their waking hours, trod the arduous roads of social reform and human betterment, and played a notable part in industrial progress and the radical politics it generated. Iolo's own grandson ranks among the pioneers of modern heavy industry, yet he cherished the memory of his erratic forebear who had moved in such a different world. It was an ironmaster's wife, Lady Charlotte Guest, who was responsible for the first English translation of the *Mabinogion* tales. Lady Llanover, another fervent English convert to Welsh patriotism, even went as far as inventing a national costume, which is still inflicted on little girls until they get big enough to put their foot down, but she did such a lot of other good things that this lapse may be forgiven her.

One of the heroes of these old romances spent half the year in this world and half in the Other World, and a wander through Wales is still a bit like that. Even the most obvious practical necessities have had to be canvassed in somewhat exalted terms. Robert Owen, the Utopian Socialist, one feels, could not possibly have been born anywhere else. Did we need to emigrate to America because we were starving here? Not a bit of it. We had a mission to fulfil, variously interpreted in religious or social terms. Perhaps we would even discover those Welsh Indians.

You can imagine how acceptable the apocalyptic message of Karl Marx must have been in its time. In Wales he was the successor not so much of Robert Owen as of Geoffrey of Monmouth. We have cooled off a bit since those heady days, and our eyes for the most part are more sensibly focused on our own corner of the earth. But the note is still to be heard. Do we need devolution for sober, technical administrative reasons? Yes, perhaps, but that is not all there is to it; oh no.

There is still that august destiny beckoning us, boyo. Nobody's quite sure what it is by now, but it's there all right. That note had been sounded over the centuries by the bards and by the evangelists and hymn-writers after them, and by the political leaders of Wales, whether liberal, radical, socialist or nationalist. And it won't be switched off overnight. Anyway, I'd rather have it like that than have everything explained in terms of the price of spuds.

Radio Times (28 February 1976)

The Arthur of the Welsh

John Heath-Stubbs, *Artorius*.

One of the most important negative decisions ever taken was Milton's when he rejected Arthur as the subject of his epic 'not knowing whether any such existed in history'. English readers (and non-readers) acquired instead an uncanonical cosmic drama which has attained scriptural status, and were spared a King Arthur forever on guard on the Chinese wall (in Eliot's phrase) of Milton's mighty line. The paths of the imagination have remained open back to Malory, to Geoffrey of Monmouth and the Matter of Britain and the almost invisible nucleus of historic fact. The present work stands high in the succession of those who have benefited from this freedom.

The most recent specialist opinion, as expressed at this year's Arthurian Congress at Exeter, is that a *dux bellorum* called Arthur flourished about 500 AD whose activities checked for fifty years the extension of the Saxon hegemony. Everything else is accretion of ancient tales and myths around a folk hero, or much later literary invention exercised in the interests of decidedly unromantic power-politics. This in turn engendered a purely literary and romantic phase. One could add, I suppose, a vast literary industry and the ingenious scholarly speculations of even more recent times. By now none of this matters very much. Every age is entitled to remake Arthur according to its own imaginative needs (David Wright, a close associate of John Heath-Stubbs, retitled Tennyson's version 'Morte d'Albert'). Every age gets the Arthur it deserves.

In strict historic logic, Arthur belongs more to the Welsh than the

English. But, like the Tudors, who were inspired by his example, he emigrated and quickly became naturalised. He typified *unbeniaeth Prydain* – what, today, many Welsh people, taught by J.R. Jones, recognise and reject as *Prydeindod*. In discussions with the leading Welsh Arthurian, Professor Bedwyr Lewis Jones, it has become obvious to me that we are well rid of him. After the Act of Union he faded out of the Welsh imagination. Arthur II was never crowned, and his younger brother Henry VIII ruled in his stead, with what consequences we know. He re-appeared briefly during the Cymru Fydd period, but changed into Lloyd George, despite T. Gwynn Jones's magnificent, but characteristically evasive poem which opened the century. Subsequently his most potent invocation was by Saunders Lewis. In inviting us to follow Arthur (his seminal collection of nationalist writings was entitled *Canlyn Arthur,* from the *Mabinogion*) he seems to have exorcised him. Quite instinctively, Welsh poets in both languages have stopped writing about him. I don't suppose I am the only one who got him out of my system at school. Now we write about the hard-pressed, harrassed men of the *Hengerdd,* of the House of Gwynedd, of Glyndŵr, not romantic, half-known figures, but men whose dilemmas were concrete, urgent and painful, men we can evaluate in terms of our own experience. Glyndŵr, perhaps one can make the point, was a master of psychological warfare with the natural flair that led him to unfurl the dragon of Cadwaladr, bear the arms of the House of Gwynedd, summon parliaments according to the precedents of Hywel Dda, and boldly manipulate the ancient prophecies. And at the end, a disappearance rather than a death, which must surely have been modelled on Arthur, to keep alive the hope of return, as if to salvage from myth what there was in it of survival value for Wales.

In England, Arthur still lives because he is needed, and not only by the poets. There is a huge cult, much of which would not be very disconcerting to Tennyson and Malory. Odd-ball patriots, flying saucer watchers, cranky scholars, British Israelites, believers in the Pyramids, readers of Tolkien are all drawn to Glastonbury to commune with him, a sad, squalid parade of the moral and intellectual collapse of a once proud and self-confident culture. It seems a wretched end, but the present work restores our confidence in the continued validity of this magnificent theme in the purely English context. Mr Heath-Stubbs belongs to a small, civilized group of luminous and literate poets (one associates them with *Agenda* and *Aquarius*) who stand apart from the Gaderene antics to which Anglo-English poetry has for the most part degenerated. This poem is the best thing that has come out of *Anglia Pura* for some time. He is not David Jones, of course, but covering something like the same territory, he displays a humour, a humanity, a feeling for social context, a sharp but not unkind wit, which David Jones lacks. Typically English qualities perhaps.

The poem is about 5000 lines long. It will take you all of a summer's day to read. It is constructed within an elaborate frame of reference drawn from history, anthropology, mythology and astrology, and divided into cantos for each sign of the Zodiac, beginning, like English poetry itself, in the sign of the Ram. At once, we are obviously one step at least away from realities of a brutal age of conflict. The Battle of Mount Badon is much less interesting to the poet than the speeches and arguments. Cerdic's address to his troops contains references to Aristotle and Anaximander, and the issues are debated also by the bards of the rival armies, who reappear in various guises throughout the story. Artorius's first duty, having secured peace, is to convene a synod at Oxford under the sign of the Bull! The heretics, who all recognizably belong to the silly 'sixties of our own century, are confuted, and we are taken to the Other Place for some more fun at the expense of some equally recognizable personalities. One of them is transparently named Ianto. When he goes out in a hurry the stage direction reads 'Exit Ianto, full pelt'. I am dazzled by this example of our poet's omniscience. Does he really remember Dai Lossin? If you want to open this book at random, do so at page 25, where the two poets, intruding on a bleak seminar, proclaim their credentials in a glorious 55-line romp through English Lit, modelled on the transmigrations of Taliesin, or, perhaps more proximately, on the boast of Dai from *In Parenthesis*. It is written with the gusto of a true lover of literature for its own sake and I would not be surprised if this passage assumed a life of its own. In the fourth book, under the sign of the Crab, Artorious is initiated into a series of shamanistic experiences. Malory is lost to sight here, this is Mircea Eliade territory, with a compelling macabre atmosphere.

Then, in a short, formal-stanzaic canto, the hero is crowned in the sign of the Lion. In the sixth book, a mixture of verse and prose as befits the hundrum Virgo, Mordred is sent to escort the *Ymerawdwr*'s bride. Uncanny birds sing of the coming disasters. 'And Mordred delivered to Artorius his KORE, his corn-dolly, his fairie queen.'

In the sign of the Balance, Artorius codifies the laws, and is persuaded to re-establish their authority over Europe. Mordred decides to take advantage of his absence. Under the Scorpion we have a dialogue between a learned professor and a shape-shifting old woman, the prophetic ghost of the queen, and the next short canto, the

Archer, is a jumble of all the objective correlatives. Saturnalia-Christmas is celebrated in the sign of the Goat. Revelling satyrs are revealed as disguised invaders (a dramatically successful moment) and Mordred abducts the queen (there is no Lancelot in this story). Camlann occupies the eleventh canto and the sign is the Water Carrier. Finally the Fishes witness the hero's committal to the sea and to another cycle of rebirth. The location is Cornwall. Just before the end,

> As they passed by
> The holy place of Morwenstow, an old priest
> In a fisherman's jersey and heavy sea-boots,
> And the green headgear of an Armenian archimandrite,
> Looked out and blessed them.

The reference, characteristic of many throughout the poem, is, of course, to Hawker, remembered today as a ripely Anglican eccentric and proto-Cornish Nationalist, but an Arthurian poet also, with a still readable *Quest of the Sangraol* to his name (the footnotes to it alone are a sheer joy). The exequies are constructed at Zennor by an archetypal lady, who is the well-known sea-maiden of the place. There is no reference that I can detect to Zennor's most famous, albeit temporary, literary resident, and this is such a contrast to the punctilio with which the vicar of Morwenstow, a very minor figure, is acknowledged, that it can only be interpreted as a devastating dismissal for poor Lawrence. Like *Finnegans Wake,* the poem ends with its first line repeated, and for the same obvious reason. It offers a temptation to read it again and many times, one which I do not propose to resist.

As I have said, it is a very *literary* poem, it takes place in the head, but we need that sort of poem as much as we need the other sorts. The poet's verse form, one characteristically his own, contributes here to strengthen an effect which is not so much archaic – with its alliterations, its grammatical inversions, its hovering between four-teener and hexameter – as learned and literary. He sees himself,

> As a poet, perhaps, in the future predicament
> doubtfulness and dullness of a third Dark Age.

Well, it is not as bad as that, not yet, anyway. The libraries are still unburnt, and we can all enjoy the Alexandrine erudition of a Hellenistic twilight. I suppose you could say *Artorius* bears the same relationship to its predecessors as Coventry Cathedral does to York Minster or St Paul's, a great success in terms of what can still be done. And great fun too. I hope it is not too eccentric a compliment to say that I would like to see an imaginative stage version. In the mean time, I hope you will read it, and enjoy it as much as I did.

Poetry Wales (11.3, Winter 1976)

Not Mexico

Glyn Jones (ed.), *Poems '76*.

The Gomer anthologies are by now punctual summer visitors, like twin swallows. They are nicely produced by today's impoverished standards, hardback publication for this type of volume obviously belongs way back with real beer and real bacon. But why, oh why must the soft covers once again be so light-toned and so easily soiled? *Poems '76* is after all a book you will want to read more than once.

Glyn Jones is this year's selector, which inspires confidence. He is big enough to be modest, his brief introduction flies no kite, trails no coat, grinds no axe. He gives us fifty poems by thirty-four poets. The predictable First XV (yes, literally) get two poems each and R.S. Thomas gets three because he's the skipper. There are six new caps, but the team-building formula is tired and trusted. Here are the seasons, the horses, the problems of the motorist and the householder, the birds (the feathered variety of course, where do you think we are?), the myths, the surface minutiae of things rendered with a scrupulous fidelity that has its own eloquence, the virtual absence of any point of view or of strong or immediate feeling, emotion recollected not so much in tranquillity, as Wordsworth would have it, but in the clinic – though John Ormond's elegy is a moving exception. It is all legal, decent, honest, truthful, like the advertisements. Nobody curses God or the Government, asks awkward questions, loses his temper – except John Tripp, just a teeny bit – or lusts after his neighbour's wife, or even his own. Well, what did you expect? This isn't Mexico. But confronted with the severe handicap of living in a country which is small in every possible way, they don't fare too badly and will no doubt do much to relieve the tedium and frustration of which life in Wales largely consists.

Dannie Abse, kicking off briskly, punctures pretentiousness in a Cardiff parlour as well as in literary Florida. Alison Bielski hunts the cutty wren through the longest poem in the book, a romp through *The Golden Bough*, but Anthony Conran makes a more concentrated use of the same type of material in an epithalamium. Much of his work is intimately social, addressed to close friends; this is what gives it an immediacy too rare in our field. Ruth Bidgood speeds an unwanted guest, for our muse has always been sensitive to domestic irritants. Roland Mathias offers a typically complex meditation on his ancestry, otherwise there is not much of that, except the fluent 'Search for Identity' by Edward Lloyd, a name new to me. Tom Earley, Robert Morgan and John Stuart Williams provide the obligatory ration of Valleys nostalgia. Raymond Garlick is excited by trains (how lucky to be him), Jeremy Hooker goes camping but does not camp it up, weekenders Gillian Clarke and Leslie Norris stumble about in the mud. It is all, one must say it, rather cosy. John Ormond, in 'Design for a Quilt', even manages to assimilate nature itself into a piece of needlework. The editor has, I think, caught literary Anglo-Wales going about its business with some exactitude, and if none of us are going anywhere particular just now that is not his fault. Only in one instance he may have stumbled. I have seen better poems by S.M. Pugh than the one printed here, but they may have been published after his deadline. And Tony Curtis's poem is rather 'literary' for him: 'I am tempted by images from Ted Hughes', he says. Resist, Tony bach. The only poem that, to me, conveys the immediate feel of real life as lived by ordinary people is Meic Stephens' 'Ballade for Spring'. It is always a difficult task and here it is achieved in the most archaic and formally strict verse-form in the book. There may be a lesson here for some practitioners.

Somewhat uncharacteristically the editor makes the large claim 'that it seems unlikely that finer poetry in English could have appeared anywhere in our period than the best in this anthology'. Leaving this for posterity to decide, we can confidently recommend it as fulfilling the more modest aim of providing the reader with a representative selection of the best English poetry produced in Wales in recent years.

Welsh Book News (Winter 1976)

The Historical Context of Welsh Translation

A poet's European reputation, said Housman with characteristic asperity, is only relevant if he writes in Esperanto. And that language has indeed produced its poets, though, rather unfairly, they do not appear to have attracted much European attention except possibly among other Esperantists. Housman was among the last of the Latinists and nobody could have been more conscious than he of the great changes which had taken place in the relative position of languages, so that the language he loved and served at least as much as his native English had completely lost its former supremacy and lingered on as nothing much more than a status symbol. The tone of his reference to Esperanto expresses not merely his habitual malicious wit, it is a comment of some profundity; it says a lot not so much about Esperanto (a harmless, well-meaning substitute for Latin, doomed to impotence) but about the nature of a fragmented culture, searching around for reputations which were but a poor substitute for the genuine fame and achievements of the authentic European poets, those who had written in Europe's only common language and who were, by his day, an extinct breed. Thomas Gray is considered to be the last Englishman to write Latin poetry that rises above the level of mere exercises. Since Housman's day Latin has lost its last relevance, when the most conservative of institutions, the Roman Catholic Church, abolished its use in the Mass. The vernacular revolution has stormed the last fortress. That movement's first identifiable manifesto seems to have been Dante's *De Vulgare Eloquentia*, but it only began to make headway with the invention of the printing press, the Protestant Reformation (with emphasis on 'language understood of the people') and with Renaissance scholarship's lively interest in and exact scientific knowledge of 'diversity of tongues'.

Nowhere was this revolution more complete than in England, already in the late Middle Ages the home of a rich, assertive, self-confident and self-sufficient middle class who, neither practically nor psychologically, needed any other language than their own. Indeed, it is probably the majority opinion in England still that to speak any other language is no good thing. The vernacular movement tied in nicely with political and economic expansionism, with English as its instrument and symbol against the other countries and cultures of the British Isles. French and Italian had their prestige, of course, but not as learned languages like Latin. They were, and they remained, social accomplishments, the fruit of conspicuous leisure. And, with older vernacular literatures than English they were a rich source of entertainment material – Boccaccio rather than Dante. An intriguing relic of this attitude down to our own day is the preference that many English intellectuals used to show for French and Italian films as against English-language ones from America, which by any objective standards were far better. It is interesting to note that the first English poet to achieve a European – or at any rate a French – reputation, was Chaucer, hailed by one of his contemporaries as '*grand translateur*' – of their own poetry, naturally.

But the medieval genius, as seen typically in Malory, was not so much for translation as for creative adaptation. Exact verbal fidelity was not as esteemed as it was to be under the influence of later teaching. Originality too was of no great importance, this being essentially a romantic doctrine. The aim of the translator was to assimilate and annex. Dryden was to speak for them all when he said that his duty was 'to make Virgil speak such words as he would probably have written if he were living and an Englishman'. By the time of Dryden there was already a tradition which justified his attitude. Vigorous idiomatic English translations existed of Montaigne and Plutarch, Don Quixote in his English guise was thought of as almost a native product, there was Marlowe's Ovid and Chapman's Homer, and all these can still be admired as good English writing of their period. But this was a point of view that could not be maintained indefinitely. The romantic shift of sensibility included a new appreciation of historical perspective and a greater appreciation of variety and diversity. Virgil obviously was not a modern Englishman, and the great original writers of the other vernacular languages of modern Europe had to be accepted and appreciated on their own terms, French or German as the case may be, however universal their message. So Carlyle translated Goethe into conscientiously Germanic English. And Victorian translators generally accepted the doctrine of exact verbal fidelity in translations from all periods – except of course for the bawdy bits. The exotic was now an experience in itself. The nineteenth century explored the world and explored history and antiquity. It stuffed its museums with the loot of the remote past and remote places. Its most perfect expression is its diversity of architectural styles, from all ages and all parts of the world, imitative, derivative and often tasteless, but often flaring out into something striking and with all the marks of originality. So with the literature. Near the beginning of the period there is Moore's *Lallah Rookh*, near its end is Fitzgerald's *Rubaiyat of Omar Khayyam*, the one unjustly neglected, the other still running. The one is purely original work masquerading in Oriental fancy dress – and it attracted as much attention from the reading public of several generations as did Moore's longer surviving poems inspired by his study of Irish. The other, we are assured by experts, is almost equally original, a pastiche which bears little resemblance to anything in its alleged source. Obviously the *mystique* of translation has a strong appeal. Most authors strive to be original but some quite popular works make their effect by pretending not to be. The appeal of the exotic is never exhausted.

It is against this background that we must examine the literary relationships of the English language with its nearest neighbour. It is just as discouraging a story as many other aspects of the relationship. Despite a vague knowledge of the Welsh tradition of minstrelsy, very few of even the keenest and most sensitive minds in England have ever shown the slightest interest in the mere existence of Welsh literature, let alone any desire to exploit its riches. The sad fact must be faced that we are even more boring to the English than they are to us, which is saying a great deal. The Act of Union was supposed to bring the two peoples together on terms mutually beneficial to both, but the very basis of this union was the supremacy of the English language and this was acted on to the very letter. Individual Welshmen were accepted, typically, as lawyers, soldiers, divines, their mannerisms were tolerated, sometimes mildly satirised. Their history and antiquities attracted the attention of the appropriate specialists as did the Welsh language from the purely philological point of view, but the idea that there was any such thing as a Welsh literary culture worth serious study was not accepted. As usual the Welsh did very little to help themselves. The Tudor and Stuart London Welsh do not appear to have done much to enlighten their fellow-subjects of the Crown as to its existence. The bards who stayed home ignored even the invention of the printing press and went on circulating their manuscripts from hand to hand and dining at the tables of the few surviving patriotic gentry until the whole tradition nearly died on its feet. To be quite fair, it was a body of literature which presented, and still presents, formidable difficulties. The language of the oldest poets, the *Cynfeirdd*, demanded the attention of patient scientific scholarship which even today has not solved all its mysteries. The poets of the early middle ages, the *Gogynfeirdd*, spoke out of a vanished system of social relationships with its own technical vocabulary, some of it obsolete beyond recovery, and with its own emotional attitudes which, even expertly rendered, do not register as sincere to later ears. Then came the *cywyddwyr* who for centuries maintained a remarkable continuity and homogeneity of poetic style which tends to mask the individuality and originality of its greatest practitioners. These are genuine difficulties even today. It has been my privilege to hear Mr Saunders Lewis lecture on Guto'r Glyn, and to have been taken by Mr Myrddin Lloyd through some of the poems of Cynddelw Brydydd Mawr. In each case there was revealed a real and living voice, communicating, even out of a very different world, human emotions that made sense in personal terms. But also in each case one was only too clearly conscious of how much help was needed, what equipment of scholarship and what intuitive emotional sympathy above and beyond scholarship, were necessary to rectify the distortions of time, of social change and of changes in language. Neither of these essentials existed in the first centuries of union between England and Wales. In 1757 John Parry of Rhiwabon, the blind harpist, played at Cambridge. He 'scratched out such ravishingly blind harmony, such tunes of a thousand years old with names enough to choke you' that Thomas Gray was prompted to re-commence work on a poem he had had by him since 1755. He called it an 'Odikle', we know it as 'The Bard'. There is nothing in this famous poem that Gray could have derived from English books on Welsh history or from the metrics of his own time. But the scholarly recluse of Peterhouse had intuitively anticipated one of the major changes in literary taste and in the life of the imagination. 'The Bard' with its extravagantly dramatic action, its wild scenery, its 'raptures', its element of prophecy and supernatural foresight, was what a sated urban public was looking for. Only a few years later they were to get it in full measure when Macpherson published the first of his Ossianic poems. The controversy which raged about Ossian is relevant to the whole question of translation. If the high-bourgeois reading public of England and much of Western Europe besides had not craved so intensely for the exotic antithesis of its own standards and values, the authenticity or otherwise of Ossian would have mattered very little, at the most been a subject of specialist dispute between scholars. But it became a question of wide public interest, on which everyone felt entitled to state their views, and it was not a question which was to die down overnight either. Well into the nineteenth century the vogue continued, with Napoleon himself numbered among Macpherson's faithful followers. In the circles immediately concerned, the antiquarians and the early folklorists, activity was stepped up. The success of Macpherson encouraged Evan Evans, Ieuan Fardd, to bring out *Some Specimens of the Poetry of the Antient Welsh Bards* in 1764. One wonders if without this impetus the dissolute and disorganized Ieuan would have been moved to publish at all. Gray and Percy were his correspondents. Gray visited Wales and had ample opportunity to hear Welsh spoken and to know what it actually sounded like. Described as 'the most learned man in Europe', there is no reason to question his sound knowledge of the language, one of the many he knew. He was also, which is not unimportant, a great English poet. His translations therefore must be expected to rank high in fidelity at least. And indeed they do. They are spirited and move with pace well suited for declamation and convey much of the feeling, as well as most of the sense, of the originals. Yet his own original composition, 'The Bard', written before his interest was fully engaged, and while he was still reliant on English sources, surpasses them in every respect, not least in continuing popularity. Which then in poetic or imaginative terms is the more authentic achievement? 'The Bard' and Ossian surely have achieved their own authenticity independent and irrespective of their alleged originals, and led the way to a wider appreciation of the alien cultures that had inspired them, which is presumably the overall aim of any translation.

The nature of this interest, of course, can sometimes be suspect. Gray wrote to Percy about this time, 'the Welsh poets are coming to light'. They had been available for study at any time since the Act of Union, but until the eighteenth century not the slightest interest had been displayed in them. They only 'came to light' because they happened to satisfy an emotional, imaginative need among a section of urban society. It may be doubted if they were really accorded any substantial reality in their own right. Percy wrote about them in conjuction with 'Erse, Runic, Chinese, Arabic, Hebrew, East Indian, Peruvian, Lapland and Greenland poetry', a strikingly Poundian, even Penguinish catalogue. Another full title of Ieuan Fardd's pioneer volume ends with these words: 'in order to give the Curious some idea of the Tasks and Sentiments of our Ancestors, and their manner of Writing ...' There is a whiff of the museum about it.

But Ieuan's generation stood at one of the great watersheds in our history. The Methodist Revival was already gathering strength, and this was to inspire its own literature, unlike anything seen before. And it can be no coincidence that a revival of national consciousness was also taking place There was a literary renewal, associated with the patriotic societies based in London, the Gwyneddigion and the Cymmrodorion, there were the tireless and many-sided activities of the Morris brothers, notably Lewis, the eldest of them, and their hosts of correspondents and co-workers, who included in the field of creative writing the poets Ieuan Fardd and Goronwy Owen. The latter studied the forms of classical Welsh poetry, which were still being practised in a feeble and debased manner, and put new life into them. He is the refounder of Welsh poetry in the strict metres and his direct influence was powerful well into the nineteenth century. The old tradition may be taken to have ended with the death of Siôn Dafydd Las, 'the last of the bards', in 1694, but this man's nephew, David Jones of Trefriw, was among the early printers on Welsh soil which the printing press did not reach until 1718 under evangelical auspices. The whole general movement was essentially middle-class and heavily influenced by the only accessible models and precedents, which were English. It cannot be too much emphasised that a very high proportion of what had been published in Welsh since the six-teenth century had been translations from English, some of them of great elegance and classics of the Welsh language. At a certain level the integration of Wales with England had gone very far. But the growth, at last, of a native middle class, even if a high proportion of the most active and creative of them were in London, was bound to re-invigorate a sense of national identity. The religious leaders preached middle-class virtues to all sections of the community, including the very poorest. That influence has persisted until our own day and is by no means exhausted as yet. Our own idea of ourselves, as we are or should be, is still basically this idea however transcribed or transposed from spiritual to social or political terms. Good or bad, we cannot escape from it. It expresses the national condition as no other set of ideas could. But its literary expression was in the nature of things unoriginal in form and content. Its masterpieces are hymns and fall inevitably under the strictures pronounced by Dr Johnson on all forms of pious literature. Translation of the vast bulk of Welsh religious writing into English is hardly worthwhile and has rarely been undertaken. Thus William Williams of Pantycelyn, whom many consider to be our greatest poet, must remain inaccessible to anyone who does not know the language, and the same is true of many of the lesser practitioners in the same vein. Reduced to the basic sentiments they express, they are mere hymns.

The purely literary revivers, Goronwy Owen and his successors, notably the poets of Eifionydd, are not open to the same reproach. But in the revealing title of Saunders Lewis's book about Goronwy Owen and his immediate associates they are *A School of Welsh Augustans*. Quite apart from the difficulties of translation from the strict metres, the basic sameness of Augustan modes of expression in Welsh and English makes it almost impossible to convey anything of what originality and personal tone of voice there is in any of them. Anthony Conran, perhaps the most wide-ranging and ambitious of the modern translators, gives comparatively little space to them in *The Penguin Book of Welsh Verse*, and what comes over of Goronwy Owen there is not very exciting in substance, for all the translator's virtuosity.

The eisteddfod movement, beginning modestly in the eighteenth century, became in the nineteenth a powerful force for popular culture. Its aesthetic was conditioned by its social function, its poetry subject to obvious limitations. It was didactic and declamatory, at its worst intolerably verbose and jejune, disfigured by cloying sentimentality and an exasperatingly bogus-sounding (though no doubt sincerely intended) patriotism. Little of it stands up to translation and indeed little of it has been translated, though the indomitable Mr Conran has had a go at Eben Fardd, whose *awdl* (typically and magniloquently) on the destruction of Jerusalem is considered to be about the best of a dismal period, and may be inspected, fragmentarily, in the Penguin Book. It is rather a solemn thought that the eisteddfodic style prevailed until the beginning of the present century almost unchallenged for the treatment of serious subjects. It is a pity really that it is neither translatable nor worthy of translation, for it offers its own perverse pleasures. The last purely eisteddfodic poet of any consequence was Dewi Emrys, whose last major award (in 1948) coincided happily with Euros Bowen's first. Whatever the subject, he had a whole body of verse at hand which with minor modifications could be transferred *in toto* from one title to another. There is perhaps something to be said for a literature in which such achievements are possible. On a higher level stand the nineteenth century's lyric achievements, but these do not stand up to translation. Welsh song lyrics are not alone in this, of course. Some of the verses of Ceiriog have the same sort of absolute perfection in their medium as have those of Heine, and this is the least translatable quality of all. At the opposite pole stands the more cerebral poetry of Islwyn. His is undoubtedly the most unmistakable personal voice of the century. On first reading one gets something of the flavour of Browning, but Mr Saunders Lewis has shown that the major influence on Islwyn, especially on his psychological epic *Y Storm*, was none of the enduring English poets of his day, but one Bayley, whose long poem *Festus* went through many editions in its time, but whose reputation has now sunk irretrievably into oblivion. (In fact the wider the reading audience the more likely this sort of thing is to happen. Nineteenth-century English literature is full of stranded hulks that will sail no more, and one wonders, does one not, about some of the more influential reputations of more recent times.)

Meanwhile the older literature continued to be studied in Wales, and to a limited extent in England, for its own abundant rewards. But in both countries students were misled by the fantasies of Iolo Morganwg and by the defective scholarship of his successors as authorities on Welsh literature, Owen Pughe and John Williams (ap Ithel), and by the whole romantic climate in general and the yearnings of a rational, industrial age for bards, chieftains, clouds, raptures, etc. And of course there was plenty of genuine material in the older literature that did make for a mystification easy to confuse with mysticism: the obscurity of the language and many of the references to places and people, the element of political propaganda in the mediaeval 'prophetic' poems, meaningless as soon as the immediate occasion for them had passed (Dr Thomas Parry has admitted none of this stuff into the *Oxford Book of Welsh Verse*) and the novelistic nonsense that gathered quite understandably about the outstandingly individualistic figure of Dafydd ap Gwilym. In fact much of this translation concentrated on clarifying the meaning of what was doubtful; it was more of an exercise in textual accuracy than in poetry as such. Freer translation had even less fortunate results: bowers of verdant hue, flow'ry meads 'neath the welkin, and (one matchless touch) the swarth excretion of the night. Mrs Hemans, the leading lady-bard of her day, who spent most of her productive life in Wales but who has mysteriously escaped enrolment among the apocryphal ancestors of Anglo-Welsh poetry, thus translated '*Stafell Cynddylan*':

> The hall of Cynddylan is gloomy tonight,
> I weep, for the grave has extinguished its light,
> The beam of the lamp from its summit is o'er
> The blaze of its hearth shall give welcome no more.

This if anything is better than the average level of nineteenth-century translations. *Wylaf wers, tawaf wedi* seems the only appropriate comment. I find it in some way significant that Welsh made its most notable appeal to the marginals, the eccentrics and the loners among the English poets: Borrow, Barnes, Peacock and (avoiding the complexities of a vexed subject) Hopkins. The first three turned out agreeable and spirited minor verse in their translations – or, in the case of Peacock, pastiche-parodies. As for Hopkins, the case is far from proven. English too has its alliterative ancestors.

To our own ears originality and individualism in Welsh poetry only really begin with the present century. At last here is a wide range of subject-matter treated in a variety of moods and techniques. Sir John Morris Jones has always seemed worth the attentions of a major translator because of the urgency with which he addressed himself to the problems of national identity and survival, and to his lyric gifts. He is more like a German Romantic or a French Parnassian than any English poet. He represents the wider horizons that were beginning to open up before the nation and he still awaits justice to be done to him. The same can be said of a succession of non-eisteddfodic poets up to the present day (this is not to dismiss the eisteddfodic poets, of course; the Welsh-speaker will know what I mean and it is not a point of much interest to those who come to Welsh from the outside): W.J. Gruffydd, a man of many reputations, Robert Williams Parry, whose deceptively Georgian idiom hides a spirit akin to Hölderin, T.H. Parry-Williams, sparse and ironic, Saunders Lewis the reigning monarch, Gwenallt and Waldo, cult figures among the nationalistic young with whom the future both of the nation and its literature now rests. Here indeed are urgent individual voices and a growing body of at least competent translation. Most prominent and productive of the translators is Anthony Conran, but this is not to disparage Gwyn Williams or Joseph Clancy as close contenders, and a number of others with occasional successes to their credit. And by now the literary and social function of the translator has changed. Gwyn Williams dedicates *The Burning Tree, Poems from the First Thousand Years of Welsh Verse* to his daughters 'in the hope that they may grow up to read both sides of the book'. Today most of Wales, even educated Wales, is monoglot English. And every Welsh-speaker is, effectively, bilingual. The translator's role today is not to satisfy 'the curious' in Evan Evans' phrase, nor to interest the English – though of course it is not an unwelcome fact that more and more of them are beginning to take an interest, as the constant reprinting of some of the best volumes of translations demonstrates. He has now to enlighten his own countrymen about some of the treasure that has been stolen from them. Not everybody agrees with this point of view. We Welsh are a vicious lot, among whom *tradutore, tradittore* threatens to take on a new shade of meaning. My own few efforts have provoked a reaction – and significantly, from friends who like myself have had to acquire the language in later life – that by translating from Welsh one is somehow selling the pass, passing off an *erzatz* article as the genuine thing, and thus in some way diminishing the drive to learn the language of the original, that reaction of the disinherited which is now the main hope for the survival of Welsh. This is a case which must be argued in a wider context. I do not think it will stop translators translating. The impulse to translate is not readily distinguishable from that which urges one to write original poetry in one's own language. Today, in Wales, there are more translations, and by better poets, than ever before, with more responsibilities, both to Wales and to England and to a wider world whose attitude to 'minority' languages is rapidly changing for the better. Being Welsh, however, he will encounter the peculiar difficulties implicit in the peculiar situation of a peculiar people. My own feeling is that we can't have enough of it, and my advice is to get on with it. But be careful how you handle Dafydd ap Gwilym.

Poetry Wales (11.3, Winter 1976)

Spending the Week

How am I going to spend the week? Being a writer, I shall spend most of it at my desk. Nothing spectacular, I'm afraid. An author composing a passionate poem or inditing an eloquent piece of prose does not look very different from his accountant working out his tax for him, a task which often seems to require just as much in the way of passion and eloquence. There are few Byrons today who feel moved to go off and liberate somewhere, few Dylans to lend bohemian colour to the scene. Indeed, when I meet one engaged on a crusade or a debauch, I have doubts about the quality of his writing. Neither do I feel impelled to go anywhere special to do my thing, Cornwall or Capri or wherever. Any crusades or visions must strictly relate to one's own patch, otherwise they are just bogus rhetoric. So here I sit in Cwmbach, surrounded mostly by paper of one sort or another, like a winter sheep in a snowdrift, and jars full of defunct ballpoints and all the other dreary débris of clerical activity. There are the magazines that keep me in touch, and those I hopefully write for: *Poetry Wales, Planet, Penderyn, Rebecca, Y Faner, Y Saeth, Taliesin* and the *Welsh Nation*. To keep these supplied there is my typewriter – and the view. This begins at the willow-tree just outside my window, its twigs tapping the panes, planted there by the hand of nature herself when I wasn't looking. Across the road there is a tall oak-tree. Beyond all these branches, there is the village, and the Cynon Valley stretching up to the spire of Aberdare and bounding the view to the north, the dark slope of Foel Penderyn and, on a good day, the Beacons.

Not far away, in place though not in time, lived Edward Ifan of Toncoch, whom that old liar Iolo Morganwg claimed to be the last of the Druids, and Telynog, the runaway from Cardigan town to the coalfield, after whom we have named a row of houses, who died young and left behind a handful of remembered lyrics, Bob Coe, the last man to be publicly hanged in Wales, whose tale is still told, and the unknown heroes of the working class who, in the course of a long and bitter strike, set up the first co-operative on Welsh soil, in an old building that only the other day fell to the bulldozers of progress.

I am still at my desk, but my mind moves actively through these scenes and associations. Wales is a small country only in a geographical sense, you can travel far in time and achievement simply by looking out of practically any window in the land. And this is what I shall be writing about, in the magazines I have mentioned and perhaps others. I have only one appointment this week, no readings to schools in Gwynedd, no political meetings in workmen's halls, no film-scripting sessions in Chapter, no big match. But there is the Book Fair at Pontypridd Polytechnic, the south-eastern session of the annual Welsh Books Fair. My part in the proceedings is to deliver a lecture on the literary history of Pontypridd, from the bridge-builder himself, to the lively Pontypriddians of our own day, iconoclasts and no-nonsense debunkers to a man, Alun Richards, Meic Stephens, John Lewis Hughes, but all, in their own ways, bridge-builders too. I shall tell my audience that their town is just as interesting and just as rich in its associations as anywhere else in Wales. And that, I hope, will be my good deed for the week.

Previously unpublished, 1977

Some Pontypridd Writers

In his *History of Pontypridd and the Rhondda Valleys*, published in 1903, Owen Morgan, more widely known as the journalist Morien, proclaimed his intention of relating the history of a flourishing industrial district with its remote past. 'Down to 1850,' he writes, 'its pastoral character had only been disturbed at Dinas and slightly at Hafod and Cymmer.' He invokes Tacitus and the Silures, he tells us that the Common Fair was held on the second Sunday of July and that this proves that it was the remnant of the Summer Solstice ceremonies that were held there in ancient times. That it was a convenient time and place for such an activity, dictated by common sense and practical considerations, is a mean and philistine thought, perhaps. But Morien's imagination soared above such details: he was using his imagination to throw a bridge across time, just as William Edwards had used his skill as a builder to throw a bridge across a dangerous and turbulent river, the Taff.

Pontypridd, like everywhere else in Wales, is its own place. It is of course intimately linked with the surrounding areas, bound particularly to the Rhondda by the closest of umbilical cords, receiving also the tribute of Taff and Cynon, as well as an important contribution from the Vale of Glamorgan. Its growth as a market-place was achieved at the expense of the old hill-town of Llantrisant. There is a distinct feel about Pontypridd, one which I hope it is not too fanciful to see as having generated a special mental climate which can be detected in the work of its writers.

Only a few yards up in the direction of Porth the hills begin to cast their shadow, and a short distance downriver one becomes aware of the pull of the cities of the plain. But the mart of many valleys, Ponty has a completely different atmosphere from any of them. It is a place where transport and communication have loomed large. It once had the longest railway-platform in the British Isles and this has always seemed to me a more important fact than the town's use as a setting for the exhibitionism of the quack Dr William Price. I always think of Pontypridd because of its station in the days of trains – 'the Gateway to the Valleys' used to be the GWR's proud boast here-abouts, and now as a convergence of routes in the age of the motor-way and urban flyover. Ponty's fame, for many, lies in its open-air market. But the town's monument is not a castle or a church, but a bridge. Its best writers have been aware of movement, of passing through, on the road to somewhere else, even if some of them were not too sure in which direction they were heading. I have no time to go into the differences between the feel of their work and that of other writers, but I think of the gloom of the Rhondda, the manic euphoria of Merthyr, the lyricism of Aberdare, and Pontypridd's writers seem something else again.

Pontypridd was a place but thinly populated until the beginning of the nineteenth century, when the coal of the lower Rhondda began to be raised by the first mine-owners. One of these was Dr Richard Griffiths, who died in 1826, achieving some local notoriety by arranging a farcical funeral for himself at Llanwynno. Although no writer himself, he thus struck a note of characteristically macabre humour which later writers have found to their taste.

The Taff Vale Railway began operations in 1841 and, in the decades that were to follow, Pontypridd acquired something of the ambience of a frontier town, the uneasy meeting-place of an old rural community and the new raw age of iron and steam, of cut-throat capitalism and brutal exploitation. The fantasies for which some of its leading citizens became famous can only be properly understood against this background. Their imaginings were part of a reaction to a dislocated, frenzied world, an attempt to make sense of and impose some sort of pattern on a scene that was changing too fast for com-fort and sometimes seemed to make no sense at all. This was partic-ularly true in the place where the traffic was thickest. While Pontypridd could not challenge the older towns of Aberdare and Merthyr as cultural centres for they had their own printing and pub-lishing facilities, it was nevertheless a lively place and it attracted some lively minds. The clanking of trucks, the shrill whistles of the engines, and the clouds of steam are echoed and reflected in the excited imagination of the poets and visionaries, whose over-heated minds often generated clouds of vapour that eclipsed the Sun of Reason itself.

They arrived with the first trains. By 1844, Evan Davies, known by his bardic name Myfyr Morganwg, had set up as a watchmaker, one of those crafts that keep cropping up in the history of Welsh literature. By 1847, with Iolo Morganwg's son Taliesin dead, Myfyr was claiming the vacant archdruidical throne, which he was to occupy until his death some forty years later. During these decades Pontypridd was the metropolitan see of the druidic cult. The Rocking Stone on the Common, still there today but no longer rocking, alas, became a focus of ritual and pilgrimage, rather like the Kaaba at Mecca for Muslims, I suppose. Four times a year at the appointed solstices and equinoxes, the rites were held, much to the scandal of the more orthodox faiths. Not only did Myfyr outrage the devout, he offended against the canons of scholarship and played a leading part in the disgraceful proceedings at the Eisteddfod held in Llangollen in 1858, where the Sanhedrin over which he presided, together with even less reputable men (including an Anglican clergyman who was also a bishop in a Celtic Church of his own invention) ganged up with the unscrupulous John Williams (ap Ithel) against the new scholarship being pioneered by Thomas Stephens in his chemist's shop in Merthyr's High Street. Ap Ithel distributed the prizes among members of his own family, while Stephens's classic work proving the fabulous nature of the story of Prince Madoc's discovery of America was disqualified because it ran counter to patriotic legend. This was the first Eisteddfod of modern times. Like Pontypridd, it was the product of the railway age, so it was appropriate that the Myfyr should be there, taking advantage of the excursion tickets now being issued for the first time. There was a first-class row about it all, just as there has been since, such as last year at Cardigan. The Myfyr, who claimed to have discovered the secret of wisdom and kept it in an egg-shell slung around his neck on a piece of string, was of the same breed as the most eccentric eccentric of them all, another local man, Dr William Price, who built the Round Houses at Treforest as the gates to a Kubla Khan he was planning further up the hill above Glyntaf, and who later achieved notoriety as a pioneer of cremation. It seems fitting that he has been celebrated in a ballad by Meic Stephens, another Trefforest man, which has proved so popular that it is now often reprinted as 'traditional'.

But they were not all like that, far from it. At the diametrical extreme from this parade of sham and folly, we hear one of the most sincere and authentic voices that the nation has ever heard, one which speaks for the nation. Evan James was one of the first settlers in Pontypridd after the discovery of coal. He was from Gwent, and had brought with him his wife and son. The story of '*Hen Wlad fy Nhadau*' I have told on another occasion. When we read, in the pages of gifted writers, of the polluted river that flows through Pontypridd, we do well to remember that from those waters there arose a song that gave the Welsh people what little of pride and dignity they have. The father and son, both weavers, the one a poet and the other a musician, exemplify perfectly the pattern of life and culture that was growing up in the new town.

The poets of Pontypridd were prolific, they wrote for the public, they worked closely with musicians, and their work was recited and sung in both chapel and tavern. The most prominent musician in town was John Thomas, known as Ieuan Ddu, a Carmarthenshire man, who started a school at Pontypridd in 1850, later moving to Trefforest where he spent the rest of his life. He is credited by some as being the creator of the Welsh Choir as we know it today. His grave at Glyntaf seems to me to be a worthy place of pilgrimage. Ieuan Ddu knew Thomas Rees (Alaw Ddu) and all the other musicians of the district and the boost he gave to the town's musical life must have been important in the background of other musicians, such as Morfydd Llwyn Owen of Trefforest, whose premature death in 1918 is said to have been one of he most serious losses ever suffered by Welsh music. Then there was John Hughes, from nearby Tonteg, who gave us one of the most famous hymn-tunes of all, 'Cwm Rhondda', which he composed for one of Pontypridd's chapels, Capel Rhondda. I have not exhausted the list but I think I have said enough to suggest the rich cultural life of Pontypridd.

An almost exact contemporary of Ieuan Ddu was John Jones, who with a name like that had to be better known as Ioan Emlyn. He began his career as a preacher in the chapels of Pontypridd. He was a man of considerable scholarship but he is remembered as the author of a single poem, '*Bedd y Dyn Tlawd*', still one of the most popular in the Welsh language. Ioan was buried at Ebbw Vale and when the National Eisteddfod was held there in 1958, I paid a visit to his neglected grave, marked by a leaning obelisk in an overgrown cemetery. Nobody from the Eisteddfod knew it was there or bothered to visit it. I was younger then and this graphic evidence of the fading of literary fame had me worried for a day or two.

No such worries troubled the minds of *Clic y Bont*, a group of poets who gathered regularly in Pontypridd in the latter half of the 19th century. As individuals they do not seem to have had any lasting significance and most Welsh-speakers today would be hard put to mention any of their names, even if they have heard of them as a clique. Their social role, however, was important. They gave Pontypridd a literary identity at a time when it needed one. The town was still only a random assembly of industrial undertakings of one sort or another, and of hastily thrown up houses deemed good enough for the working population, most of whom were incomers. Local government was still embryonic, politics was still in the feudal stage, there were few institutions to give stability or dignity to the place. But there was this little group of poets who met regularly to discuss and practise their craft. It is an inescapable conclusion that the group included some inveterate and assiduous self-publicisers, not unlike some we know in our own day. Their work may remain unread, but their collective existence is still spoken of as one of the town's claims to fame, so they must have had some significance while their group lasted. Who were they? First there was Thomas David, or Dewi Wyn o Essyllt, a native of Dinas Powys who moved to Pontypridd in 1874 and lived there until he dropped dead in the Hewitt Arms in 1891. Of him it was said that 'even in an age of eisteddfodic zeal he was considered to have over-indulged his competitive instincts'. His book *Ceinion Essyllt* run to more than six hundred pages. In 1883 he submitted no less than three full-length *awdlau* the Eisteddfod. His post as Poetry Editor of the *Western Mail* was a great help in boosting his reputation and that of his associates.

Another bird of the same feather was Owen Morgan, the journalist Morien, who lived until 1923. He too worked for the *Western Mail* in a long line of highly literate men who have been associated with that paper. He was no poet, unless we regard his historical theories as flights of creative fancy. Do not be misled by the prosaic title of his book which I mentioned earlier. It is the most astonishing mish-mash of information and nonsense that you are ever likely to read. The really amusing thing about Morien was the lofty attitude he took towards his fellow-mystagogues, Myfyr Morganwg and company, for what he regarded as their credulous folly. He reports the Myfyr's dying words, 'Who, now that I am gone, will fight the battles of the True God?' The answer was obviously 'Morien', who, however, had some different gods of his own. The basic principle of his fantasies seems to have been that a purely fanciful version of the derivation of placenames or an unsubstantiated account of a historical event should always be preferred to the obvious or straightforward. Thus Bristol, which is Early English for 'Bridge Town', must be explained as 'The Town of the Britons', and Wells, which means just what it says, is derived from 'Wales'. His history sprouts with far-fetched etymologies that have all the charm of bad puns. Compared with some of Morien's high-flown speculations, the relatively modest claims of the Myfyr pale almost into sense. One of his titles is 'The Battles of Wales, the Unconquered Country of the Empire', possibly the most extreme mis-statement of them all. We see in it a type of perverted nationalism that was characteristic of the period, trying to have its cake and eat it, anxious to share the glories of the Raj and at the same time laying claim to a separate identity that would seem, logically considered, to point the nation in another direction altogether. It is a stange country whose history we are asked to consider where there are mysterious noises under Barry Island, whose Boadicea fought her last battle near Rhyl and where King Arthur and St David are both solar myths. Reading Morien, one feels that *Clic y Bont* had no need for the more routine intoxicants on offer at the Llanover Arms or the Maltsters.

In a different league altogether stands William Thomas, Glanfrwd, historian of the nearby parish of Llanwynno. Although he spent many years as one of the clergy of St Asaph's Cathedral, he took a detailed mental map of his native place with him and lovingly described it in his best-known work, *Hanes Plwyf Llanwynno*, a minor masterpiece describing not so much a place as a state of mind. The book, which has been translated into English, is the only product of the group which has kept its charm and importance.

By the time the National Eisteddfod was held in Pontypridd in 1893 it had become as respectable as it is ever likely to be. By then its scholarly standards were no longer those of the cheerful humbugs of Llangollen and if its arch-druids practised druidical rites on the *Maen Llog*, there were those among them who did not really believe in them. But the lunatic fringe had not completely died out. They now organized themselves into a hermetical or schismatic Gorsedd under the leadership of Gwilym Cowlyd (William John Roberts), who had appointed himself Chief Bard Positive in a ceremony held on the shores of a lake in North Wales which he claimed to be the birth-place of Taliesin. He comes into our story because he erupted onto the stage during the Eisteddfod at Pontypridd, angrily challenging the adjudicators who in his opinion had awarded the prize to the wrong poet. There was quite a scene and the Chief Bard Positive had to be dealt with in no uncertain manner by another doughty son of the district, Judge Gwilym Williams of Miskin, whose statue stands outside the law-courts in Cardiff. After that things went quiet.

By the 1920s, Pontypridd, like the rest of industrial Wales, was in for a bad time. It no longer had the resilience of its first youth. The old popular culture succumbed to the ravages of the Depression, to unemployment and depopulation The cultural impoverishment wrought by anglicization and the economic distress were in fact two facets of the same process. By 1930 *Clic y Bont* were in their graves and the society that had produced them had also passed away. Perhaps the last literary manifestation of a Welsh-speaking way of life were the short stories of J.J. Williams, written about Ynysybwl, which although it belongs administratively to the Cynon Valley, is closely linked with Pontypridd. The republication of his stories about 'Y Gilfach Ddu' is long overdue, if only because they were written in the authentic dialect of the Glamorgan valleys. From now on the writers of Pontypridd were to write in English.

[The lecture ended with an appreciation of the work of three more writers who were born in Pontypridd, namely Alun Richards, Meic Stephens, and John Lewis Hughes.]

Extract from a lecture delivered at the Polytechnic of Wales during the Books Festival held there in March 1977.

Webb's Progress (II)

It is a day in the late 'thirties, Auden's 'dishonest decade'. A cold, grit-laden wind is blowing tattered newspapers along Swansea High Street. One of them wraps itself round my legs. I kick it away. Its headlines proclaim the fall of Madrid to the Fascists. The way is clear for the greater storm that is soon to break, the war that they say the men in the dole queues are praying for, the war that I and all my generation was born for, as we understood more clearly than our rulers.

In most other matters, though, I had been fortunate. A family background deeply rooted in a seemingly stable and relatively unchanging society, English Gower, one moreover of great beauty and full of tangible history, castles, churches, bone caves and standing-stones. A home that had not known unemployment or deprivation, in perhaps the last years when to belong to the working-class was to belong to a complete culture, with its own absolute and re-assuring standards. Good parents and good teachers who between them had made it possible for me to reach Oxford. An experience, not of the lost enchantment of the Middle Ages, but of Edwardian England. Another country, another world, to be enjoyed, but not to be seduced by. An Anglican upbringing, decently devout but charitable and tolerant. An inherited, long-inherited possession of the English language. An interest in language for its own sake that prompted a positive and sympathetic attitude towards Welsh. Towards its literature, however, a certain ambivalence. The prominent druids of the day were clearly not to be taken all that seriously, but still there was something there if you dug for it. And there was Saunders Lewis, the mad arsonist, but he belonged to the same scenario as the anthracite miners, nearer home, who had burnt the blacklegs' buses. All of it irrelevant in comparison with the coming war.

The Bessemers of Dowlais had long since been sold for scrap. The nights they used to light up the Gower sky were a fading memory. Older and colder were the ruins of Landore and Plasmarl, and the grass was just beginning to grow again on Kilvey Hill, on earth long poisoned by zinc and lead and copper smoke. But the town in its lovely natural setting was still a place where life flowed, as the tankers, trawlers, colliers and big beautiful banana-boats steamed across the bay. I was aware of its history only in a confused, uninformed way. Such things were not taught. One picked it up from gossip, from a neighbour who had rounded Cape Horn under sail, from the tall tales that were told about Cwmfelin works (I was to find exactly the same tales about Dowlais), from men who could remember Gipsy Smith (his autobiography was one of the few books in our house) storming through the slums of The Strand with his flaming gospel. I too wanted to go about into the streets and speak to the people and arouse them into an awareness that they were worthy of something better than their present lot, not in the next world, but in this, their own corner of the earth. It had nothing to do with nationalist fire-raising, a remote, cranky episode, nor yet with the various political creeds preached from the soapboxes on the sands, all of which seemed to belong to the same order of holus-bolus universal salvation as the evangel of Gipsy Smith (as indeed they still do). It was a simple desire to see my own people appreciate themselves at their true worth. This perhaps had been my greatest good fortune of all, a vocation which I cannot readily assign to any external circumstance in my background or education or upbringing. Uncovenanted, it makes it easy for me to understand why Hugh MacDiarmid, for all his tribulations, entitled his autobiography *Lucky Poet*.

But there the luck seemed to run out. Where to begin? I had no means of entry into the literature that included Gwenallt, who would have been – as he was to be much later – very much to my purpose. Some of Dylan Thomas's first output, the early surrealist prose, had been passed around in ill-duplicated sheets during my last years at school, and his first, coterie reputation was already beginning. Powerful stuff of its kind, but all so personal and introverted. I came across the productions of Huw Menai and Idris Davies. These erred in the other direction. They said the right things, but, alas, not very well. Then, of course, there were those early numbers of *Wales*. Well, here at last was a group of people aiming in the right direction. But weren't they all being just a bit too esoteric? I liked the technical versatility of Keidrych Rhys and the authors he collected around him, their wide horizons, their cosmopolitanism, their apparently deep and varied knowledge of Wales and the world, their 'Modern' idiom, the manifest love of country displayed by many of them and, best of all, their complete lack of respect for all literary and political establishments. They taught me more, perhaps, than I suspected at the time. For somehow, none of this seemed quite to my purpose. I was studying the literatures of France and Spain, the products of markedly different cultures, different historical circumstances. This helped me to understand that the literature of England, too, for all its accessibility, was equally the product of a people completely differently circumstanced from our own and, overwhelmingly, of one class of that people. Its working-class authors, such of them as there were, all went mad or committed suicide. Meanwhile, the sky was falling.

I have written very little about the war, and am unlikely ever to consider it as more than a tedious and irrelevant interruption in my life, and the immediate post-war years were also barren, as if one were still falling through space. One day in 1948, on impulse, I joined Plaid Cymru. I didn't realise till afterwards that it was St George's Day, but there is no significance in this. Not long afterwards, as a result of correspondence with him, I found myself working for Keidrych Rhys, in premises above various shops in Carmarthen, looking down on the life of the rural capital as it flowed along Lammas Street. Not for long. The fates were unkind, and the magazine, and the publishing imprint which issued the first work of R.S. Thomas, the still unrecognized genius of Nigel Heseltine and work by Richard Hughes, John Cowper Powys and Eirian Davies had to come to an end. It was an incomparable introduction to every aspect of life in Wales. When many now-famous names have been forgotten, Keidrych Rhys will be remembered among the great men of our time in this land. It would be impossible for me to tell a fraction of all I saw and heard and learnt in that brief period of my life. I will settle for one circumstance. On the same day, I met, for the first time, both Dylan Thomas and Gwynfor Evans. My own path was to follow neither, and I chose political activity of an unorthodox character, with the Welsh Republican Movement, rather than any but the most occasional and contingent literary activity. Not that I have ever been able to make much of a distinction. The poetry that 'makes nothing happen' is something we cannot afford. I do not claim that all writing should have an explicit social programme. Such dogmatism is the prerogative of the thought-police, the critics. I can only say that in my case I never wrote anything of worth before I became a political activist. It was a long, slogging stint and the story of it is probably of little general interest by now. On St David's Day 1954 the first Hydrogen bomb was dropped on Bikini Atoll, and most of our problems were solved, only to be replaced by a new set of problems, as is the way of things. Coincidentally, on the same day, I began work as a librarian in Dowlais, and stayed there for ten years, in defiance of any rational career structure, absorbing myself at last into the national experience.

In the early 'sixties I began to receive letters from someone who had the same ideas about poetry and society, a young man called Meic Stephens. I met him in one of those old-fashioned central Cardiff pubs now tarted-up out of all recognition. For a time, he and I and a lot of other miscellaneous activists inhabited a cavernous and ramshackle house in Merthyr Tydfil which did not seem to belong to anybody. That was where he started the Triskel Press and *Poetry Wales* while I was editor of the *Welsh Nation*. Another leap forward, and I like to think that I gave it a leg up, if only as a link between Keidrych Rhys and Meic Stephens. Together we warred upon what we saw as the inadequacies of Plaid Cymru as it then was, against servility and anglomania, against the absurd pretensions of the London Welsh, against provincial prejudice, and for mutual recognition and respect between the writers of both languages in our land. It has been a long haul. The very first time that I heard the late, revered, D.J. Williams was at the Plaid Cymru Conference in Cardiff in 1960. He asked one of the lecturers to explain why so many Anglo-Welsh writers were so antagonistic and contemptuous towards the Welsh language and indeed, to the nation itself, which they could only use as a subject for savage and grotesque caricature. I wanted to get up and protest, but realised that a contrary case would be difficult to argue. Only a few years later it would be the same D.J. who was chiefly instrumental in opening the doors of Yr Academi Gymreig to the English writers of Wales of a newer and healthier generation than those he had castigated. In the mean time it had somehow fallen to me to organise a petition among these writers, dissociating ourselves from an ill-inspired campaign to dethrone the Welsh language from its paramount status in the National Eisteddfod. I was astonished and touched to see some of the signatures, and I have never done anything that I will be more proud of.

One of the milestones in this progress was an interlude of black farce. In 1964 it was somebody's bright idea to hold a Commonwealth Arts Festival. Entering into the spirit of the event, India and Pakistan went to war, and things were not much better in Cardiff, which had been chosen as the location of the Commonwealth Poetry Conference. (If you want to know what Commonwealth Poetry is, don't ask me, I am still none the wiser). Some of the visitors, notably the Australians and Canadians, were very pleasant people who talked sense when they were allowed to talk at all, but they were hardly representative of most of what went on. Decent language cannot describe the vile rabble of petty criminals who descended on Cardiff in the guise of poets. To be fair, one of them turned out to be quite a major criminal, the murderer Michael X, who was hanged in 1974. This obscene circus, recruited from the literary slums of the English-speaking world (it included some ripe horrors from the U.S.A., which had presumably been re-annexed to the Commonwealth for the occasion) was a shocking eye-opener, and must have done a lot to emphasise the separate status of the English writers of Wales. That we shared a common language with these degenerate freaks was an undeniable fact. But we obviously belonged to a completely different culture, one in which it was not necessary to carry on like a demented juvenile delinquent in order to prove that one was a poet. Indeed, it was only a few months later that *Poetry Wales* was founded. The two events were not unconnected.

Loneliness is a burden every poet must carry with him, for it is, after all, a bleak, miserable business, scratching out verses far into the night. But still, nothing is free. And writing poetry is the nearest mortal man ever comes to pure creation – something out of nothing. One does not even need pen and paper, let alone all the instruments and implements and materials necessary for the practice of the other arts. And you cannot learn from teachers, only from other poets. But what if there aren't any? Keidrych Rhys's pioneer achievement was to create, almost single-handed, a sense of community among English-language writers in Wales. From then on, isolation of the wrong sort began to dissolve, there began a change for the better in the way these writers looked at their country. The nastiness and the bitterness that disfigures the work of certain older writers, and has led them to pervert great talents, is found no longer. The personal and social situation of the writer, his whole relationship to his audience, to other writers, his view across the language barriers have quite simply changed out of all recognition, and the pace of the change seems to be accelerating. Although we do not live in one another's' pockets – there are, in fact, some quite healthy hatreds blowing around – there is something of a community, perhaps even the beginnings of a tradition, and one which, in the Welsh way, is open to all.

In considering the present position it would be totally unrealistic, a sort of aesthetic prudery, not to mention the Welsh Arts Council, as its arrangements have existed since 1967. Its mere existence in its present form, quite irrespective of anything it may do, is a factor for the good. Not simply because it accords public recognition or makes available public funds, but because, in the circumstances of a bilingual country, it imposes Equal Status in practice and for obvious practical reasons. And because language is – or has been – a sensitive area, it defuses the situation simply by being there, and under an obvious duty, which not even the most bigoted extremists can challenge, to deal out even-handed justice. Indeed, as far as the writers themselves are concerned, I don't think one can talk of 'sides' any more, though doubtless a few coelocanths still lurk. I can testify, after four years' arduous service on the Arts Council's Literature Committee, that everybody falls over backwards to be fair, and there has never been any of the old tension and bitterness.

And because life is never free of problems, official benevolence has now itself become one of them. We are not unique in this. From Canada, Mordecai Richler writes about 'Maple Leaf Culture' which he describes as 'an era at once embarrassingly grandiose, yet charged with promise. We are smitten with an unseemly hasty tendency to count and codify, issuing definitive authologies of a hundred years of poetry and prose, as if by cataloguing we make real, by puffing, meaningful, especially when mere publication is taken as a licence to enshrine the most ephemeral stuff .... What characterises Canadian culture today is not so much energy and talent – it is there at last, a real but tender shoot – as an astonishing affluence and benevolence. Our cultural plan is vulnerable to the charge of staking just about all the alienated kids to committing their inchoate but modish complaints to paper or canvas .... Lesser writers, all of them world-famous in Canada, are blowing the dust off early manuscripts and digging old letters out of the attic, mindful of the burgeoning market in raw Canadiana. Book-length studies of just about everybody in the house are threatened, operas are being commissioned, ballet companies subsidised, and townships sorely in need of tolerable restaurants and bars are being paid to erect theatres instead. If Canada was once loosely stitched together by railroads, such is the force of today's culture boom that it may be re-knit by art palaces coast-to-coast, though there hardly be the plays or the players, not to mention the audiences, to fill them'. Another Canadian, Northrop Frye, has written, 'such is the obvious and unquenchable desire of the Canadian cultural public to identify itself through its literature there are so many medals offered for literary achievement, that a modern Canadian Dryden might well be moved to write a satire on medals, except that if he did he would probably be awarded a medal for satire.'

Despite some obvious similarities in detail, things have not quite reached this stage in Wales yet. Canada is a much richer (and much nicer) country. Our native philistine meanness will save us from many of these excesses. But if we do become a rich country – as a self-governing Wales undoubtedly would be before the end of the century – then we'll have to watch it. The Welsh-language writer is of course free of the temptation to write for the market, and would be even if everybody suddenly started speaking Welsh and reading Welsh books; the market is simply too small to be worth manipulation by modern capitalism. It has, as Ned Thomas has pointed out, some of the characteristics of the 'alternative society' which is beginning to grow up on the crumbling edges of capitalism, so the Welsh-language writer is *free* in an absolute sense. But the temptation to belong to a comfortable official culture is common to writers in both languages, and must be resisted. Man, after all, is a wild animal, and if the poet is to speak for his own section of mankind, he must guard his independence, not only from the capitalist and the commissar but from even the most benevolent demo-bureaucracy. When the Sherman Theatre was inaugurated in Cardiff not long ago, the first play was *The Government Inspector*, a happy choice in many ways, one might have thought. But the programme note was at pains to point out that it all happened in Russia a long time ago. Today all governments are honest, and there is no such thing as corruption in public life! Is it really possible for a healthy, socially responsible literature to flourish in that sort of atmosphere? There is far too little satire as it is, and far too little humour. This is a sympton of social anaemia. What humour there has been is often sick and nasty. Anthony Conran put his finger on one of the more obvious weaknesses of Anglo-Welsh poetry – 'the horrible feeling that every *mot* has got to be *juste*'. Even our best editors remain incorrigibly po-faced when humour and satire or anything even mildly bawdy is submitted to them. You can't even get it on to the telly without a top-level decision having to be taken behind the scenes. Humour, after all, springs from self-confidence, laughter from strength. Anxious, insecure, neurotic, petit-bourgeois Anglo-Wales is not yet ripe for it. In Welsh there is plenty of it, in proletarian South Wales there is Max Boyce, but one of the pervading weaknesses of the Anglo-Welsh generally is ghastly good taste. Closely allied with this problem is another, identified by B.S. Johnson, the only English *avant-garde* writer of any consequence, and a good friend to Wales, whose death was a loss to both countries. 'There is,' he once wrote, 'a serious problem of form facing Anglo-Welsh poets, for while their material is marvellous, and they have reasons to write which are virtually unknown to English and American poets, the forms they have used so far are almost without exception traditional, to sometimes deadening effect. Simply, their forms do not do their material justice, and while they should not necessarily imitate or take up advances made in English outside a Welsh context, the problem of form must be faced with more courage than hitherto. Perhaps it can only be solved by a poet of the calibre of Yeats who has yet to develop or appear. The last ten years have produced achievements which were hardly thought possible, the next ten years may just see the impossible.' Kind and encouraging words, relevant and timely. But the difficulty as I see it is this. *Avant-garde* itself is by now *vieux jeu.* What passes in English for experimental writing is usually something the French were doing a generation previous. And for the moment even France seems to have run out of steam. I am not too worried personally. My job is to communicate to as wide an audience as possible, and traditional forms help rather than hinder my task. The formal break-through, which I agree is necessary, may not come through poetry at all in the first instance. As Johnson himself showed, there seems to be more scope for innovation in the novel. David Jones, too, set a promising precedent for prose-writers to follow. Or perhaps it could come through the performing arts. This is what happened in Ireland. Literary archeologists will of course be able to unearth various fossilised relics of attempts to repeat the Irish success story in a Welsh context, but a straight crib rarely comes off. But the theatre is in such a state of chaos just now that absolutely anything seems possible. And despite the astringent remarks of Mordecai Richler, it is good to have at least the buildings. Some think that television, too, offers its opportunities. It is significant that one of our best poets, John Ormond, works in the medium. And perhaps it is here that the future glories will be born.

But even when all this is on the way to being achieved, yet another obstacle lurks. A certain species of critic. The thought-police, the classic collaborationist *milice.* Like sharks, because they have tough hides and snapping teeth and small brains, they are difficult to kill; like Struldbrugs, because they are so feebly animated, they take a long time to die. Dimly aware that things are not going the way their political masters would wish, they have begun swinging their truncheons menacingly, and laying down the law that there is only one permissible 'authentic Anglo-Welsh dilemma'. Now it happens that I am more authentically Anglo-Welsh than most, with more generations of English-speakers behind me than the majority of indigenous Welsh people and am, moreover, by upbringing a down-town Swansea Jack, and I do not need Shoni Hoi from Cwmscwt or Dr Hengist Horsa from Hogs' Norton to tell me how to think or what to write.

I would not want to end on a sour note, however. There is some genuinely constructive criticism that is worth repeating and emphasising.

Meic Stephens has said, 'The big danger threatening Anglo-Welsh verse as I see it is that it may continue to be peripheral, both in Wales and England ... while so many of us acquiesce in the anglocentric organisation of life in Britain today, I think our literature will remain in much the same position as Scotland's before the 1920s: parochial, disorientated, minor, conservative, dull, and without one critic or poet of Hugh MacDiarmid's stature. Like him our poets must "strive to break their living tomb".' Since those words were written in 1967, the grip of the grave has slackened noticeably. No Yeats, no MacDiarmid yet, but I am sure that one is around somewhere. And when there is talk about being peripheral, one must now ask, peripheral to what? England, and there has been a referendum to prove it, is not the centre of anywhere or anything any more, except to the anglomaniac politicians who are already becoming obsolete. Its literature has gone to pieces, and very little of it is now worth reading, much of it has become so alien to us as to be meaningless anyway. It no longer commands or deserves our loyalty. We have to do our own thing, cultivate our own garden. We could be due for a bumper crop.

Artists in Wales (3, 1977)

The First Seven Hundred Years

A.O.H. Jarman and G.R. Hughes (eds.), *A Guide to Welsh Literature, Volume One.*

This is the first of an intended series of six volumes covering the whole history of Welsh literature. It is aimed at a wide readership, not confined to the colleges and not confined to Wales. Such a concept is not only a credit to the publishers who have always been enterprising and ambitious anyway, it is of wider significance in a world where attitudes to 'minority' languages and cultures have changed dramatically, and more pertinently still, it betokens a change for the better in the attitude of Welsh-speaking Wales, a community which has always guarded its treasures jealously and has never shown much readiness to share them. In a reciprocal melting of attitudes, the philistine contempt of the outside world (a polite euphemism for England) and the correspondingly sullen silence of the insiders have now been modified to a point at which communication is at least possible across the most formidable of all iron curtains. The point must therefore be made that the present work is radically different from the English translation of Dr Thomas Parry's standard history, and no useful purpose is served by making comparisons between the two volumes. The one was originally written in Welsh, with all the inbuilt attitudes and assumptions which that implies, and the translation into English is therefore not free of a certain bumpiness. The present volume is engineered for the English market and, ideally, should be judged from the standpoint of the reader who comes fresh to the subject. That does not mean to say, of course, that its credentials should not be examined, and these seem to be of a worthy standard. Of the two editors, the one, Gwilym Rees Hughes, certainly needs no introduction as an editor, and the neat organisation of the present volume must undoubtedly owe much to his expertise in a rather special field. The other editor, A.O.H. Jarman, Professor of Welsh at Cardiff, is an authority on the period covered here. There is among the contributors a heavy preponderance of Cardiff-based scholars; one must presume that our other seats of learning will have their opportunity in subsequent volumes.

The editors explain their intentions in a short preface. Their brief is to cover the first seven centuries of Welsh literature, from the earliest recorded beginnings in the sixth century up to the end of the thirteenth century, roughly the first era of Welsh independence, a period which is generally considered to be self-defining, and no one is likely to quarrel with it as an entity. For a volume on the present scale, however, it presents problems. It covers, after all, half the lifetime of our literature and recorded history, a period which saw a lot of action, from the fall of Rome to the fall of the House of Gwynedd. Conservative our ancient society may have been, but I suspect that its conservatism, like that of most societies, has been exaggerated, and that people at all times have been just as uncomfortably aware as we are today of living in a world hell-bent on perdition. The editors have to deal with this long period in one volume, whereas the subsequent seven centuries will have five volumes in which to spread themselves. How do they handle it? Quite dexterously, I think, though with some sacrifice of symmetry in chapter-length. The book opens with a long chapter (quite its longest) entitled 'The Historical Background of Early Welsh Verse', by Professor Ceri Lewis, a lot more history than verse, usefully setting the historical, social and linguistic context in which our literature first emerged, taking the story from prehistoric times up to *Armes Prydain*, a tenth-century Celtic League manifesto, rousing stuff and a historical as well as a literary landmark. The reader will require some familiarity with the typographical conventions of comparative philology, but otherwise the exposition is lucid. Three subsequent, much shorter chapters (by Jarman) deal with individual names prominent in the early part of this long period: Taliesin, Aneirin and Llywarch Hen, and the respective bodies of verse traditionally associated with them. There is an inevitable dependence here on Sir Ifor Williams, whose theories are presented to the general reader in English for the first time (if one excepts Kenneth Jackson's treatment of the *Gododdin* in a Scottish rather than a Welsh context). Next, three substantially longer chapters, the later Cynfeirdd, up to the tenth century (Jarman still) then The Court Poets, Their Function, Status and Craft, Lewis again and with this scholar's social emphasis (he is a disciple of the great G.J. Williams), a fascinating exposition of the *servitudes et grandeurs* which were the crucible of a complex and esoteric craft. The same body of verse is then surveyed again from a different angle by Myrddin Lloyd, a subtle master of the close reading, especially of his obvious favourite, the torrential Cynddelw. The two chapters together provide a stereoscopic picture. The poetry of this period was by intention hieratic and difficult, made more so by time and change, it can only be fully apprehended and understood by a scholarship given to few. These two chapters taken together give us as good an insight into its essential spirit and tone as we are likely to get.

Next, two chapters on the prose literature of the period. *The Mabinogi*, as the national classic, must of course have a chapter to itself, by Glyn E. Jones. The title is here properly restricted to the Four-Branches Tale. Its genesis and its relation to oral tradition are discussed, but no account is taken of Mr Saunders Lewis's persuasive correlation of certain passages in the narrative with actual historical events in the reign of Henry II (his *Meistri'r Canrifoedd* is not in the bibliography either, a rare lapse), but the emphasis is equally on the literary artistry of the tale as we have it in its final form. A longer chapter deals with the other stories usually included, since Lady Charlotte Guest's day, under the made-up title of *The Mabinogion*, with a preview of the material in a wider context, by Brynley Roberts. He is fascinated by the enigmatic aspects of *Peredur*, he considers *Culhwch and Olwen* to be a picaresque novel that does not come off and doubts whether the modern reader is responsive to the wild humour in the enumeration of Culhwch's unlikely entourage. Well, at least one modern reader thinks that this goonish, surrealist roll-call is still funny today, but a more solemn age may well be on the way when it will be out of favour again. This whole chapter is full of good things. The richness of the material evokes a correspondingly lively enthusiasm in the treatment. Mr Roberts also contributes a very brief chapter on Historical Writing, in which he makes a useful point about the superiority, at that date, of Latin. Morfydd Owen ends the volume with a survey of Functional Prose. This we need reminding about. Non-literary writers were important in shaping our prose to the precision and elegance it is capable of. Devotional writing in Wales is older than Puritanism, and some of the medieval stuff is just as morbid as any of the later wallowings in masochism, but fortunately there were also treatises on more useful subjects – agriculture, science, medicine, geography. And of course, there were the Laws, closely related, under the conditions of their day, to a vivid oral tradition.

A reader coming fresh to the subject will have, from this volume, an accurate and comprehensive picture in general terms, of the first seven hundred years of our literature. I have no doubt that it can be criticised, perhaps even torn to pieces, by the appropriate specialists. But on the whole a formidable task has been well handled both by the editors and the individual contributors, and nicely presented by the publishers. There is no scholarly apparatus of footnotes or references, but bibliographies at the end of each chapter are a rare convenience. There is a lot of repetition from one to the other of these, but this the reader will readily forgive. They seem comprehensive for most purposes this side of advanced study, and are up to date to 1974. The illustrations are a welcome embellishment, the price is reasonable, and we look forward to the next five volumes in the series.

Poetry Wales (12.3, Winter 1977)

A Nation's Chief Glory

Doctor Johnson, who made many memorable pronouncements, once said the chief glory of a nation is its authors. He was one himself of course, but he was quite right, because in the nature of the case, the authors have always the final say. In the Gospels that we will soon be hearing for Christmas we are told 'In the beginning was the word'. A sage of our own time has assured us that 'the medium is the message' which amounts to much the same thing. And for over five hundred years, ever since Guthenberg invented the press with moveable type in 1450, that word has been the printed word. The immediate result was the Renaissance, the Reformation, the Age of Discovery and the distant beginnings of modern science and democracy. Once people could freely communicate by means of the printed book, everything was possible. And today we live with the potential of an equally stupendous revolution. Like all revolutions, we take it in our stride: the ubiquitous transistor, the television that is by now an essential of life. The most recent edition of the *Encyclopaedia Britannica* tells us that for the first time in five hundred years the monopoly of the printing press has been broken – by the electronic media, of course. And you could add, as part of the same process, films, records, cassettes and other developments still in the experimental stage.

As a former public librarian I saw the reading habit reeling under successive body-blows as these developments established themselves, but I also saw shelf after shelf-ful of books being added to the stock of the libraries under their stimulus. The communications revolution of our time, I am convinced, is the real revolution. Not the political or economic ideas. Most of these have by now been exposed as romantic nineteenth-century myths. But Dr Johnson was still right. For so much of what we absorb through the media is ephemeral and transient. By its nature it is designed to catch the attention by hook or by crook. and demands the confirmation of more considered judgement. It has to be checked, supported and confirmed by an authority we can turn to and consult after we have switched off. We are still, in the last resort, dependent on the printed word, even though it is now but one among many of the resources available to us. If I were asked what was the real choice that faces the generation that will have to grapple with the implications of the communications revolution, I would say that it consists in holding the balance between the superficial and the permanent, between a mass of brightly presented but obsolescent snippets of fact and pseudo-fact, and the more enduring verities. One of the things that will soon be engaging the attention of some of us will be the compilation of an important work of reference, to be published simultaneously in both English and Welsh, which will be *A Companion to the Literature of Wales*. It will contain information about some two thousand authors in both languages. It is going to take some years, and represents a considerable investment, in every sense. Those who have undertaken this task are obviously convinced that it is not only desirable but necessary. Because in Wales perhaps more than in most countries, our authors are not just our chief glory but our only glory, our only claim to any attention from the outside world. We are fortunate to have so many of them, and of such a high standard. What I would like to know is what sort of readership will they be able to count on in an era which offers so many counter-attractions.

Sixth Sense (BBC Radio Wales, 16 December 1977)

208

Compulsory Reading

Duncan Glen (ed.) *Akros*, vol. 12 nos. 34-35
Special Hugh MacDiarmid Double Issue;
Philip Pacey, *Hugh MacDiarmid and David Jones:*
Celtic Wonder-Workers.

In August 1977 'Hugh MacDiarmid', Christopher Grieve, 'Auld Chris', celebrated his eighty-fifth birthday. On Palm Sunday 1974 a group of us stood with him under the yew at Ystrad Fflur to honour another *prifardd*. For some of those present, this will be a memory they take to their own graves. He was, and remains, the greatest poet any of us would ever know. If the nations of Britain competed for a Triple Crown in poetry, Scotland, since the 'thirties at least, would have been permanent champions, and the whole diversely brilliant generation of literary talent which has spearheaded the broader Scottish national revival of our day, gladly acknowledge him as their progenitor and inspiration. *Sangschaw* and *Penny Wheep* belong to 1925 and 1926. In this celebratory number of *Akros* (and other literary magazines of 1977) it is possible to read delightful short poems that are still fresh and lively, and the final section of the issue is a recent bibliography of W.R. Aitken showing a record of continuous activity into the poet's ninth decade. "The days of our needing to defend or propagandise 'Hugh MacDiarmid' are over," says Duncan Glen, and here he has collected seven essays that illuminate the massive achievement.

When, in 1974, MacDiarmid addressed Yr Academi Gymreig at Lambed, he quoted with obvious gusto his own comment on his own work: 'A volcano belching mud as well as flame. I know that some of what I have written is considered rubbish, but I would not like to be one of those who with infinite pains bring forth a tit's egg.' The Anglo-Welsh literary magazines have always been full of tit's eggs, small, fragile, exquisite – and often *clwc*. And small, fragile, exquisite critics, neurotically preaching a doctrine of sterile, inoffensive good taste. MacDiarmid ought to be compulsory reading in Wales, perhaps he would encourage some of our poets, those who are young enough to learn, that no disgrace attaches to ambitions beyond the norm. I know that Wales is irredeemably petty-bourgeois with not much room for manoeuvre, but Scotland was in a like case before MacDiarmid. Not any more. Anyway, his tosh-content could not possibly be higher than, say, that of Yeats, and is more easily separable from his best work. And what there is of that offers an inexhaustible theme, which these seven essays set out to explore.

K.J. Annand, a good Scots poet in his own right, looks at the early MacDiarmid's vocabulary, drawn not from one district but from the totality of Scots, of all regions and all ages, at his delight in 'the obsolete, the distinctly local, the idiomatic, the unused', in Scots words with no exact English equivalent. He makes the point that the hostile critics of those days (a sorry bunch they look now) dealt not with the poems as such, but with the language in which they were written. In other words, their hostility was politically motivated (as is all literary criticism). To take these words seriously was an offence against the centralised 'British' state. But, as Mr Annand points out, these poems were much easier to understand than the metropolitan English products of the time, and have certainly lasted a lot better.

Then Kenneth Buthlay, one of the leading exegetes of our poet, analyses in some detail his interest in language for its own sake, reminding us that MacDiarmid shares a Borders background with James Murray, the great lexicographer, and Alexander Melville Bell, the phonetician, whose son invented the telephone.

Next Stephen Mulrine considers the prosody of *A Drunk Man Looks at the Thistle*, a poem of over 2,500 lines with over fifty different metrical schemes. Despite this diversity on the ear, the 'tune' of this long poem is as unmistakeable as that of *Paradise Lost*. It could have been mentioned that the poem is available to the ear on disc, read by the poet himself (Claddagh CCA 1 & 2).

John Herdman studies the much harder poem 'To Circumjack Cencrastus' which he sees as a crucial stage between the twin peaks of the earlier and later achievements. John Manson, in an essay entitled 'Water of Life', looks at five poems from the 'thirties dominated by the symbolism of water. Ruth McQuillan faces the problems presented by 'On a Raised Beach', written on Shetland in the mid-'thirties, 'which asserts no fundamental certainties, raises the fundamental problems' and which exists in at least two versions, a strange and perplexing work.

Akros is published from Preston (which thus assumes more prominence in Scottish affairs than at any time since the Forty-Five). Also at Preston, Art Librarian at the proud city's Polytechnic, we encounter Mr Philip Pacey, last heard of at St Albans, and before that at the College of Librarianship, Aberystwyth, where he gave evidence of exciting potential as a poet, and one with a feel for place, which well qualifies him to write about one of the main strands in MacDiarmid. Here, in the concluding essay, he considers the composite long poem *In Memoriam James Joyce*, a work in memory of and in praise of not only Joyce (though Joyce above all) but all who have contributed to the continuity or extension of verbal expression.

Subtitled 'From a Vision of a World Language', this poem looks to a unity not to be achieved by uniformity. Soloviev is invoked, as so often with MacDiarmid, and one feels, too, in touch with the thought of Goethe, and something of the same loftiness of vision.

All dreams of imperialism must be exorcised
Including linguistic imperialism which sums up all the rest.

Otherwise only barbarism awaits the human race. The poet invokes Eliot and Pound, as well as Joyce, and Mr Pacey draws a parallel with Whitman. I think he could also have cited Pablo Neruda.

Mr Pacey has also published under the *Akros* imprint an essay on MacDiarmid and David Jones which asks us to consider the basic similarities between these two superficially contrasting writers. The differences are seen largely as accidents of temperament, as between a shy recluse and a vehemently combative public personality. The essay divides into three parts. In 'Fact and Sacrament' MacDiarmid's plea for a 'poetry of fact' is seen as congruent with David Jones's insistence on the piety of place. We recognize, surely, other voices here. W.J. Gruffydd: '*Y mae pawb a phopeth yn Llanddeiniolen*', the doctrine of '*y filltir sgwar*' enunicated by D.J. Williams. And I think we can recognize too the essence of much good writing in Wales in both languages, the *haeccitas* of Duns Scotus, what Tom Earley once defined to me as *specificity*, the things that have to be existentially experienced before they can be written about. Everything else is mere poetic diction. In 'The Celtic Front' MacDiarmid is quoted in praise of Mistral, who

... beginning with his native region
Ended by embracing all nations.

The 'world consciousness' for which he yearns can only be firmly rooted in one's own place, and is clearly related to David Jones' themes and images. Our attention is drawn to an extensive quotation from David Jones's preface to *In Parenthesis* to be found in *Lucky Poet*. (Mr Pacey says that it has escaped the attention of the indexer, but in my copy of the 1943 edition it is correctly indexed at page 185. The reference to page 399, however, is a ghost.) I would like to suggest, if someone is not already engaged on it, that a study of the plentiful Welsh references in *Lucky Poet* would have its own fascination and be immensely valuable as one great polymath's view of our culture as it appeared to him circa 1940. 'Wonder-Voyagings', the third section, deals with the significance for both writers of the image of the ship, with ample reference to the common Celtic background.

The ship of art which we must launch into the unknown, our Celtic heritage, which under threatening skies, is the Ark of our salvation.

Poetry Wales (13.3, January 1978)

A Welsh Antiquary

Exactly two hundred years ago a tall well-built man in vigorous middle life looked with the paternal satisfaction of an author at a new copy of the latest of his many books. He was Thomas Pennant of Downing in the parish of Whitford near Holywell.

Today we think of the area as industrial Deeside. But it was then rural Flintshire, dominated by the intermarried dynasties of substantial gentry, Salusburys, Myttons, Middletons and Mostyns. They were cultured and public-spirited.

John Salusbury, father of Dr Johnson's friend Mrs Thrale, had given the young Pennant a book on ornithology which was to turn his mind to the natural sciences. He went up to Oxford, took silk and attended to the duties of his station in life, became high sheriff and improved his estates.

But, displaying originality and initiative, he had, as an undergraduate, sought out Dr Borlase in Cornwall, the antiquary and geologist, and he subsequently visited or corresponded with most of the savants of a brilliant epoch, from Voltaire, whose command of English obscenities caused him to marvel, to Francis Grose, another inquistive traveller whom Robert Burns was to immortalize as 'a child's amang you takin notes'.

Pennant, too, took notes about everything. His published works fill eighteen volumes. Not to mention his correspondence: Gilbert White of Selborne, Buffon, Linnaeus, it sounds like name-dropping, but these men acknowledged him as of their number.

He has some claims, too, as a pioneer of travel literature, perhaps even of tourism. Johnson said of him, 'He is a Whig, sir, and a sad dog, but he's the best traveller I read; he observes more things than anybody else does.'

It was a way of life with him. The record of a youthful visit to Ireland had to be abandoned as imperfect 'such was the hospitality of the country'. For despite Johnson he was anything but a sad dog.

But a more sober visit to Scotland produced a best-seller which opened up the country to visitors for the first time. He travelled in

England, too, and wrote well about London.

He belonged to the last generation of the gentry to follow the ancient custom of fostering, so had spent much of his early life in the family of a tenant farmer. It was to be a priceless asset.

Here was a man who could speak good earthy Welsh as well as the French of high cosmopolitan culture. He could talk on his travels not only with learned clergymen and antiquarian squires, expert in archaeology and heraldry, but with the people.

And from talking with shepherds and husbandrymen he learned a remarkable oral tradition. It was the story of Owain Glyndŵr still living in their minds. Gone underground since the Son of Prophecy had disappeared into the mountain mist, forgotten or ignored by the literate and well-informed, it ran like a buried stream.

Pennant put the tales together and correlated them with written history. It was rather like Jacques Cousteau reassembling fragments found on the seabed into a masterpiece of ancient art. Most subsequent accounts of Glyndŵr depend on Pennant, to whom, in Sir John Lloyd's words, belongs the credit of restoring 'the lineaments of a great national hero, whom literature had agreed to belittle, but whom folk memory had never forgotten'.

The well-read country gentleman has always been an important figure in European culture, from Montaigne to Lenin. Wales, with its usual luck, produced one who gave back to the people the memory of their proudest hour and their greatest man.

The famous traveller never travelled to better purpose than through the scenes that were familiar to him from childhood. He died a celebrated man, honoured by learned societies throughout Europe. His contribution to many branches of knowledge was considerable.

He was, perhaps, the famous Welshman of the past that one would most like to have met, and he deserves our special thanks for having rescued a tradition that has played a vital part in the way that Welsh people have thought of their country ever since. His *Tours in Wales* is one of the half-dozen most important books we have. Its anniversary deserves to be commemorated.

Western Mail (26 August 1978)

Pure Propaganda

T.S. Law and Thurso Berwick (eds.),
The Socialist Poems of Hugh MacDiarmid.

In 1972 the present publishers gave us *The Hugh MacDiarmid Anthology* which corrected many of the shortcomings of various comprehensive editions that had been appearing since the 'forties. It is currently rumoured that the definitive Collected Works is on the way at last. Here, in the mean time, *tamaid i aros pryd*, are sixty-seven pieces selected from the vast achievement that lies between *Sangschaw* (1925) and *A Clyack Sheaf* (1969). In a solid foreword of biographical and analytical commentary, the editors provide a balanced and useful survey of a continent of marvels which, encountered at random, could baffle and confuse. Writing firmly from the viewpoint (however defined) expressed in the title of the volume, the editors identify with the poet's own attitude, even when this has seemed contradictory and paradoxical. Their selection clusters heavily around the *Second Hymn to Lenin* (1935) and work from *Lucky Poet* which, although not published until 1943, seems to belong mostly to the same period. The earlier lyrics are sparsely represented, and there is only one extract from the most impressive of his longer poems, *A Drunk Man Looks at The Thistle*, represented here, unsurprisingly, by 'The Ballad of the General Strike' when

> The thistle like a rocket soared
> And cam' doon like a stick.

Disappointingly, there is little from *A Kist of Whistles* (also 1943) and containing fine poetry about working people actually at work, and only a representative scatter from later books, but including material not in previous collections.

'We no longer know where history is going, if indeed it is going anywhere at all,' says Richard Marienstras. The philosophies of determinism have been undermined if not discredited. But our poet, like everybody else, is influenced by the events, personalities and attitudes of his youth, when ambitious schemes for human betterment, involving the extension of freedom in all directions, could be hailed with what now seems naive enthusiasm. There were prophets then, of a vanished breed. Lenin and John Maclean kindled the imagination of the young firebrand. To MacDiarmid as to James Connolly, Socialism and Nationalism were two faces of the same coin. Fifty years later, with the coin having come down on its edge, and probably a dud anyway, poor Maclean now exists only in MacDiarmid's own verses in his praise, and Lenin can be seen to have founded a system in which the perennially dissident poet would have been unlikely to achieve an honoured ninth decade.

But good writing outlasts its immediate occasion. Milton survives his theology, Kipling his Raj. And there is still a lot of mileage in the preachments of one whose thinking has always been genuinely dialectical rather than merely and meanly mechanistic like the Anglo-Left in general. His robust anti-clericalism now seems to have much the same self-confident tone as the systems he attacked, but his onslaughts on humbug, royalist hysteria, Billy Graham-type religion, political cant, anglomania, municipal philistinism and pouf-pastry literature are as relevant as ever, and his observations on the ugliness and futility of urban proletarian existence seem to have gained force as the century wears on. I take it that the aim of the present anthology is to emphasise certain aspects of the *content* of his work. His technical mastery, his status as a Lord of Language (more than one language) we must take on trust. The arrangement of the selection is not strictly chronological nor clearly thematic, it seems more of a lucky dip. But with such a bran-tub, why worry? From the *Second Hymn to Lenin* I pick this:

> A pretty tribute to the old rural scene
> Can mask a base betrayal of mankind:
> The mellowest religious reference conceal
> The Kruschen spirit of Fascism behind,
> In short, any utterance that is not pure
> Propaganda is impure propaganda for sure.

Planet (45/46, November 1978)

Gwyl Ddewi

The most successful St David's Day that I ever heard of was described to me by a cousin serving in one of the Welsh regiments in the Italian campaign.

They got hold of the carnival dragon used in the local fiesta of a small town and cavorted around the piazza with it, breathing smoke and fire provided by squibs and crackers. An immensely enjoyable time was had by all and the *trattoria* ran out of *vino*.

Then they got on with the war and won it. It came near, I think, to what must have been the earliest celebrations of all.

An extrovert knees-up by hard fighting men, the dark, dangerous Silurians often more appreciated in action than in their rowdy relaxation from it, the scruffy, undisciplined, invincible soldiery who collected more jankers and more battle honours than most.

To commemorate their pint-sized patron saint (I always think of him as about the same dap as Gwenallt or Saunders Lewis) they hoised 'the green and gritty leek, Saint David's frugal dinner' as John Heath-Stubbs has called it, a pungently defiant parody of the plumage and panache of chivalry.

Shakespeare captures the atmosphere in *Henry V* when the bombastic Pistol is forced to eat the leek by the Welsh sapper Fluellen (although the battle of Agincourt took place in October).

There must have been many memorable wearings of the unlikely emblem. One of them is captured for us by Hogarth. Taffy with a huge leek in his hat is one of the passers-by as The Rake is being arrested for debt and dragged out of his sedan chair just as he is on his way to a levee at St James' Palace, while the lightning strikes White's Club and the vicious pavement life of the metropolis swirls around. An ugly customer with a cudgel eyes the Welshman askance, but he too has a truculent air and the leek is as prickly-looking as any thistle. To judge by his good clothes, our Hanoverian compatriot is likely to have been one of those merchants or professional men who were beginning to foregather in London as the old broils died away and Britannia began to rule the waves.

Only a few years after The Rake met his exemplary end in Bedlam, it was men like these who would come together to form the first Cymmrodorion Society, dedicated to convivial and charitable ends and taking the state of Wales much as they found it.

And for some two centuries the decorous celebrations of the Honourable Society and its successive incarnations set the tone for hundreds of dinners throughout the land, some, no doubt, more sober than others.

Nonconformists honoured a saint, solid citizens consumed carnivorous banquets in memory of an ascetic vegetarian and drank the health of the teetotaller in heaven with deep draughts he would not have approved during his sojourn on earth. It was all slightly absurd, like so much in our story. But it got things done.

Between the beanfeasts constructive work went on, cultural activities were encouraged and co-ordinated, eisteddfodau were organised, the nation began to wake up. The annual celebration could look back, in some years, to the beginnings of the university to serve the people, to a museum that would house that people's treasures and to a library that would house its memory. Not inconsiderable achievements by any standards.

It was a phase, the Cymmrodorion era one is tempted to call it, which deserved well of us all and it was to endure from Georgian times until blown away at last by those winds of change that whistle about our own ears. Its final substantial benefaction is likely to have been the *Dictionary of Welsh Biography*, the formidable volume that reached the bookshops for Saint David's Day 1953.

The date does not vie with Christmas and Eisteddfod week in the publishers' and booksellers' calendar but an attempt is made to observe it nevertheless. The University Press punctually produces its bilingual booklet every year, and some of these have proved to be of interest to those who like to read about the activities of our people, from David Samwell, who sailed with Captain Cook, to John Hughes, who founded the Donetz steel industry.

The translation of the New Testament into the language of today was presented to the nation with some formality, not on any of the major festivals of the Christian Church, but on Saint David's Day 1975, and this was felt to be altogether appropriate.

It is hoped that the new version of the entire Scriptures will be completed in time for the four-hundredth anniversary of Bishop William Morgan's monumental translation of Elizabethan times – and Saint David's Day 1988 will indeed be a day to remember.

In the wider public mind, Gwyl Ddewi has had a rather less secure lodgement. At best a half-holiday in some schools, with the morning given over to entertainment of a vaguely eisteddfodic character, followed by a free afternoon at just the least hospitable time of the year. The weather is usually dreadful (this, one must suppose, is what Saint David died of) and most of us keep our heads down.

Except, of course, for little girls who never need any excuse for dressing up, and cheerfully brave the elements in various versions of the costume devised by an over-enthusiastic English lady in the high tide of Victorian taste. The charm of their years and breed usually carries them through. Little boys are subject to similar trials, but draw wooden swords and don cardboard armour with great brio all over the land. Then they go home and forget all about it until next year. Or do they?

It's like Christmas perhaps, even if, as Thomas Hardy sourly commented on the battle of the Somme, 'After two thousand years of mass, we've got as far as poison gas.'

It could be argued that the solemn and emotional observance of Armistice Day after World War I did nothing to prevent the second one when the pressure-cooker blew its whistle.

But the artificial poppy and the plastic leek have both kept alive a flickering flame of genuine belief that can only be repudiated by falling into the utter despair that is the ultimate sin. As the witty Frenchman said, hypocrisy is homage paid by vice to virtue. The once-a-year patriots may be doing better work than they know.

And, as the temper of Wales, which is difficult to gauge but disastrous to misjudge, changes once again, as it has over these last few exciting years, observances change too. Our unofficial festival, unrecognised by the State, has emerged in a characteristically oblique manner almost by stealth at another level.

The Government and the Welsh Office time the publication of White Papers and Green Papers (but no Red Papers as yet) with the auspicious day in mind. There is usually a debate on a Welsh topic somewhere near the Day. Welsh M.P.s in the House of Commons, shy and modest men as a rule, sport daffodils. Well, you wouldn't expect them to eat leeks, would you?

I doubt that anything like it could have been observed even in the headiest days of Cymru Fydd and the young rebels Tom Ellis and Lloyd George, not to speak of the supine centuries whose weight was to be too much even for such fiery crusaders.

Like the commercial observance of Christmas, there seems to be more of this sort of thing with every year that passes. Recently somebody referred to Saint David's-tide, the season when there is always an 'll' in the month.

Hard-line hegemonists and even harder-line separatists will dismiss all these manifestations as superficial tinkering.

While the one faction rallies to defend the last bastion of the Raj and the others toil to deepen Offa's Dyke, the tides have already begun to flow that are going to change our political and constitutional topography out of all recognition, and there are those who, euphorically perhaps, are beginning to refer to themselves as post-nationalist.

The second-order adjustments, the minutiae, the nuts and bolts are unlikely to be sorted out to everyone's satisfaction, and we should not confuse a referendum with revelation, or an Assembly with an Apocalypse.

But still the European and world dimensions of the future are already beginning to take shape and now even the immediate familiar past begins to look small and strange.

All our pomp of yesterday is one with Nineveh and Tyre, and none too soon. It is one of those irresistible and irreversible shifts forward that take place in human affairs from time to time, and it can be dated as precisely as the first run of Trevithick's locomotive.

On March 1, 1954, the first hydrogen bomb was dropped on

Bikini Atoll. Previous atomic bombs had been dropped in the heat of the war, and there had been dancing in the streets. Not this time. The dance has been postponed indefinitely.

We are still trying to come to terms with what Churchill called 'The Balance of Terror'. When the news reached Paris, a Breton said to Jean-Paul Sartre, 'At last the Breton question exists.' All sorts of questions could now be put. All sorts of other questions ceased to be asked.

Speaking for Belgium, Paul-Henri Spaak said that Europe now consisted of two types of small nation, those which knew that they were and those which didn't.

The Suez affair, with all its traumas that still give a twinge, was a messily-scrawled postscript to a story that had ended. It takes a long time for a big truth to sink in. Twenty-five years ago today we lived through the most momentous Saint David's Day ever.

As the space-anchorages and spy-satellites prowl the sky, the world is, paradoxically, not getting smaller but expanding to accommodate the great transformation of our times.

It has nothing to do with any clash between Left and Right or black and white or whatever. Pervasive everywhere, it has been hailed as 'The Revolution of Expectations,' that almost messianic sense of the infinitely possible that is common to all the diverse unrests of the day.

And one of its manifestations, surely, is the emergence, against every possible suasion, of a loyalty for what the Spaniards call *la chica patria*, the homeland of the heart, uniquely precious and not to be lightly surrendered.

It is right and proper, some of us may think, that the birthday of this new era in human history should also be the birthday in heaven, as the Christian Church has always reckoned these matters, of the saint whose last well-remembered charge to his people was that they should be mindful of the little things.

Western Mail (1 March 1979)

A Visit to the Waterworks

Today, said my father, we are going to see the waterworks. Our summer holidays in those inter-war years consisted in staying home and catching a bus or train to somewhere new and interesting every day. Or at any rate, somewhere new. Sometimes I was allowed to choose. Once I chose Banwen. For no other reason than that it was right at the top of the South Wales Transport Company's route map. I do not say a word against Banwen. But as a place to go for a day out it has its limitations. It took me a long time to live that one down. But our visit to the waterworks belongs to an even earlier period of my life, when I had no say in what was going to happen, and every new day fell like an apple from a tree. Neither had I quite mastered all the intricacies of the language. Because in my own mind I had a pretty fair idea of what we would see when we got to the waterworks. Like fireworks, only made of drops of water instead of sparks and lights. There was a precedent to go by, the Illuminated Fountain at the Drill Hall.

Besides its military function, the Drill Hall housed in the course of the year many social functions and trade exhibitions. These latter were another typical family outing in those days. One came away with free samples of miscellaneous junk, colourful promotional leaflets, mostly unintelligible, and, if it was a really good exhibition, i.e. one concerned with food, there were also miniature samples of all the popular brands, faithful replicas of the familiar tins and boxes containing minute samples that you could actually eat. There were marvels too. One year there was a real Robot. I knew he must be real because he spoke with an English accent, like the wireless. But the marvel of marvels was the Illuminated Fountain. At a given moment the lights in the hall were lowered, and a complicated pattern of silver jets would shoot high into the air and then start changing colour as they danced up and down to an accompaniment of oohs and ahs. It was always the same, but it never failed to thrill. Did you see the Illuminated Fountain? we would ask in school next day. It is almost impossible now, after decades of technicolour films and colour television, to recreate that particular excitement, but in its day the Illuminated Fountain, believe it or not, was one of Swansea's main attractions. I suppose the local T.A. must have included a more than usually enterprising section of the Royal Engineers, and that the almost hallucinatory spectacle was produced by nothing more mysterious than Sappers turning on taps and manipulating searchlights. Never mind, there were wonders in the world in those days, and this was one of them.

So I knew exactly what to expect when we got to the waterworks, and asked no tiresome questions as my mother prepared paste sandwiches and currant cake to put into father's tin, which was also having a day off from the power station. And I was rather mystified when he remarked, 'The right sort of day for it anyway'. But then I reasoned that under these threatening skies the waterworks, as I pictured them, would show up all the more colourfully. How my imagination ran riot as we boarded the bus and set off through the slums at the top of the town, Landore, Morriston, Clydach, the ravaged and rotting lower Swansea Valley, then further on still to Pontardawe with its groves of chimneys and tall narrow church spire, and on and on into real *terra incognita*. I hardly saw any of it that grey morning. We were accustomed to that desolation, anyway. It was a shame, people said, something should be done about it. And that was as far as it went. From Clydach onwards and up through Ystalyfera and Ystradgynlais passengers boarded the bus who spoke Welsh among themselves. This was an added bonus, increasing the interest of the trip. I wished I could understand it. And that was as far as *that* went. But all that really exercised my mind was the imagined wonders we were soon to see, pinwheels and rockets of colourful rain, perhaps. And would there be pictures made of water, too, like sometimes there were pictures made of fireworks in Singleton Park on Hospital Carnival night? Of one thing I was certain – this was going to be big. For I had enquired, and my father, who knew everything, had assured me that this was a very big waterworks, one of the biggest in Wales, perhaps a mile from end to end. A mile of waterworks! No wonder it was such a long way from anywhere, such a spectacle obviously needed plenty of space. Do a lot of people go to see them, I had asked. Oh yes, people come from all over. And no wonder, I reflected. There would surely be crowds. I vaguely assumed that the steep hills now beginning to loom up on either side of the road had been selected as a location because they afforded natural terracing to accommodate the hordes of spectators, and would give them a good view.

After Ystradgynlais it is a long haul to Cray, a boring bus-ride at the best of times, but I was still held in an inward trance of expectation, not fidgeting, asking no questions, unaccustomedly quiet, unbelievably well-behaved. I was given a slice of currant cake. At Craig-y-Nos the talk was automatically of Madame Patti. I was not particularly interested. I knew that she was a great singer and took it for granted that she had sung in Welsh, like everybody else in these parts. Did she, I wondered, sing at the waterworks? Were her soaring notes accompanied by soaring luminous jets of silver rain? Did she sing against a background of coloured cataracts?

I think my mind must still have been actively engaged in this fantasy when I heard the words, 'There's the waterworks' and the bus pulled in at the dam of grey stone. As I have said, it was a dull morning. The hills were dull, too, as they are on such days. And here was a dull-looking pond, big but nothing sensational. After all, I could reach the shores of Swansea Bay within five minutes from the tea-table if I ran, as I often did, and see right across to Devonshire. Neither were there any ornamental ducks, like there were on the much smaller pond in Brynmill Park. A wet slab of still water, between grey hills under a grey sky. I looked. I looked dutifully, as I was told. I looked for a long time. And said not a word. This was it all right. There it was on a noticeboard: Swansea Corporation Waterworks. There was no possibility of a mistake. Where were all the leaping and glittering cascades and fountains that I had conjured up in my mind? I had no appetite for the sandwiches and sulked ferociously all the way back, which seemed a lot longer journey than I remembered. I don't know what's got into the boy, they said, he was so good on the way up. Perhaps he's sickening for something.

Planet (48, May 1979)

A Chronicle of Decline

The National Coal Board closed Big Pit earlier this year. A chapter in the history of Blaenavon had come to an end, and an epoch in the history of Gwent. Over a hundred years of large-scale mining had come to the inevitable closure that must face every mine, however prosperous and profitable in its day. Perched 1,400 feet up at the top of the Torfaen, the celebrated Eastern Valley of Gwent, Big Pit was the last colliery on the Northern Crop, where the coal, iron and limestone surfaced together to furnish the raw materials for two centuries of high profits, high wages and high risks.

Blaenavon lies snug in a green valley. As in so many of the old iron-working towns of north Gwent, it is possible to discern some of the rudiments of town planning in its layout, some spaciousness that survives the frantic, often squalid improvisation that is the signature of the coal boom years. But it has the inescapable topography of a cul-de-sac. All around loom the dark hills that seem an appropriate setting for the dramatic episode in human history that has been called 'The Rape of the Fair Country'.

Ironically, as the collieries decline, archaeology takes over as the latest growth industry. The Blaenavon Colliery Museum was planned as the last shift came up in the cage. Ideal for such a project in many ways, it is accessible from the Heads of the Valleys Road and the motorway network. Although lacking a towering pithead, the solid Victorian stonework monumentally proclaims the golden reign of King Coal as the unchallenged monopolist of energy, and some of the royal swagger was communicated to even the humblest of his subjects.

A pit with a shallow, easily-drained, gas-free shaft, with no intractable maintenance problems, it adapts well to its new role. Soon it will be possible for the visitor to go down in the cage, board a journey of drams, inspect displays portraying the history of coal-mining, with all that there is of pride and courage in the tale of blood and tears.

Big Pit is mercifully free of some of the more shameful chapters in the story. The Iron Company which owned it does not rank high in the role of tyrants; Blaenavon is not a name immediately associated with disaster; it has none of the resonances of Gresford or Senghennydd; the visitor may tread its galleries untroubled by intolerable recollections. Nor, by the same token, does it invoke memories of some passionate act of defiance or historic strike. And Blaenavon's later history was one of slow, uneventful decline until, some years ago, the last of the specialised steel plant was sold off at the behest of distant debenture-holders, and the whole place was written off. What happened here was happening all over the coalfield, but nowhere in such final and absolute terms.

Still, it cannot be considered in isolation from the wider picture, the crowded and colourful decades when a small, difficult, mountain coalfield bunkered the world's navies; when prodigies of ingenuity and engineering were called for to get the jolting truckloads of black diamonds down from the hills where the precious stuff was mined to the docks where the freight was loaded for the outposts of empire.

The present programme glances – it can only glance – at the headlong development of the narrow upland valleys, the social tensions and bitter confrontations of which Rhondda and Aberdare were the battlefields, the coalfield docklands with Cardiff in the colourful lead (a different place entirely from the sedate minor capital of today), the endless ferment as a whole new breed of humanity, the Welsh industrial worker, grappled with a harsh environment, hostile social conditions and a trade that is dangerous and dirty under any circumstances.

The most recent chroniclers of this struggle, the historians of the South Wales Miners' Federation, are Hywel Francis and Dai Smith, the conscientious custodians of a vast collection of archive material.

The Miners' Institutes, now mostly converted to more convivial activities, housed libraries, lodge records and minutes, and a wealth of other material, much of which has been preserved and is now housed in the South Wales Coalfield Library at Swansea. The programme makes extensive use of this treasure-house, the documentation of an epic. Other museums and libraries tranquilly preserve memorials of what was seen in its day as a clash of Titans, an embattled confrontation between right and wrong.

The Industrial and Maritime Museum at the end of Cardiff's Bute Street rises in a different world from the old Tiger Bay. The similar colliery museum in the hills above Port Talbot is thinking of reactivating a steam-driven train, something that will presumably compete with the established attractions of the northern tourist belt, puffing and clanking with nostalgia, an activity which is undoubtedly profitable and gives a lot of pleasure to a lot of people. But one does not have to be a particularly dour Puritan to question whether it may legitimately be reckoned as an industry to strengthen the moral fibre of a nation.

For generations men poured into Glamorgan and Gwent in search of a livelihood, and a future for their families. Time's whirligig seems to have decreed that future generations will again take the same path, this time in search of the past.

Radio Times (22 November 1980)

Bibliography

This list, far from being exhaustive, consists only of those items of Harri Webb's literary journalism which were considered for inclusion in this book but which, in the end, had to be excluded for lack of space. Another list, though not a complete one, will be found in John Harris, *A Bibliographical Guide to Twenty-four Modern Anglo-Welsh Writers* (1994). See also the selection of Harri Webb's political journalism, *No Half-Way House* (1997).

'The Anglo-Welsh Writers', a letter to the editor of the *Western Mail* (28 March 1949) taking Professor Gwyn Jones to task for his criticism of Saunders Lewis for failing to recognize the existence of an Anglo-Welsh literature.

'An Iscariot's Life of Judas', a review of Thomas Jones, *Lloyd George*, in *The Welsh Republican* (Dec. 1951 / Jan. 1952).

'Aneurin versus Bevan', a review of Aneurin Bevan, *In Place of Fear*, *The Welsh Republican* (June / July 1952).

'Sut Daeth Merthyr Tudful yn Fwrdeisdref', an article on how Merthyr Tydfil became a borough, in *Y Faner* (23 Tach.1953).

'Great Events, Great Places', an article about Richard Trevithick's steam-engine's first run at Penydarren, Merthyr Tydfil, in 1804, in *The Welsh Republican* (Oct. / Nov. 1953).

'Nemesis', an article about the Irish patriot Roger Casement, in *The Welsh Republican* (Dec. 1953 / Jan. 1954).

'Welsh Wizards who Went Wrong', a review of Frank Owen, *Tempestuous Journey: Lloyd George, his Life and Times*, and Richard Aldington, *T.E. Lawrence*, in *The Welsh Republican* (Feb. / March 1955).

'Atgof am Ambrose Bebb', a memoir of the writer and Nationalist Ambrose Bebb, in *The Welsh Republican* (June / July 1955).

'Remember and be Proud', an editorial about Dic Penderyn and Keir Hardie, in *The Welsh Republican* (Aug. / Sept. 1956).

'Dic Penderyn', a letter in reply to Chris Rees confirming the writer's membership of the Labour Party, in *Welsh Nation* (17 Nov. 1956).

'A New Welsh Artist and a Great One', an article about Cyril Ifold, a Swansea Valley miner and painter, in *The Welsh Republican* (Dec. 1956 / Jan. 1957).

'Letter from Wales: Merthyr Tydfil, the Neon-lit Sheep-track', in *The London Welshman* (Dec. 1959).

'Llyfrau'r Flwyddyn', an article on Welsh books published in 1960, in *The London Welshman* (Jan. 1961).

'Dewch Adre o Lundain', a letter to the editor of *Y Faner* (19 Ebrill 1962) appealing to the London Welsh to return to Wales.

'He Learnt Welsh: his First Book', a short notice of Gerald Morgan, *Yr Afal Aur*, in *Welsh Nation* (Sept. 1963).

'National Hero or Rebellious Magician?', an article about Owain Glyndŵr, in *Welsh Nation* (Feb. 1964).

'Phew!', a letter to the editor of *Welsh Nation* (April 1964), signed 'Tudor Pritchard', one of HW's pseudonyms, about Goronwy Rees.

'Un Babell Lyfrau', an article about the need for a Books Pavilion at the National Eisteddfod, in *Llais Llyfrau* (Gaeaf 1964).

'Bristol Channel Challengers', an article about the rivalry between Cardiff and Bristol for commercial supremacy, in the *Western Mail* (19 March 1965).

'The Summer Scene', an article about the pleasures of the National Eisteddfod held at Newtown, in *Welsh Nation* (Sept. 1965).

Untitled review of Gerald Morgan, *The Dragon's Tongue*, in *Cilmeri* (1965).

'Mountain Ash, a Local History', compiled from various sources, published as a cyclostyled booklet by Mountain Ash Public Library (1966).

'A Hero for our Time', a review of Glanmor Williams, *Owen Glendower*, in *Welsh Nation* (July 1966).

'Mapped', a review of L.G. Bullock, *A Historical Map of Wales*, in *The London Welshman* (March 1967).

'Libraries and the Arts', an address delivered at a symposium held at the College of Librarianship, Wales, in September 1969 and published in D.E. Gerard (ed.), *Libraries and the Arts* (1970).

'The Moggie I See in my Dreams', an article about *inter alia* the idiosyncrasies of the Cardiff bus-service, in *Welsh Nation* (Oct. 1969).

'There Was an Amazing Gap on that History Shelf', a review of Gwynfor Evans, *Aros Mae*, in *Welsh Nation* (Sept. 1971).

'Webb on Thomas', a review of Gwyn Thomas, *The Sky of our Lives*, in *Welsh Nation* (5-11 Jan. 1973).

'Galicia', an article about the cultural situation of Galicia, in *Planet* (24 25, Aug. 1974).

'Nid Serch Pethe Ifanc', a review of Gwilym Rees Hughes and Islwyn Jones (eds.), *Storiau '74*, in *Taliesin* (30, Gorff. 1975).

'Hynafgwyr yw ein Beirdd Gorau?', a review of T. Gwynn Jones (ed.), *Cerddi '74*, in *Taliesin* (31, Rhag. 1975).

'Preview', a monthly column on Welsh television programmes for the Wales edition of *Radio Times*, to which HW contributed 44 columns between September 1976 and July 1980.

'Canmlwyddiant Trychineb', an article on the Tynewydd pit disaster of 1877, in *Y Faner* (10 Meh. 1977).

Untitled review of Gwyn Williams, *The Land Remembers*, in *Resurgence* (May / June 1977).

'Portread o Hanes', a review of Alexander Cordell, *This Sweet and Bitter Earth*, in *Y Faner* (12 Awst 1977).

'By the Light of the Czar's Jewels', an article about the jewels that Fabergé made for the Russian royal family, in *Welsh Nation* (Aug. 1977).

'Llyfrau Dwy Ganrif yn Ol', an article about Welsh books published in 1977, in *Y Faner* (11 Tach. 1977).

'Stori Antur', review of Lynn Hughes, *Hawkmoor: Adventures of Twm Siôn Catti*, in *Y Faner* (2 Rhag. 1977).

'A Journey through One Man's Mind', a review of David Cole, *Mount of Angels*, in the *Western Mail* (6 July 1978).

'The Twelve Days of Christmas', a short radio-talk about the festive season, broadcast by BBC Wales on 26 December 1978.

'1979: Pethau sy'n Llenwi'r Cof', a short tribute to Hugh MacDiarmid who died in 1979, in *Y Faner* (21 / 28 Rhag. 1979).

'Cymry ar Wasgar', a radio-talk about the Welsh overseas, broadcast by BBC Cymru on 19 August 1980.

'Coalfield Art', an appreciation of the work of the painter Jack Crabtree , in *Radio Times* (13-19 Nov. 1980).

'Then and Now', an article on the inter-war years in Wales, in *Arcade* (2, 14 Nov. 1980).

'Disestablishement: a View from the Pew', an unpublished article about the Church in Wales (1981).

Untitled review of Dai Smith, *A People and a Proletariat*, in *Welsh Republic* (1, Jan. / Feb. 1982).

Untitled review of K.O. Morgan, *Rebirth of a Nation: Wales 1880-1980*, in *Welsh Republic* (6, Dec.1982).

'Eisteddfodau Abertawe', a memoir about the visits of the National Eisteddfod to HW's hometown of Swansea, in *Barn* (234/235, Gorff. / Awst 1982).

Untitled tribute to Saunders Lewis, in *Barn* (Hydref 1982).

'Llew Llywel, dawn a anghofiwyd', an article about Llew Llywel (Rhys Davies, 1844-99), in *Y Faner* (10 Rhag. 1982).

'Local Boyce Makes Good', an article about the singer Max Boyce, in *Radio Times* (23-29 April 1983).

'The Friendly Festival', an article about the Llangollen International Eisteddfod, in *Radio Times* (16-22 July 1983).

'Lampeter's Eisteddfod', an article about the National Eisteddfod held at Lampeter in 1984, in *Radio Times* (4-10 Aug. 1984).

'English? That's the Dying Language', an interview given to Mario Basini, in the *Western Mail* (2 April 1985).

About the Editor

Meic Stephens teaches Journalism at the University of Glamorgan and at the Centre for Journalism Studies at Cardiff University. New editions of his *Companion to the Literature of Wales* appeared in 1997 and 1998, and he has also edited *A Cardiff Anthology* and *A Rhondda Anthology* for Seren. He is an accomplished translator as well as editor, poet and journalist, and among his published translations are the memoirs of Gwynfor Evans, a selection of essays by twentieth-century Welsh writers, and *Monica*, Saunders Lewis's first novel.